JASPER TUDOR
GODFATHER OF THE TUDOR DYNASTY

Debra Bayani

M

MadeGlobal Publishing

Jasper Tudor: Godfather of the Tudor Dynasty

ISBN-13: 978-84-943721-0-0

New Fully Revised Edition 2015
First Published in 2014

M
MadeGlobal Publishing

For more information on
MadeGlobal Publishing, visit our website:
www.madeglobal.com

For Kawa, Didar, Adair & Kara

Important Sites in
England and Wales

SCOTLAND

Bamburgh
Alnwick

York

ENGLAND

Penmynnedd
Denbigh

Harlech
St Davids
Barmouth

Bosworth

Coventry
Warwick

WALES

Hereford

Sudeley

Mill Bay
Pembroke
Tenby

Carmarthen

Raglan
Gloucester
Minster Lovell

Chepstow
Thornbury

Windsor
London

Keynsham

Dover

Salisbury
Portsmouth

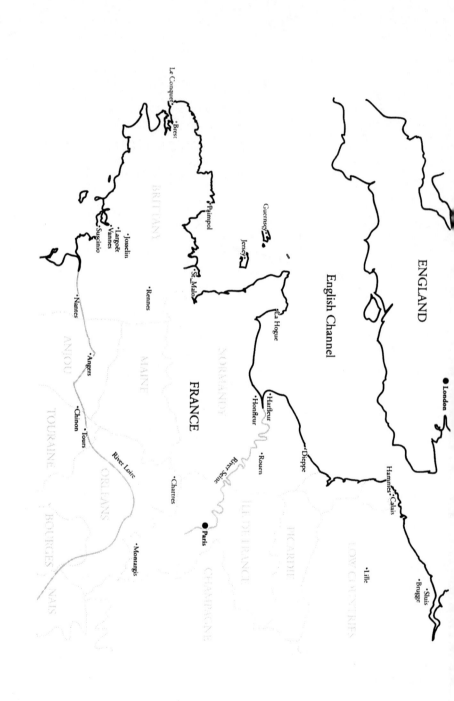

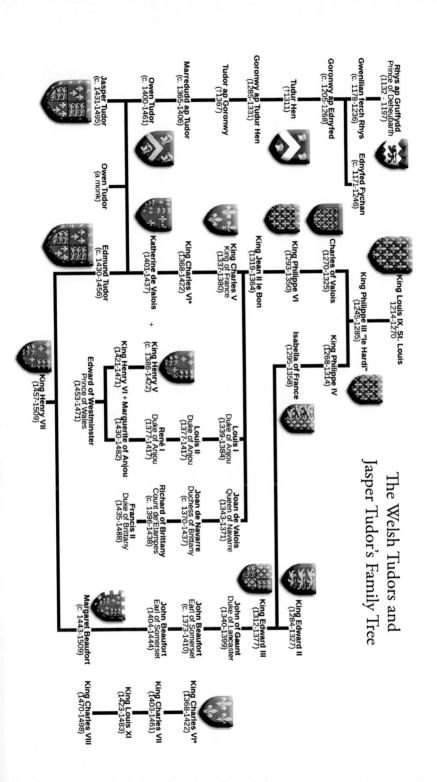

The Welsh Tudors and
Jasper Tudor's Family Tree

CONTENTS

ACKNOWLEDGEMENTS

I am extremely grateful for the kindness of helpful people in the course of the incredible journey of researching and writing Jasper's story. Without the help of the following people this book would not have been possible, first of all Mary Murphy my editor, who helped me to turn this book into something I am proud of, Eurig Salisbury, translator of Welsh Medieval poetry and a research fellow at the Centre for Advanced Welsh and Celtic Studies, who found the time to translate nearly all the poems in this book, Brooke Westcott, for kindly translating the Latin and old English documents. Thanks also goes to Mark Lewis, from Tenby Museum, Tony Cherry, an expert on Thornbury Castle and the now vanished manor house, Susan Chrich and Alison Talbot from Boots, and also Angie Morgan, who kindly showed me around in the cellar in Tenby.

I owe much to the scholarship of others,- Roger Stuart Thomas' thesis 'The Political career, estates and connection of Jasper Tudor, Earl of Pembroke and Duke of Bedford (d. 1495)' has been of particular help. I must also acknowledge the influence of professor Ralph A. Griffiths, Howel T. Evans and Chris Skidmore.

I would also like to thank a gentleman, who helpfully pilot me to and through St. Gredifael's Church in Penmynedd but whose name I unfortunately cannot remember.

I have also been very lucky to have made some helpful, knowledgeable and amazingly supportive friends online, especially Susan Higginbotham, whose unlimited knowledge about the period has often been of great help and Mr. David Durose who kindly took the time to share his knowledge about medieval Brittany in the time of Jasper and Henry's exile with me. I would also like to thank the followers of my Facebook page 'The Wars of the Roses Catalogue'.

I would like to say a big thank you to Claire for her support and her husband Tim Ridgway from MadeGlobal Publishing, for their encouragement and the chance they have given me to re-publish this book.

The last word must be reserved for my family, I would like to thank my husband Kawa to whom I owe more than I can possibly say and my children Didar, Adair and Kara without whose love, support and patience I could not have written this book. This is for you, with all my love.

DEBRA

February 2015

PREFACE

It was three or four years ago when I was reading a novel about the Wars of the Roses that my attention was first drawn to Jasper Tudor. This, to me, shadowy but heroic Welshman was fascinating and soon I found myself starting to gather as much information about him as I could. Somehow, once I had started, it was as though I had no other choice. The secondary sources were scarce but what I did find was interesting and encouraged me to dig deeper. Discovering Jasper had not yet been given the honour of at least one biography surprised me. How was it possible that no one had ever accorded this man the recognition he deserves?

On an early April evening in 2011, six months after I began researching Jasper Tudor's life, I found myself on a plane to Bristol, leaving my family in the Netherlands for a few days. On the train through beautiful South Wales, with the late afternoon sun shining on the coast and the many castles that went by, I realised that these places I was seeing were the same places that had been familiar to both Jasper and his older brother Edmund. This gave me a real emotional jolt and a sense of connection that became the driving force for my continuing research. That first trip was followed by many more, and visits to archives. It has been an incredible journey – from the small town of Keynsham in Somerset, where now are visible only the foundations of what was once one of the most important and splendid religious houses of the region and the burial place of Jasper, to the cellar in Tenby in South Wales, where tradition has it both Jasper and his nephew Henry hid before their flight to France, and from Ty Gwyn, the house in Barmouth reputed to have been used as a headquarters by Jasper and his supporters prior to his exile in Brittany in the 1460s, to the many remote castles in Brittany where Jasper and Henry were imprisoned during their long exile between 1471 and 1485. Despite all this, I have to admit that the sources that do survive are insufficient to permit a full biography. Nevertheless, it is my hope that this study may offer the means to an understanding of Jasper's importance during the Wars of the Roses and, afterwards, for his nephew Henry VII, and of his key role in the foundation of the Tudor dynasty.

I should state here that it has never been my intention to become Jasper's definitive biographer. My only aim was, and is, to have people get to know Jasper and to understand the times he lived in and the difficulties he faced.

1

IN THE BEGINNING
A French princess

KATHERINE DE Valois was the youngest surviving daughter of King Charles VI of France and Queen Isabeau of Bavaria. She was born in Paris on 27 October 1401 in the royal palace Hôtel Saint-Pol. Katherine's eldest surviving sister, Isabella (1389–1409), had been Queen Consort of England as a child bride to Richard II from 1396 until her husband was murdered in 1399. Despite her high rank, it is believed by some that Katherine's early years were largely miserable and impoverished. At the time of her birth, France was in chaos and her family in turmoil due to her father's recurrent bouts of insanity – a foreshadowing of the fate in store for England under Charles VI's grandson Henry VI five decades later.

Charles VI had been a well-loved and widely respected monarch, but as far back as 1393 the French king had suffered attacks of insanity. As time went on these had increased in both frequency and length.

By the time Katherine was three years old, in 1404, it was decided that, for the sake of the king's well-being and dignity, he should retire from public life. The Hôtel Saint-Pol, a secluded royal residence, was chosen as the place best-suited to house the unfortunate king. It was also the home of Katherine and her siblings. In total, Charles VI and Isabeau of Bavaria had twelve children, but by 1404 their two eldest sons, both named Charles (the first born in 1386 and the second, Dauphin of France, in 1392), and a daughter named Jeanne (b.

1388) had already died in early childhood. The royal children now numbered seven: Louis du Guyenne, the 2nd Dauphin of France (7); Jean (6); Isabella (15), who returned to France in 1400 after the mysterious death of her first husband Richard II; Jeanne (13); Marie (11), who had entered the convent of Poissy in 1397; Michelle (9); and Katherine. Two more sons would follow: Charles in 1403 and Philippe in 1407 – the first would later become King Charles VII of France and the latter died soon after birth.[1]

With the king now shut away and heavily guarded in Saint-Pol, the political consequences of the lack of a strong and determined leader became apparent. Disorder quickly grew within the French government. In this situation, tensions mounted between the king's younger brother Louis I, Duke of Orleans, and their royal uncles - Philip the Bold, Duke of Burgundy; John, Duke of Berry; and Louis II, Duke of Bourbon - who took advantage of the king's illness to seize power, establishing themselves as regents. Queen Isabeau found herself in the centre of all this and so, by 1402, Charles allowed her to mediate the growing dispute between the Orleanists and Burgundians. He also turned over to her control of the treasury.

Jasper's maternal grandmother, Isabeau, who was born in around 1370, was the eldest daughter of Stephen III, Duke of Bavaria (in modern-day Germany), a descendant of Charlemagne and from the house of Wittelsbach, and his wife Taddea Visconti of Milan. Apart from Charles's bouts of mental illness, the marriage between Charles VI and Isabeau appears to have been happy. It used to be suggested that Isabeau was a shamelessly unfaithful wife, who was known for her arrogance and ruthless ambition and viewed her husband's misfortune as her opportunity for self-advancement, but this assessment is quite possibly due to the tendency of some male historians to malign strong medieval women. One nineteenth-century exception with regard to gender was sometime novelist Agnes Strickland, who had a rather hostile opinion towards Isabeau and asserted that the queen seriously neglected her children and shut them away at the Hotel de Saint-Pol, 'nearly starved and loathsome with dirt, having no change of clothes, nor even of linen'. More recent opinions about the biased nature of contemporary sources have changed, and modern historians now see Isabeau as playing an extraordinarily astute and effective role when her husband's illness forced her to assume his responsibilities and, in

1   Monstrelet, pp. 4–5, 12.

particular, to safeguard the monarchy from being despoiled by his powerful male relatives.

After Philip the Bold died in 1404, he was succeeded as Duke of Burgundy by his son John the Fearless, who continued his father's strife in an attempt to gain access to the royal treasury for Burgundy. The Duke of Orleans believed Burgundy intended to seize power for his own interests and Isabeau took sides with Orleans to protect the interests of the crown and her children. John the Fearless accused Isabeau and Orleans of financial misconduct and demanded money for himself and raised a force of 1,000 knights to enter Paris in 1405. Orleans and Isabeau swiftly withdrew to the fortified castle of Melun, leaving her household and children behind. The queen ordered her brother, Louis of Bavaria, to follow with the royal children, Katherine and her sister Michelle and possibly Marie, but most importantly of all the heir to the throne, the Dauphin Louis, and his brothers Jean and Charles. However, Burgundy immediately set off in pursuit and intercepted the party of royal children. According to the French chronicler Monstrelet:

> When the duke of Burgundy approached the dauphin, he made him the most respectful obeisances, and supplicated him to return and live in Paris, where, he said, he would be better than in any other part of France; adding, that he was desirous of conversing with him on many points which touched him personally. After this conversation, Louis of Bavaria, seeing the dauphin was inclined to comply with the request of the duke, said, 'My lord duke of Burgundy, suffer my nephew the dauphin to follow the queen his mother and the duke of Orleans, as he has had the consent of his father for so doing.[2]

Despite this, the dauphin and the other children were quickly returned to their father in Paris by Burgundy.[3] The whole episode almost caused a war between the dukes of Burgundy and Orleans, and it is said that Isabeau attempted to mediate in the issue, but to no effect.

---

2   Monstrelet, p. 38.
3   Monstrelet, p. 293.

It is thought that, while Katherine's brothers remained at court and her sister Michelle was given to the care of the Duke of Burgundy, with no sign of an end to the power-struggles at court, the princesses Katherine and Marie were sent to the convent at Poissy. There they would be removed from their mother's influence and could receive the education suitable for princesses of their status.

While Katherine was spending her days in the seclusion of Poissy, far from the disorder that had marked her childhood years, France was on the edge of civil war. Despite his brief recovery, the king's health remained unstable and it was not long before he was forced to retreat once more to the shelter of Saint-Pol. This initiated a bloody fight between the rival forces of John the Fearless, Duke of Burgundy, and Louis I, Duke of Orleans, the latter of whom was supported by his ally Bernard of Armagnac. Each brother was eager to take advantage of the king's malady by grabbing control of the throne of France. After Orleans was assassinated in Paris in 1407 by followers of the Duke of Burgundy, he was succeeded by his son Charles, who had married Katherine's eldest sister Isabella the previous year. Both the Burgundians and the Orleanists tried to gain control over Isabeau and her children, and Isabeau found herself forced to frequently change sides.

By 1413, Princess Katherine had been called back to court. The only princess left who was neither betrothed nor destined for the convent, she was now a valuable asset to her struggling family and had already come to the notice of Henry IV of England. In that year Henry, who had previously made fruitless proposals regarding Katherine's sister Isabella, the widow of Richard II, and perhaps also her sister Marie, proposed a match between the young princess and his eldest son, Henry of Monmouth. While the outcome of negotiations for Katherine's hand was awaited, Henry IV died and his son came to the throne as Henry V. Young and full of life, it soon became apparent that he was determined to have his French match.

Although his initial approaches were refused by the French, who were outraged by the excessive dowry he demanded and fearful that a match with their princess might encourage Henry to renew his own claim to the French throne, he was not to be discouraged. Using their reluctance to agree to the match as his excuse to take action, Henry began preparing for an invasion of France. To show he was serious, he sent a letter to the French king before his departure, repeating his demands for two million crowns, the restoration of Normandy and the southern provinces, and the hand of Princess Katherine. Henry V launched his invasion, and on 25 October 1415, a battle occurred near modern-day Azincourt. Henry V's decisive and somewhat unexpected victory at the battle threw all of France into disorder. The large numbers of French noblemen who were slain or taken prisoner very much boosted Henry V's cause and weakened the already divided country still further. Henry returned to England a hero and, for a while at least, appeared to have given up his quest for Katherine.

While Henry was in England, Katherine and her family were cast into chaos by the sudden death of her eldest brother, Dauphin Louis, on 18 December 1415. When Louis' death was followed only sixteen months later by the sudden death of the new dauphin, his brother Jean, all France was gripped with fear and, according to several contemporary accounts including that of Monstrelet, both deaths were due to poison.[4] Charles VI and Isabeau's youngest son Charles was now, at the tender age of twelve, his father's sole heir.[5]

For his part, the ill-fated king was unable to deal with these latest developments and his mental condition deteriorated once again. By the spring of 1417, Count Bernard VII of Armagnac had been raised to Constable of France by Charles and the dauphin was married to Armagnac's daughter Marie and therefore favoured the Armagnacs, making their power significantly stronger. It was during this time that Armagnac imprisoned Isabeau and her sister-in-law, the Duchess of Bavaria, and had them taken to Blois and from there to Tours.[6] Burgundy and the Armagnacs, including the new Duke of Orleans, continued their feud and at the end of the year the queen seized her opportunity to regain her freedom with the help of John the Fearless. With the aid of her new ally Burgundy, she swiftly took control and declared herself regent. Soon she was to share the regency with Burgundy and together they eliminated her son's government. Burgundy took control of Paris and killed Armagnac. Eventually, Dauphin Charles negotiated a truce with Burgundy and requested a private meeting with the duke in 1419 at Montereau. The meeting, however, was a plot and Burgundy was murdered by the dauphin's companions.

---

4   Monstrelet, p. 349.
5   Strickland, p. 120.
6   Monstrelet, pp. 265–6.

It appears that, while all this was going on, Katherine gained great influence over her mother, whose maternal feelings, according to Strickland, 'seemed centred in her [Katherine] alone, to the unjust exclusion of her other children'. If true, this was probably due to the fact that Katherine was now the most valuable asset the House of Valois possessed. From that point on, Isabeau appears to have decided that the path to success lay in devoting her energies to securing her daughter's future rather than her son's throne.

According to Agnes Strickland's account, 'Katherine had very early set her mind on being queen of England, and it will soon be shown how completely her mother entered into all her wishes.' Isabeau sent ambassadors with Katherine's picture, to ask Henry V 'whether so beautiful a princess required such a great dowry as he demanded with her?' Although Henry admitted that Katherine was 'surpassingly fair' he was not prepared to lower his demand.[7]

By the end of 1418, Rouen had fallen into English hands and the next spring a peace conference was held at Melun.[8] Confident that her daughter's personal charms would succeed, the determined queen made sure that Katherine was included. In the richly ornamented enclosure prepared for the conference 'Henry seated himself opposite to Katherine, and gazed at her most intently'.[9] Henry appeared to be quite taken with the French princess, who is said to have had an oval face with a clear ivory complexion and large dark eyes. After the conference had finished they took 'most respectful leave of each other'. This scene was evidently depicted in a painting commissioned by Henry VII for his chapel at Sheen. In the painting Katherine wore an arched crown and some kind of veil to the shoulders which was trimmed to the sides with ermine. After it was taken from Sheen, this painting was in the Arundel Collection and sold at Tart Hall in the early eighteenth-century. In 1782, it was in the collection of Horace Walpole and was on display at Strawberry Hill at Twickenham.[10] Unfortunately, its whereabouts are now unknown.

The queen, outraged that Henry still would not lower his demands, decided to take action and at the next meeting three weeks later, Katherine did not join them. Henry was angry and it was clear

7   Strickland, p. 121. Monstrelet, p. 407.
8   Monstrelet, pp. 215–16.
9   Strickland, p. 122.
10 Strickland, pp. 122–3. Horace Walpole and George Vertue, *Anecdotes of Paintings in England*, (London, 1782), pp. 55–6.

that he 'was desperately in love'.[11] After a few days he impatiently demanded another meeting, but on arriving at Melun discovered the tents and banners had all been taken down and the French royal family had already departed for Paris. His anger seems to indicate the extent to which the queen's plan had worked. Turning on the new Duke of Burgundy, Philip, the only French representative present, Henry said, 'Fair cousin, we wish you to know that we will have the daughter of your King, and all that we have asked, or we will drive him and you out of his kingdom!'[12]

Isabeau now schemed furiously to ensure the match went ahead. The dauphin was eager to separate himself from his mother, who seemed determined to put his sister's future before his own. The terms of the treaty, besides the provinces Henry already had demanded earlier, now included the reversion of the whole sovereignty of France, with the immediate possession of the name of regent. If this treaty was accepted it would disinherit Katherine's older sisters and, most of all, her only surviving brother, Dauphin Charles.[13] After the murder of John the Fearless, the duke's outraged son and heir Philip was anxious to avenge his father's assassination and punished the dauphin by instantly concluding an agreement with the English and offering Henry V his full support.[14] These terms, which overturned the sovereignty of France and disinherited the dauphin, who surprisingly was supported by the Duke of Burgundy, were made official at the Treaty of Troyes by April 1419.[15] The dispossessed Dauphin Charles retreated to Bourges, while Isabeau and Charles gave the treaty their unreserved consent.[16] If Katherine had any objections against the disinheriting of her brother they were never documented. But it seems she was as eager about the match as her future husband. Whatever her motives, from the moment of their first meeting the princess 'had passionately longed to be espoused to King Henry'. Henry and Katherine were betrothed on 21 May 1420, and were married on 2 June in a magnificent ceremony at Troyes Cathedral. Their marriage not only made Katherine Queen of England but, in accordance with

11 Strickland, p. 123.
12 Monstrelet, p. 416.
13 Strickland, p. 124.
14 Monstrelet, pp. 408–9.
15 Monstrelet, p. 415.
16 Monstrelet, p. 431.

his previous demands, Henry was now named as heir to the French throne.

After performing a tour through France and celebrating Christmas in Paris, Henry V and his queen made their way to Calais where they set sail for England on 1 February 1421, soon arriving at Dover where the new Queen of England was splendidly received with a warm welcome.

On 23 February, in a magnificent ceremony, Katherine was crowned at Westminster Abbey and, afterwards, an elaborate feast and banquet was held in her honour. In June, Henry returned to France to continue his military campaigning, leaving his wife in the care of his brother John, Duke of Bedford. It was during this time that Katherine discovered she was pregnant with what would be their one and only child.

It is said that Henry V had made Katherine promise that she would not let the baby be born at Windsor, and that when news was brought to the superstitious king about the birth of his son he repeated the following verse:

> I, Henry, born at Monmouth,
> Shall small time reign and much get;
> But Henry of Windsor shall long reign and lose all;
> But as God will, so be it.[17]

It was in Windsor, on 6 December 1421, that the future Henry VI had been born.

In the spring of 1422, with no sign of her husband returning, Katherine wrote a letter, 'declaring that she earnestly longed to behold him once more'.[18] Before long, having received permission from Henry, Katherine left her infant son in the care of his uncle, the Duke of Gloucester, and set sail for France for a reunion with her husband.

On 21 May 1422, Katherine landed at Harfleur accompanied by the Duke of Bedford and 20,000 men at arms to reinforce the English army.[19] Katherine then travelled to Rouen and from there to the castle of Vincennes, where she and Henry were reunited. On 30 May the royal party advanced towards Paris, where great celebrations were held in honour of the arrival of the queen and the birth of an

---

17   Strickland, p. 275, digital edition, ed. R. Kaufman (Boston, 2007)
18   Strickland, p. 151.
19   Monstrelet, p. 477.

heir. Some time after her arrival, however, it became clear that the constant battles of the past few months, and the siege of Meaux in particular, had broken her husband's health and the once strong and lively warrior king was now gravely ill with dysentery. It was obvious to all who saw him that he would not recover.

Henry's final hours were almost entirely passed in selecting a protector for his son and heir, the eventual choice being the king's uncle, Thomas Beaufort, Duke of Exeter. On 31 August 1422, shortly after consigning his young queen, who must surely have been in a state of absolute despair and sorrow, to the care of his brother Bedford, Henry V died at the age of thirty-five. The twenty-year-old Katherine was now a widow with an infant son.

Although the royal Tudors were a mixture of Welsh, English and French blood, their paternal ancestors were from North-Wales, and they, in turn, claimed direct descent from the great Welsh kings.

Owen Tudor – in Welsh, Owain ap Maredudd ap Tewdwr – was a direct fourth great-grandson of Ednyfyd Fychan, a Welsh warrior and seneschal of the kingdom of Gwynnedd under Llewellyn the Great and his son Dafydd Llewellyn. Through his fourth great-grandmother, Ednyfyd Fychan's second wife Gwenllian ferch Rhys, Owen was a direct descendant of Rhys ap Tewdwr, also known as Lord Rhys, who was Prince of Deheubarth until 1093, and through him a descendant of Rhodri Mawr (in English, 'Rhodri the Great').

Owen Tudor was born around 1400 as probably the only son of Maredudd ap Tewdwr ap Goronwy Fychan and Margaret ap Dafydd Fychan ap Dafydd Llwyd. The circumstances surrounding the early part of Owen's life are very obscure, but it is alleged that as a young man he became a servant in the household of Henry V. Owen's uncles – Rhys, who was escheator and sheriff of Anglesey, Gwylliam and Goronwy – were supporters of Richard II and, after his death, stalwarts of the revolts of Owain Glyndwr, to whom they were related by marriage. Eventually, both Rhys and Gwylliam were executed. Owen's father Maredudd, a fourth son, is a more shadowy figure about whom many stories have arisen. In one of these he was the shieldbearer for the Bishop of Bangor and, either deliberately or by accident, killed an important person and was forced to flee into the mountains of Snowdonia with his wife Margaret. Tradition has it that their son Owen was born there and the mighty Owain Glyndwr was the child's godfather. Maredudd is said to have later left for London

with his family and presented himself and his only son Owen at the
court of Henry V, where they both are supposed to have become the
king's servants.

The young Owen Tudor is said to have belonged to the group
of Welshmen, under the command of Davy Gam 'the one-eyed',
Glyndwr's brother-in-law, with whom Henry V was on good terms
after the death of Owain Glyndwr. Tradition also has it that Owen
was rewarded by Henry V after he played a significant role in Alençon
and Agincourt, and was appointed as one of the squires of the king's
body and made an armiger (he was entitled to use a coat of arms)
around 1420. He may also have obtained a position in the household
of Henry V's queen.

We will probably never know for sure which of these suggestions
are fact and which are fiction but what is certain is that the Welshman,
Owain Tewdwr, and the French princess, Katherine de Valois,
eventually found each other.

Figure 1   Tombs of Jasper's grandparents Charles VI and Isabeau (in
the back) and Charles V and Jeanne de Bourbon (front) in
the Basilica Cathedral of St. Denis. *(© 2015 Debra Bayani)*

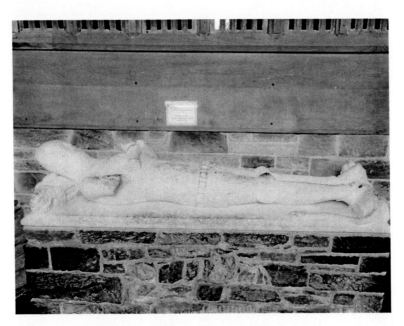

Figure 2   Tomb of Lord Rhys in St. David's Cathedral.
(© 2015 Debra Bayani)

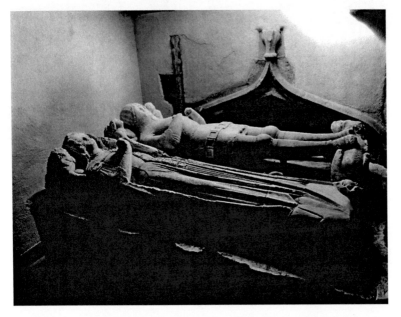

Figure 3   Tomb of Goronwy Fychan, uncle to Owen Tudor, and his
wife Mevanvy in St. Gredifael's Church, Penmynedd.
(© 2015 Debra Bayani)

Figure 4   Marriage of Henry V and Katherine de Valois.
              (Image © British Library)

2
KATHERINE THE FAIR
AND HER 'BRILLIANT
GOLDEN MAN'
c.1429 – December 1449

AFTER HENRY V's sudden death on 31 August 1422 at the Château de Vincennes near Paris, his widow, the twenty-year-old dowager queen Katherine de Valois, often called 'the Fair', was much occupied with her baby boy. Nearly two months after losing her husband, Katherine also lost her father, who died on 21 October. Her child, who had never seen his father, was now not only King of England but, in accordance with the Treaty of Troyes, at the age of ten months had also succeeded to the French throne. Katherine spent most of her time with her son in his early years at Windsor and took him often to her castle at Hertford and her manor at Waltham.

The possibility that the queen might remarry was of great significance, and as she was still a very young woman it was only natural that she might desire to do so. The two most powerful men in the realm at the time were the lord protector and the late king's brother Humphrey, Duke of Gloucester, and Henry Beaufort, Bishop of Winchester. When rumours arose that Edmund Beaufort, Count of Mortain and the future Duke of Somerset, was courting the dowager queen and that they were thinking about marriage, Gloucester grew alarmed at the prospect. Edmund Beaufort was a nephew of Henry Beaufort, Bishop of Winchester, who was Gloucester's arch-enemy. Gloucester reassured the Privy Council that a law had been put in place by parliament in 1427/28 forbidding a dowager queen to remarry without permission from the king.[1] This law, for which Gloucester was responsible, also stated that if the queen remarried without the king's permission, the husband would 'be punished in the forfeiture of all goods and in the death penalty as a traitor to the King',[2] although any child of the marriage would still be a member of the royal family and would not suffer punishment. Furthermore, it specified that the king's permission could only be granted once he had reached his majority. As Katherine's son was only six years old at the time, the new law would prevent her from marrying again for at least another ten years.

At some point not long after the queen dowager was forbidden to get involved with any kind of man, she became passionately involved with the Welshman Owen Tudor, who was, according to Polydore Vergil, 'adorned with wonderful gifts of body and mind'.[3] From different contemporary accounts, and also a poem from 1437, it seems that the spark between Katherine and Owen was struck at a feast where he, by accident, fell into her lap and from that moment on their romance was kindled:

> […] on a feast day,
> showed his affection, fearful business,
> to the king of the wine-country' daughter,
>   who was a beautiful, worthy, gentle and tall maiden;
> if my brilliant, golden man touched the maiden's skin,
> it was by her consent.[4]

However, according to the Welshman Elis Gruffydd, Owen came to Katherine's attention when she came upon him swimming naked.

1   Leics RO, BR II/3/3.
2   Giles, p. 17. R.A Griffiths, 'Queen Katherine of Valois and a Missing Statute of the Realm', *Law Quarterly Review* 93 (1977), pp. 249–58. Hall's Chronicle, p. 185.
3   Camden Society Old Series, vol. 29 (1864), p. 62.
4   Ieuan Gethin 1437, 'In praise of Owen Tudor in gaol' (1437), in *Y Flodeugerdd Newydd.*, ed. W.J. Gruffyd (Caerdydd, 1909), pp. 119–22). Exclusively translated for this book by Eurig Salisbury.

It was probably during this time at court that Katherine met some of Owen's cousins. A surviving account describes her as eager to meet some of his kinsmen and comments that:

> [...] for being a French woman, she knew no difference between the English and Welsh nation. Upon which sir Owen sent for, and brought into her presence the said John ap Meredith and Howell ap Llewellyn ap Howell, his near cousins, Men of goodly Stature and Personage, but destitute of all learning; for when the Queen had spoken to them in divers languages, they were not able to answer a word, which caus'd her to say, they were the goodliest dumb creatures ever she saw. [5]

From around the mid-1420s, Katherine's appearance is noted several more times. She had a crucial role to play during the king's minority and it is reported that Katherine sat near the seven-year-old when he was crowned as Henry VI King of England at Westminster on 9 November 1429.[6] It is also recorded that she continued to live in her son's household and be involved in his upbringing until at least the end of 1430.[7] The statute intended to dissuade her from considering marriage to Edmund Beaufort did not forbid her from associating with his uncle and Cardinal Beaufort, who was with her at Waltham soon after Christmas 1430. During this time Katherine granted in survivorship the stewardship of Oxfordshire, Bedfordshire and some Berkshire lands to William de la Pole, Earl of Suffolk, and Thomas Chaucer, a relative of his wife Alice.[8] This may point to an earlier association with Suffolk and explain why Katherine's children were put in the care of Suffolk's sister after her death. It may even suggest that, prior to her death, Katherine had decided that would be the best place for them. Her absence from the coronation in Paris of her eldest son as king of her native France in December 1431 is particularly notable, as this is unlikely to have been an event that she would have willingly chosen not to attend. The most probable reason for this is

5   *The Baronage of England*, Sir John Wynne, London 1720, p. 2 p. 286.
6   PRO, E28/56/26; GEC XII, i, p. 56.
7   PRO, E101/408/6; /9m. 2.
8   Amundesham, I, 56. CPR, Henry VI 1436–1441, p. 14.

that she was either heavily pregnant or had just given birth to either Edmund or Jasper.

It seems that Katherine continued some of her public activities as, on 30 November 1431, she is recorded to have had a discussion with the treasurer of England, Lord Hungerford, again at Waltham, and in July 1433 she successfully negotiated a readjustment of her dower grant. She is also recorded as present at the court's Christmas festivities of 1435 in Gloucester.[9] After this, Katherine seems to disappear from the public eye, as she does not appear again in the official records until her death in 1437.

It may be assumed that Owen and Katherine withdrew from court at some time during 1430 and that only a few trusted people were aware of their romance, since Owen was granted the rights of an Englishman by parliament in 1432, something that would not have happened if their relationship was commonly known. According to the earliest known reference to their romance (1484), it was in 1427 that Owen became a chamber servant of the queen.[10]

Probably around the time they withdrew to the countryside in 1430, Katherine became pregnant with their first child and nine months later a boy called Edmund was born in Much Hadham Palace, which belonged to the Bishop of Ely, Philip Morgan (he would later be called by the name Edmund of Hadham). Some modern historians have suggested that Edmund was actually Beaufort's son rather than Owen's, and that Owen helped Katherine by marrying her to prevent her child being declared illegitimate and to avoid a scandal.[11] Among the reasons put forward to support this theory is the choice of Edmund as the baby's name as there were no Edmunds in either Katherine or Owen's family. However, it may simply have been that Edmund Beaufort was his godfather. Also, the coats of arms of Edmund and Jasper looked very similar to that of Beaufort, and nothing like that of Owen. Other supposed evidence for these rumours are an allegation that Katherine had difficulty 'curb[ing] fully her carnal passions'[12], the rumour that Edmund Beaufort sought to marry Katherine, and that a century later Owen Tudor's body was not saved from the Dissolution of the Monasteries. This is all quite flimsy as evidence goes and there

9   PRO, E28/57/96. RP, IV, 459-60.
10   John Rylands Library, Latin MS 113.
11   John Ashdown-Hill, *Royal Marriage Secrets: Consorts & Concubines, Bigamists & Bastards*, The History Press (Stroud 2013)
12   Giles, p. 17.

is enough opposing evidence to prove the contrary. It is quite true that the Tudor brothers' coats of arms do not look in any way like Owen's, but they did not receive them until after they were knighted by their half-brother and theirs look very similar to that of Henry VI. Also, if they had been illegitimate then surely Richard III would have seized upon this fact to blemish Henry Tudor's reputation in 1485. Instead, Richard wrote 'the said rebels and traitors have chosen to be their captain one Henry Tydder, son of Edmund Tydder, son of Owen Tydder'; neither did any contemporary mention the issue of this supposed illegitimacy. There is also the fact that Owen Tudor's illegitimate son David Owen, born three years after Edmund's death and so could never have known Edmund in person, asks in his will for masses to be said for Edmund's and Jasper's souls. Why would he remember Edmund if he had no blood ties with him? It seems that the arguments that are supposed to prove the illegitimacy of Edmund and also Jasper, and that the Tudor dynasty should be renamed, are at the least ill-founded and groundless. It is also sad to see how Katherine's reputation is blemished this way.

Owen and Katherine's second son was born a year later, probably in 1431, and was named Jasper, or Siasbar in Welsh. Having been born at a manor in Hatfield belonging to the Bishop of London, Robert FitzHugh, he was therefore known as Jasper of Hatfield. Jasper was followed by a third son Owen, who, unlike his two older siblings, would serve God and become a monk at Westminster Abbey. It would appear that Jasper and Edmund were raised by their parents while their brother was raised by monks. Owen the younger, who was known in the abbey as Edward Bridgewater, was shown favour later in his life when he was given the sum of £2 from the royal privy purse by his nephew Henry VII in 1492, his name being recorded for posterity as 'Owen Tudder'. When the monk Owen passed away somewhere between 1498 and 1501, donations were also paid to Westminster Abbey for prayers for his soul as well as to have the bell rung. There may also have been a daughter called Margaret and possibly another one called Katherine, but if so the first probably died young and it is speculated that the latter became a nun, possibly at Barking Abbey.[13] However, although her existence has often been suggested, no contemporary source confirms those rumours. According to John

---

13 Hall's Chronicle, p. 185.

Burke, Owen and Katherine may have had another daughter, Tacina, who in the future would marry Reginald Grey, Lord de Wilton.

> Reginald Grey, 7th Baron, Summoned to parliament from 13 January 1445 to 14th October 1495 as 'Reginaldo Grey de Wilton, chevalier'. His lordship married Tacina, daughter of Sir Owen Tudor by the Queen dowager Katherine, widow of King Henry V, and younger daughter of Charles VI of France and dying in 1495 was ... by his son. Their son John Grey, 8th baron, summoned to parliament as 'Johanni Grey de Wilton', 16th January 1497 in the last year of Richard III this nobleman obtained a grant from the crown of the manor of Wilsamstede, in the county of Bedford. And in the 11th year of Henry VII, he fought stoutly at Blackheath against the Cornishmen and in rebellion under James Lord Audley in the wars of Scotland under Giles Lord D'Aubeny. He married Anne Grey, daughter of Edmund Earl of Kent, Lord-treasurer, and dying before 1506.[14]

There is, however, no contemporary evidence that this Tacina was actually a daughter of Owen and Katherine, nor of the existence of other daughters.[15]

What does seem certain is that Katherine and Owen, 'no man of birth neither of livelihood',[16] were happy together. Owen had put himself at great risk by marrying Katherine, for even conceiving children with her was to jeopardise his life. Nevertheless, they put their love first and chose to quietly live a retired life together, near London but away from disapproving eyes at the court. Unfortunately, their happiness did not last long. In 1436, Katherine developed some serious and lingering illness and presumably became bedridden, for the will she made on 1 January 1437 refers to 'this long, grievous malady, in which I have been long, and still am'.[17] She died two days

---

14   John Burke, *A General and Heraldic Dictionary of the Peerage of England, Ireland and Scotland* (1831)

15   Tacina is also sometimes described as an illegitimate daughter of John Beaufort, Duke of Somerset.

16   Croyland Chronicle, Davies, pp. 228–53.

17   Strickland, p. 153.

later, aged just thirty-five, at Bermondsey Abbey in London. It has been suggested that Katherine died giving birth and that the child too died soon afterwards. These are only speculations and have nothing to sustain them. Those assigned to execute Katherine's will were Cardinal Beaufort of Winchester, Humphrey, Duke of Gloucester, and Bishop Alnwick of Lincoln.[18] Katherine's body lay in state and was finally buried, with all the pomp due to her high status, on 8 February 1437 at Westminster Abbey.

A surprising fact about her grave is that for more than 300 years Katherine's body was displayed at Westminster Abbey and visitors were able to view it. One such visitor, Samuel Pepys, wrote about this in his diary in 1669:

> I now took them to Westminster Abbey, [...] it being Shrove Tuesday; and here we did see, by particular favour, the body of Queen Katherine of Valois; and I had the upper part of her body in my hands, and I did kiss her mouth, reflecting upon it that I did kiss a Queen, and that this was my birth-day, thirty-six years old, that I did first kiss a Queen. [...] when Henry the Seventh built his chapel, it was taken up and laid in this wooden coffin; but I did there see that, in it, the body was buried in a leaden one, which remains under the body to this day.[19]

And there is also this later account:

> Near the south side of Henry V's tomb there was formerly a wooden chest, or coffin, wherein part of the skeleton and parched body of Katherine de Valois, his queen (from the waist upwards), was to be seen. She was interred in January, 1457, in the Chapel of Our Lady, at the east end of this church; but when that building was pulled down by her grandson, Henry VII., her coffin was found to be decayed, and her body was taken up, and placed in a chest, near her first husband's tomb. 'There,' says Dart, 'it hath

18 RP, V 505–6 (26 March 1437)
19 Samuel Pepys, *The Diary of Samuel Pepys 1659–1669*, ed. R. Latham and W. Matthews, HarperCollins (London 2000), pp. 456–7.

ever since continued to be seen, the bones being firmly united, and thinly clothed with flesh, like scrapings of tanned leather.' This awful spectacle of frail mortality was at length removed from the public gaze into St Nicholas's Chapel, and finally deposited under the monument of Sir George Villiers, when the vault was made for the remains of Elizabeth Percy, Duchess of Northumberland, in December, 1776.[20]

The date of burial given here as January 1457 may be just a mistake but could also mean Katherine's remains were moved nearly twenty years after her original burial.

Equally surprising is that Henry VII allowed his grandmother's grave in the Lady Chapel in Westminster Abbey to be demolished so that, albeit by accident, her remains became exposed. This was despite his intention to remain close to her as expressed in his will – 'our body is to be buried in the said monastery, that is to say, where our said grand dame lies buried'.[21]

Soon after Katherine's death, Owen found himself in trouble with the king's council and was, as he might have expected, summoned to appear before the Privy Council. Understandably wary of the council's probable reaction to his secret marriage with a queen of England and the family they had produced, and the likelihood that he would be punished by imprisonment at the very least, Owen thought it best to flee back to North Wales. He could be sure that his children, as half-siblings of the king, would be well looked after. And so he hurriedly packed all his best goods: chalices, gilt cups, silver ewers, enamelled salts, candlesticks and flagons – most of them gifts from the queen.[22] But as Owen rode west, Humphrey, Duke of Gloucester, sent in pursuit a servant, Myles Sculle, who caught up with him at Daventry in Northamptonshire. There, Owen was handed a summons to the royal palace of Westminster to appear before the council, together with the assurance that he should 'freely come and freely go'.[23] Gloucester clearly considered Owen's descendants a threat, especially to his

---

20 According to a gentleman named Dart. Diary and Correspondence of Samuel Pepys; F.R.S., vol. 3, ed. Lord Richard Braybrooke and Rev. J. Smith (London; Henry Colburn, 1849), pp. 121–2.

21 Strickland, p. 160.

22 Sir Francis Palgrave, The Ancient Kalendars and Inventories of His Majesty's Exechequer, vol. 2, pp. 172-5 (1836)

23 PPC, vol. 5, p. 47.

own position, as he reminded the king that Owen had committed a felony – 'to mix his own blood with the royal blood of kings'. Owen subsequently went into sanctuary at Westminster for several days, 'eschewing to come out thereof' and to face the council, but after he was accused of disloyalty he was eventually persuaded by 'divers persons [who] stirred him of friendship and fellowship to [...] come out' and to show his face at court.[24] He appeared before the king at the Privy Council sitting in the chapel chamber in Kennington Palace, Central London, on 15 July 1437. Also present were the Duke of Gloucester; John Stafford, Bishop of Bath; John Kemp, Archbishop of York; William Alnwick, Bishop of Lincoln; Henry Percy, 2nd Earl of Northumberland; William de la Pole, Earl of Suffolk; Lord Walter Hungerford; Sir John, Lord Tiptoft, Treasurer of England and Keeper of the Privy Seal; and Sir William Philip, Privy Councillor and the King's Chamberlain. The record of this meeting opens with:

> The King not longe agoo, that is to say soon after ye deeth of (noble memoir) Quene Katherine his moder whom God assoille desired, willed that on Oweyn Tidr the which dwelled with the saide Quene sholde come to his presence
>
> ...

In the face of this assembly of elevated gentlemen Owen defended himself boldly:

> Affermyng he hadde no thing doon that sholde yeve the King occasion of matier of offense or displaisure ayenst himself, offryng himself in large wyse as the Kings trewe liege man shold to all thing ant man cowed or wolde surmitte upon him.[25]

From their perspective, Owen had broken a strict social code by marrying the dowager queen without the king's approval.

The kind-hearted king fully pardoned his stepfather on condition that Owen appeared before the king whenever summoned. After Owen promised to do so he was promised a safe conduct to return to Wales. Despite this, Gloucester went after Owen on his return

---

24 PPC, vol. 5, p. 48.
25 PPC, vol. 5, p. 48.

journey. According to the original but separate document relating to *The Preceding Minute respecting Owen Tudor*:

> Furst reherse how he was send afr, at what tyme the King né my Lord of Glouceter were not lerned of this malicious purpose and ymaginacion of the which he enformed sithe.
>
> Als of if any lord or other be called to plemet bi the Kings auncle wher bi him owed to rejouse wich privilege that he shuld have fre goying and fre coming zit for manes of less wysthm than ben thes that the King is enformed as for surete of pees the moche more greter.'[26]

The document goes on to give unclear justifications for Owen's arrest by Gloucester, who was obviously not sent by the king but had the power to do so if he considered it justified. According to this account, Owen did not respect the rules imposed on him at the Privy Council meeting. On his way back to Wales, Owen was arrested, together with his priest and servant, and his possessions, worth more than £138, were taken. All three men were sent to Katherine's former royal castle at Wallingford under custody of the Earl of Suffolk, possibly a place that Owen knew well.[27] By July it was found convenient to commission them to Newgate Prison (see Appendix B).

Eventually, before 29 July 1438,[28] all three men made their escape, apparently after 'wounding fouly their gaoler'. Once again Owen and his faithful adherents were captured and recommissioned to Newgate and probably very quickly brought to Windsor Castle, where Edmund Beaufort was the newly appointed constable. He remained there until July 1439. If Owen had angered another king this might have been the end of him, but Henry VI, now an adult, showed mercy and decided that Owen should be released at a bail of £2,000 on condition that he would appear before the king on 11 November and at any other time he might be summoned.[29] On 12 November, Owen was fully pardoned for all of his offences committed and, on New Year's Day 1440, all processes against him were annulled and withdrawn, including his substantial bail, possibly as a New Year's gift from the

---

26 PPC, vol. 5, pp 49-50.
27 Griffiths, R.A., The Reign of Henry VI, p. 67, note 72.
28 Foedera vol. X p. 710.
29 CCR, Henry VI 1435-1441, pp. 284-5, 225.

king.[30] It is said that King Henry later felt sorry for the treatment his stepfather had suffered and that he blamed Gloucester for it. By 1444, Henry regarded his stepfather as 'our well beloved squire'.[31] Owen then led the life of a gentleman, kindly treated by the king, and was probably part of his stepson's household until at least the late 1450s.

In the meantime, Owen and Katherine's two older sons Edmund and Jasper had been placed in the care of the Duke of Suffolk's sister Katherine de la Pole, Abbess of Barking Abbey, where both boys would stay for roughly five years. There is no reason to think the boys were anything but well treated during their stay at the Abbey. According to John Blacman, Henry VI's biographer and chaplain (who wrote somewhere around 1485):

> [...] and like pains did he apply in the case of his half-brothers, the Lords Jasper and Edmund, in their boyhood and youth; providing for them most strict and safe guardianship, putting them under the care of virtuous and worthy priests, both for teaching and for right living and conversation, lest the untamed practices of youth should grow rank if they lacked any to prune them.[32]

As the Tudor brothers approached adolescence, the abbess took them to court to bring them to King Henry's attention. It has been said this was because no money was given to meet the boy's expenses at the abbey.

When the boys grew up Henry kept them close to him at court and, again according to Blacman, the king personally protected his half-brothers from any sexual temptation by keeping 'careful watch through hidden windows of his chamber'. On 25 August 1442, their father Owen was given lands in Surrey[33] and on four occasions in the following two years he was also given a sum of £40 from the king's own privy purse.[34] Owen was undeniably Henry's stepfather, but above and beyond that he was a true servant of the king and

---

30 CPR, Henry VI 1436-1441, p. 344. CCR, Henry VI 1435-1441, p. 285.
31 PRO, Exchequer, Warrants for Issues, 60/119.
32 *Henry the Sixth A Reprint of John Blacman's Memoir with Translation and Notes*, ed, M.R. James (Cambridge University Press 1919), pp. 30–31.
33 CPR, Henry VI 1436-1441, p. 474. CCR, Henry VI 1441-1447, p. 78.
34 PRO, Exchequer, Warrants for Issues, 59/74; 60/119; 61/26 PRO Exchequer, IssueRoll 753 (20 July)

crown. Very few accounts survive of these early years of Edmund and Jasper's life, or of their father's at this time. Owen was possibly part of the delegation that went to France in November 1444 to bring the king's bride, Margaret of Anjou, to England.[35]

England's political life had now been in chaos for at least a decade. The king was constantly struggling with the magnates and nobility whose chief priority was to enrich themselves, and this inevitably had a major impact on Henry's own finances. This in turn had an adverse effect on the quality of the governance of the realm, mainly because those who were supposed to govern on behalf of the king neglected his subjects. The perceived weakness of the king made the House of Lancaster tremendously insecure and, in 1450, after five years of marriage, Henry still lacked the promise of future stability in the form of an heir. Under these circumstances, and his only remaining close relative, his uncle Humphrey Duke of Gloucester, having died in 1447, it without doubt seemed a wise decision to elevate his half-brothers Edmund and Jasper. Partly for political reasons, and no doubt also partly out of charity and the affection Henry felt for his younger brothers, Edmund and Jasper were about to be recognized as the king's 'uterine brothers' and to be created earls, with a rank above all except dukes, granted a rich patrimony and destined to live life at the centre of English and Welsh politics during the tumultuous period of the Wars of the Roses.

35 PRO, Privy Seal Office 1/17.

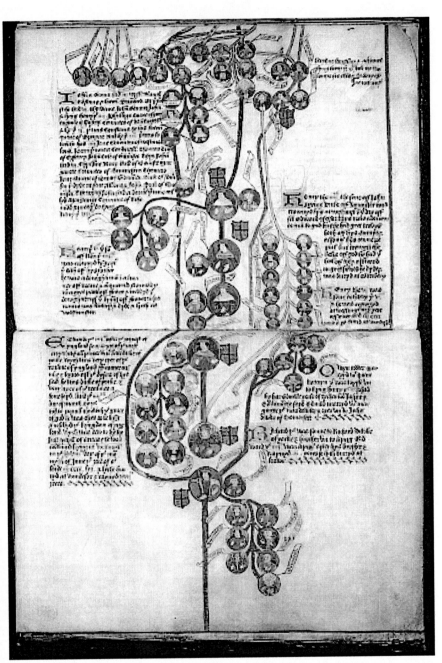

Figure 5   Diagram of the genealogy of the kings of England,
                including Henry IV, Henry V, Henry VI, Edward IV,
                Richard III, and Henry VII. Dates from the 1st half of the
                16th century. King's 395, ff. 32v-33.
                (© British Library Board)

Figure 6   Detail of the previous image, depicting Owen Tudor,
Katherine de Valois , their children Edmund and his wife
Margaret Beaufort, Jasper and the monk Edward.
(© British Library Board)

The image above reads:

> Owen Tedder married with Queen
> Katherine that was wife unto King Henry V
> and had by her Edmund the Earl of Richmond,
> Jasper, and Edward. The said Edmund married
> with Margaret that was daughter and heir unto
> John, Duke of Somerset.

3

THE KING'S 'UTERINE BROTHERS': A NEW LIFE

November 1452 – December 1453

O N 23 November 1452, Edmund and Jasper's new life officially began when they were both formally recognised as the king's half-brothers and the first step, an oral or written declaration by the king, was made in the process of their ennoblement.[1]

They were created premier earls, Edmund as Earl of Richmond and Jasper as Earl of Pembroke, and were given precedence above all noblemen below the rank of duke. These titles were significant for they were previously held by the only two of the king's uncles still alive during Henry VI's lifetime, John Duke of Bedford and, ironically, Humphrey Duke of Gloucester. By this, Edmund and Jasper became the first Welshmen elevated to the English peerage.

Then, in 1453, a year that saw many changes, the brothers were further raised from obscurity to being among the richest and most powerful men in the realm. A contemporary poem by the Welsh bard

---

1   CCR. 1427–1514, p. 122 – The Lords' Report on the dignity of a Peer, V, 293–4 – Exechequer, K.R., Memoranda Roll 231, Adhuc Communia, Recorda, Mich., M.22d. The medieval procedure of ennoblement comprised three stages: first, the King would make an oral or written declaration of the creation; the second step was the ceremony of investiture by belting with the sword of the appropriate county; and in the final stage the King would issue a charter recording and announcing the creation.

Dafydd Nanmor, who was Edmund and Jasper's dedicated eulogist, celebrates their rise (see Appendix C).

The king bestowed many generous grants on his brothers in the following seven months and they were additionally made members of the Privy Council. Edmund received the estates of the honour of Richmond, which included the manors of Frampton, Boston and Wykes, and of the sokes of Gayton, Mumby, Skirbeck and Kirton, and also the manor and lordship of Swaffham in Norfolk and some lands in Cambridgeshire. He also received, at the expense of the Duke of York, a grant in fee of the castle, lordship and manor of Hadleigh in Essex. Furthermore, the brothers were jointly granted the lordship and thirteenth-century castle of Builth in Wales, although in June that year, for reasons unknown, they surrendered Builth in Chancery and it was re-granted to Jasper alone on 27 June, together with the fee-farm of Hereford,[2] the sometime favourite residence of Edward III.

Jasper was unable to take immediate possession of the lands and estates of the lordship of Pembroke as they were in the hands of the queen, having been granted to her as part of her dowry after the death of Suffolk two years earlier. This would be settled by 6 March 1453, but in the meantime he was given £20 to support his new dignity, while the king was realising alternative sources of income for the queen. This decision to bestow Pembrokeshire's principal lordships upon Jasper gave this part of Wales stable and strong royal rule again, something that had weakened after Suffolk's death in 1450. But the king wished to elevate them in the most dignified way. In preparation the brothers were provided with a luxurious wardrobe appropriate to their newly elevated rank – velvet, cloth of gold and furs – and similarly elaborate saddles and other equestrian trappings.

After King Henry VI and Queen Margaret returned from the Christmas celebrations of 1452, which they had spent at the manor of Pleasance near Gravesend watching masquerades,[3] Edmund and Jasper were knighted at a ceremony at the Tower of London on Friday 5 January 1453, along with the brothers Thomas and John Neville, the sons of the Earl of Salisbury, Sir Roger Lewkenor, William Herbert, and Sir William Catesby of Ashby St Ledgers.[4]

---

2   CPR, Henry VI, 1452–1461, p. 50.
3   R. Somerville, *History of the duchy of Lancaster*, p. 210.
4   J.C. Wedgwood, *History of Parliament, Register of the ministers and members of both houses, 1439-1509* (London 1938), p. 163–4, 444.

The knighting of the Neville brothers may have been an attempt to retain their loyalty, given that their father, Salisbury, had just been deprived of his part of the estates belonging to the earldom of Richmond. Sources are in conflict about the exact date, but it is clear that it was either on the same day or the next (the feast of Epiphany, 6 January), and likely at Westminster, that the king, with great formality, created Edmund and Jasper earls, second stage, by belting with the sword.[5] Their elevation was given full promotion when both brothers were summoned to parliament on 20 January.[6] The final stage of the creation took place two months later, on 6 March, when parliament opened at Reading. Edmund and Jasper appeared in their new accoutrements and, in accordance with etiquette, the Commons formally presented a petition to the king, begging him to recognise Edmund and Jasper as his legitimate brothers born from the same mother, his uterine brothers. The Commons also pleaded for release of any statutory disabilities arising from the fact that their father was not English.[7] This, obviously, Henry graciously did and the king then declared them the new earls of Richmond and Pembroke.

Jasper's lands were now finally settled on him in the same way as it had happened in November to Edmund, the endowment being backdated to Michaelmas (29 September 1452). As Earl of Pembroke Jasper received generous benefactions equal to those presented to his brother, foremost among them being the castle and lordship of Pembroke, and its wind- and watermills, which had a value of £30 in 1451.[8] Also included were the lordships, towns and castles of Llansteffan, Tenby and Cilgerran, with its sub-lordships of Castlemartin, Roos, Coedraeth, Mildford, St Florence, Cemmaes, Burton, Emlyn-Is-Cach, Duffryn Bryan, Manordeifi and the forest of Cefn Drym, the lordship of Ystlwyf, Trane Clinton and St Clears in south-west Carmarthenshire.[9] Jasper also received the lordship of Aber in the Caernarvonshire commote of Arllechwedd Uchaf.[10]

When these Pembrokeshire properties had been assigned to Queen Margaret in 1447, all these lordships had a combined value of

---

5   Trinity College Dublin MS E5.10 f. 173 – *The Great Chronicles of England*, ed. A.H. Thomas and I.D. Thornley (1905), p. 163 - *Annales, or General Chronicle of England*, John Stow (1615) London, p. 392.

6   Lord's Report, IV, 932; V, 293.

7   RP, V, 250-52; Lords Report, V, 293–4.

8   RP, V, 260–61.

9   RP, 253.

10   Chancery Rolls 21/22.

£363 6s 8d a year and, when resumed by the crown in 1451, they had increased to £400 2s 8d. In short, Pembroke was the largest and most valuable of the lordships, implying Jasper had become a very wealthy and powerful man.

On 25 March 1453, Jasper was granted all manors and lordships that Sir William Oldhall, the Duke of York's chamberlain, had held before they were confiscated because of his condemnation for treason:

> Grant to Jasper de Hathfelde, arl of Pembroke, the king's uterine brother, of all manors, castles, lordships, lands, hundreds, 'wynes,' franchise, courts, markets, with knights' fees, advowsons, 'wayves,' views of frankpledge, wards, marriages, reliefs, escheats, rents, services and reversions, which William Oldehal knight, or any other to his use, had in demesne or reversion on or before the day of his outlawry for treason and felony at any other time.[11]

At nearly the same time as Edmund was appointed Master of Braydon Forest,[12] Jasper was granted, most appropriately, the former Bohun inheritance of the castle and lordship of Caldicot in Monmouthshire, which previously belonged to his mother Katherine de Valois and her first husband King Henry V. The granting of Caldicot to Jasper is a significant emotional concession and was clearly designed to demonstrate the king's acceptance of his half-brother. Other Welsh estates assigned to Jasper in tail male, on 30 March, were the manors of Cloigyn and Pibwr and the lordship of Kidwelly in the duchy of Lancaster, South Wales, lands formerly held by William Gwyn of Kidwelly before their confiscation in 1404 for his part in the Glyndwr Rebellion. On 4 April, Edmund also received the manor, castle and lordship of Ludgershall in Wiltshire and the lordship and manor of Atherston in Warwickshire,[13] and on 10 April, Jasper received the fortified manor of Frodsham in Cheshire.

The future would demonstrate that the most significant estates of Jasper as Earl of Pembroke would be the castles of Tenby and Pembroke. At first the latter was his most important military stronghold and it

---

11   CPR, Henry VI, 1452–1461, pp. 111–12.
12   CPR, Henry VI, 1452–1461, p. 60.
13   CPR, Henry VI, 1452–1461, p. 79.

was also where he created his home, making many alterations to the buildings, such as the addition of fine oriel windows to the private chambers. It is thought probable that a detached private mansion house, that formerly stood in the outer ward, and the Northern Hall were built by Jasper.[14] Nonetheless, within a few years Tenby would become his main headquarters.

In addition to the honour of Richmond, on 24 March Edmund and Jasper were jointly granted the keeping of all the possessions of the late John Beaufort, first Duke of Somerset, then in the king's hands, including the wardship and marriage of Somerset's nine-year-old daughter and heiress Margaret Beaufort.[15] When Margaret was summoned to court on 24 May, together with her mother Margaret Beauchamp, the king made her a grant of 100 marks to mark the occasion, to spend on clothes.

Moreover, in the latter part of 1443, little Margaret's father had led several military operations in France, all of which failed. Before he left for France, the duke had negotiated with Henry VI that, if he were to die, his daughter's wardship and marriage would belong solely to his wife alone. However, upon Somerset's return that winter, he was in disgrace following his blunders in France and was banished from court. Indeed he was virtually accused of treason. Shortly thereafter, on 27 May 1444, Somerset died and it has been suggested that he took his own life.[16] Soon after Somerset's death the King broke the agreement made with him concerning Margaret's wardship and marriage, instead presenting them to William de la Pole, the future Duke of Suffolk. William promptly betrothed her to his only son, John de la Pole, but at least Margaret was to remain living with her mother until both she and John de la Pole reached an appropriate age. This all changed when, on 2 May 1450, the now Duke of Suffolk, Margaret's father-in-law, who had been banished to France for five years, was brutally executed on the ship that was conveying him to Calais. By February 1453, the king had annulled Margaret's wardship and marriage to John de la Pole, the papal dispensation for which was signed on 18 August 1450, expressly so that she should be available for remarriage. This made the Lady Margaret's wardship and marriage a very desirable asset and without any doubt the king intended a

---

14 Pembroke Castle, N. Ludlow, Pembroke Castle Trust.
15 CPR, Henry VI, 1452–1461, pp. 78-9.
16 Michael K. Jones and Malcolm G. Underwood, *The King's Mother: Lady Margaret Beaufort, Countess of Richmond and Derby* (Cambridge University Press, 1993)

marriage between Margaret and one of the Tudor brothers. Since Edmund was the elder, it was he who Margaret would marry.

Margaret later told John Fisher, her chaplain and confessor, around 1494, that she was given the choice when only nine years of age whether she wished to stay married to John de la Pole or whether she desired Edmund Tudor as her husband:

> [...] as I have herde her tell many a tyme as she lay in prayer, calling upon St Nicholas, whether slepynge or wakeynge she could not assure, but about four of the clock in the mornynge, one appered unto her arrayed like a bishop, and naming unto her Edmonde, bad take hyme unto her husbande. And so by this meane she did enclyne her mynde unto Edmonde, the Kings Broder, and Erle of Rychemonde.[17]

The truth is that Margaret obviously had no say in this and that Henry VI made the decision for her, but this account can also be seen as confirmation that Margaret, either then or later in life, was content with the pronouncement. At the time she was one of the richest heiresses in England and her marriage to Edmund Tudor placed her considerable wealth in her husband's hands. Further, the lordships of Kendal in Westmorland and Wyresdal in Lancashire, which Margaret had inherited from her father at his death, became Edmund's upon their marriage.

One of the first things Jasper did in parliament was to introduce a bill in the lower house requesting the grant of the priory of St Nicholas in Pembroke, which had previously been granted to the late Duke of Gloucester. Upon this occasion the chronicler John Whethamstede referred to Jasper as: 'illustrious man, brother of the king on his mother's side, who was by the king himself raised up as the new Earl of Pembroke'.[18]

On 20 April 1453, Jasper escorted Queen Margaret when she paid a visit to Norwich. The city fathers entertained them lavishly and the earl was presented with five pounds, an amount that, compared

---

17   *The funeral sermon of Margaret, Countess of Richmond and Derby, mother of King Henry VII, and foundress of Christ's and St John's College in Cambridge, preached by Bishop Fisher in 1509*, ed. J. Hymers (Cambridge University Press for J. & J.J. Deighton, 1840), p. 58.

18   *"vir illustris frater regis ex parte matris qui de novo per ipsum regem in comitem Pembrochiae erectus"*. Wethamstede, I, 92–93.

with an annual income of roughly a thousand pounds, was a very generous gesture.[19] The benefaction did not end here – on 1 June, Jasper received, in tail male, the manors and lordships of Witley and Worplesdon in Surrey, which had a clear value of £13.[20] On 1 July 1453, Edmund and Jasper were jointly granted several estates because of their royal connections: in fee tail, the manors of Solihull and Sheldon in Warwickshire and the lordships and manor of Hyde in Hertfordshire.[21] Then three days later, on 4 July, they received the castle and lordship of Horston in Derbyshire. And, on 24 July, the manors of Mansfield and Linby in Nottinghamshire, as well as the manor of Bolsover and the office of the wapentakes of Morlesdon and Litchurch, also the lordship and splendid twelfth-century castle of Clipstone in Sherwood all in Derbyshire.[22] (Clipstone Castle, known since the eighteenth-century as King John's Palace, had long been a favourite hunting residence of the kings of England and had recently been thoroughly renovated.) Finally, bestowed upon them jointly, they received the lordship and manor of Mager in south-east Wales.[23] Jasper, like his brother, enjoyed an income of at least £925 a year.[24]

As was customary in the fifteenth-century for men of wealth and power, the new earls of Richmond and Pembroke each required an extensive household of officials to manage their finances and legal obligations and entitlements, to say nothing of actually running the great estates belonging to their earldoms. The most important part of this administrative organisation was the council that oversaw all aspects of a lord's household and estate management, and provided him with expertise and advice on different facets. Despite the importance of these councils, very little is known about them and Richmond and Pembroke's are no exception. What is known about Jasper's household council are the names of some individual members: Sir Henry Wogan, Geoffrey Pole, William Herbert, Thomas Vaughan, Walter Gorfen and John Rogger, who was receiver-general to both brothers.[25] Although the administrative workload was extremely extensive and varied, it would appear that both brothers had the

---

19   *The Paston Letters*, I, 253–4.
20   CPR, Henry VI, 1452–1461, p. 80.
21   CPR, Henry VI, 1452–1461, p. 116.
22   CPR, Henry VI, 1452–1461, p. 104. CFR, 1445–1552, pp. 239–40.
23   CPR, Henry VI, 1452–1461, p. 104.
24   Thomas.
25   Duchy of Lanc., Min, Acc. 651/10534 m.3.

benefit of a large and efficient team for the smooth running of their estates.

This glorious state of affairs would not last long. On 15 August 1453, the king had complained about not feeling well and by the end of the year this malaise developed into a mental illness that would last until Christmas Day of the following year. The king became totally unaware of the world around him and nothing appeared to change this, not even the birth of his long-awaited son, Prince Edward of Lancaster, on 13 October 1453 at the Palace of Westminster. During this uncertain time the Duke of York became protector of the realm and this would eventually lead to the first serious clashes between the houses of Lancaster and York. Within a short period, Edmund and Jasper would find themselves in a dangerous and critical situation.

Figure 7   Tower of London where Edmund and Jasper Tudor
were knighted.
(© 2013 Tim Ridgway)

Figure 8   Llansteffan Castle.
                (© 2015 Debra Bayani)

Figure 9   Pembroke Castle.
                (© 2015 Debra Bayani)

Figure 10   Cilgerran Castle.
            (© 2015 Debra Bayani)

4

'NOW UP, NOW DOWN, LIKE BUCKET IN A WELL'[1]

January 1454 – January 1457

A S SOON as it became clear that the king's mental illness was something that would not pass in the near future, Richard, Duke of York, seized his opportunity. It had been the queen and Somerset who had thwarted the duke for many years, and since the prospects of York's attempt to bring some stability to the government appealed to many, he gained a great deal of support, including that of the king's half-brothers, the Earls of Richmond and Pembroke. French-born consort Queen Margaret had every reason to be concerned about the king's condition and the threat that this might cause to Somerset, herself and the infant Prince Edward, on whom the future of the dynasty rested. Perhaps because of her familiarity with the habit of French royal women assuming power in default of the males of the family, Margaret decided, in mid-February, to lay claim to the regency of the realm herself.[2] The weeks that followed were extremely tense. The queen had her supporters but so too did York, and members of the royal household clearly feared for the safety of the king and prince, for they assembled a garrison at Windsor for their protection. There were also rumours that Somerset's supporters were seeking to release

---

1   Geoffrey Chaucer, 'The Knight's Tale', line 675.
2   Bagley, pp. 24–9 – J. Gairdner (ed.), *The Paston Letters*, Vol. 2, p. 297.

him from the Tower.

Towards the end of January 1454, Jasper and Edmund, together with Richard Neville, the Earl of Warwick, accompanied the Duke of York to London, each of them with a 'goodly fellowship'. At this point the realm divided into two factions and it is clear that both sides were preparing for conflict and were gathering resources for war. On one hand was the queen, whose supporters included the Dukes of Somerset and Buckingham, the Earl of Wiltshire, the Lords Egremont, Beaumont, Clifford, Bonville and Poynings, and also the Archbishop of Canterbury, John Kemp, who ordered his retainers to be equipped with bows and arrows and all other weapons for warfare. On the other hand were ranged the Duke of York and his son the Earl of March, the Earl of Warwick, Edmund and Jasper Tudor, and York's brother in-law the Earl of Salisbury. According to Geoffrey Pole, one of Jasper's councillors and also one of the king's servants, Edmund and Jasper were likely to be arrested on charges of treason at their arrival in London.[3] They were expected in the capital on 25 January.[4]

There is no surviving account of what happened when York and his men reached London, or even if they actually did so. According to Benet's Chronicle, York and some of his followers mentioned above, but not Edmund and Jasper, arrived a week later on 2 February. In any case, parliament assembled on 9 February at Westminster when it was decided that York should be nominated as the king's lieutenant to open the formal session on 14 February, and the Duke of Buckingham be appointed to the position of Steward of England.[5] Parliament was still divided between the queen and York, but at least Prince Edward's position was secure, for on 15 March he was created Prince of Wales and Earl of Chester.[6]

On 27 March, Edmund and Jasper and the other peers of the Privy Council agreed that the Duke of York should be lord protector while the king was ill. The death on 22 March of chancellor and Archbishop of Canterbury Cardinal John Kemp, who had been seen as a non-partisan man of wisdom, did not make the situation of the government any easier. The next day, 23 March, a number of the

3   John Stodely agent of the Duke of Norfolk, to his master, 19 January 1454,
     in J Gairdner (ed.), *The Paston Letters*, , Vol. 1, 263.
4   *The Paston Letters*, Vol. I, 266, 19 January 1454.
5   Benet's Chronicle for the years 1400 to 1462, p. 211, ed. G.L. and M.A. Harriss,
     Camden Miscellany, Vol. XXXIV (1972)
6   RP, Vol. 5, p. 249.

Lords of Parliament visited the king at Windsor to seek his opinion as to whether there should be a regent appointed, and if so whom. They were attended by the king's confessor, Reginald Boulers, some of the king's councillors, and the Earl of Warwick and some of the Nevilles.[7] Their visit was largely unproductive and all that could be reported to the Lords on 25 March was that the king showed no sign of recognition or understanding. The possibility of a regency was clearly out of the question and there was no other alternative than to appoint a defender and protector of the realm. Since York was not the king's acknowledged heir (which Gloucester and Bedford had been in 1422), he was careful not to seem too eager when the role of protector was offered to him the next day. Rather, York gave the appearance of being unwillingly and modestly dragged to the king's seat, insisting that the lords take full accountability for his election.[8] York's protectorship was confirmed formally by patent on 3 April 1454, when it was stated that his office of protector would be discontinued when the king's son became of age.[9] The duke made an attempt to bring some stability to the government. Because of the Neville–Percy feud, both Edmund and Jasper were summoned by 29 May to attend a great council meeting which was scheduled for the end of July.

On 15 October, Jasper's receiver general, John Rogger, attested that the original grant, which contained the Norfolk estates previously belonging to York's chamberlain William Oldhall, and given to Jasper a year earlier, was now invalid and these lands were legally required to be returned to Oldhall, as his felonies committed against the crown were annulled by his master the Duke of York. At this point York enjoyed unprecedented authority, and it would have been easy for him to restore these estates to his chamberlain. However, he chose not to. York recognised that his alliance with Jasper was more valuable and the political price of restoring Oldhall would have been too high. Jasper received a confirmation of the original grant.

Four days later, on 19 October, Jasper was granted, for five years, the income from the manors of Kingsthorp in Northamptonshire and Pollestedhall in Norfolk. This despite the manor of Pollestedhall having been let on a ten-year lease, on 30 July 1451, to one Robert Fouleman. Robert Fouleman later claimed that, on 25 September 1451, six local men had occupied on the property and were still

---

7   RP, pp. 240–2.
8   RP, pp. 242–4.
9   RP, p. 243 – Gairdner (ed.), The *Paston Letters*, Vol. 1, p. 146.

squatting on it at Michaelmas 1459.[10] So Jasper probably never earned a penny from these manors. On 13 November both brothers attended the meeting of the great council to discuss the reform of the royal household, Edmund as lord attendant.[11] The lords agreed that the royal household was too large and all expenses needed to be reduced. From now on both Jasper and Edmund were each to have only one chaplain, two esquires, two yeomen and two chamberlains. By the end of 1458, the king finally recovered, after eighteen months of sickness, and was again aware of what went on around him. York's protectorship was no longer necessary, so he was discharged of his duty and most of the magnates that he had appointed were replaced by Queen Margaret's favourites over the following months.

At the great council meeting of 5 February 1455, nearly all the twenty-seven peers who attended accepted that Edmund Beaufort, Duke of Somerset, should be released on bail after only fourteen months of imprisonment in the Tower of London. All the great peers present turned their backs on York, except for a few whose allegiance is uncertain. What is certain is that Jasper and Edmund did not attend this meeting, and that the king recovered and the queen and her supporters gained even more strength. Moreover, Somerset received at Greenwich on 4 March a declaration of his innocence of all criminal charges against him and York was discharged from his command of Calais in favour of Somerset. Also, York's worst enemy, the youthful Henry Holland, Duke of Exeter, was released from prison at Pontefract Castle[12] and Salisbury resigned the great seal to King Henry, only to be replaced as treasurer by York's enemy the Earl of Wiltshire on 15 March.

Clearly, York feared a reaction from the king's favourites, and even more so because he felt betrayed by the majority of the peers who had switched their support. Together with Warwick, Salisbury and Lord Cobham, York withdrew from London and went north to raise forces. Different accounts report that York expected to be punished and that he, Warwick and Salisbury feared for their lives.[13] Jasper and Edmund were facing a huge dilemma. On one hand was their generous half-brother the king, who was too weak and ill to rule

---

10   CFR, Henry VI 1452–1461, p. 113, ibid., 1445–1452 p. 213.
11   Proceedings, VI, 222.
12   CCR, Henry VI, vol. 6: 1454–1461.
13   RP, Vol. 5, p. 280, ed. J. Strachey, (1783) – J. Gairdner (ed.), *The Paston Letters* (1904), Vol. 2, p. 297.

the kingdom, and on the other the Duke of York, who offered fresh possibilities and a more effective ruling government. While York and his Neville allies were in the North, Somerset used the opportunity to take measures himself. The next step was to summon a great council meeting at Leicester which, if successful, probably would put paid to York's ambitions. By spring, York and his military adherents were slowly marching south with the intention of compelling the Council to banish Somerset. By 18 May, Somerset knew trouble was close at hand and, as York advanced yet farther south, the king's government realised that York's intentions were to prevent the king from gaining Leicester. The royal party immediately prepared themselves to meet York.

By 20 May, York had reached Royston, sending letters to the chancellor reassuring his loyalty. Edmund Beaufort, Duke of Somerset; Humphrey Stafford, Duke of Buckingham; Humphrey Stafford, Earl of Stafford (the latter's son); James Butler, Earl of Ormond (future Earl of Wiltshire); Henry Percy, Earl of Northumberland; and Thomas, Lord Clifford, left Westminster on the same day. Letters written by York in the next two days to affirm his loyalty are said to have been concealed from the king by Somerset or Buckingham.

On Wednesday 21 May, the king, accompanied by Jasper; Henry Beaufort, Marquess and Earl of Dorset; Ralph Butler, Lord Sudeley; and Lord Roos,[14] and their combined entourage of knights, gentlemen, squires and yeomen (in total around 2,000 men) left London to proceed to St Albans. Edmund was absent during the subsequent months owing to his activities in West Wales. The royal party halted at Watford for the night, while York and the Nevilles were approximately fifteen miles west of St Albans around Ware and arrived at St Albans during the evening or night of the 21st. The king left Watford the next morning, 22 May, intending, according to York's biographer P. A. Johnson, to dine at St Albans with the hope of reaching Dunstable that early evening. Johnson states that only at this point did it appear that York might attack the royal party.[15] The king's reaction was to dismiss Somerset as constable and to appoint Buckingham instead. While this was a most undesirable new development for Somerset, Buckingham chose to move on to St Albans for negotiations. According to a fifteenth-century statement, 'King

14   The Fastolf Relation, College of Arms, Arundel MS 48, folio 342.
15   P.A. Johnson, *Duke Richard of York 1411–1460* (1988), p. 156.

Harry was in harnys owne propyr person',[16] which gives credence to
the theory that the royal party was prepared for a fight, although the
nature of the wounds known to have been sustained by the king's men
suggests that he was not well-equipped with archers and that most
defenders were not wearing full armour.

On arrival at St Albans, between 9am and 10am, the dukes of
York and Buckingham immediately entered into serious negotiations,
sending messengers back and forth. However, while detailed
negotiations were developing into a standoff, one of Warwick's
soldiers, possibly on the earl's orders, broke through the barricades
and battle commenced:[17]

> Therle of Warrewik knowing therof toke
> and gadererd his meyne togeder with hym and
> brake inne by the gardyne side into the seid
> towne betweene the Signe and the Keye and
> the Chequer in Halywell Strete. And anoone as
> they were withinne the seid town they blewe up
> trumpettes and cryed with abigge voyse 'Awarwik
> Awarwik', that mervaile it was to here. And until
> tha tyme the forseid duc of Yorke might never
> have entred into the towne. And thane with
> stronge hande they brake up the barreres and
> mightily faughte.[18]

According to the Phillips Relation, there is no doubt which
soldier led the first strike against the royal household:

> [...] Sir Robert Ocle [Ogle] tok 600 men
> of the marchis and tok the Marketplace or ony
> man was war; than the larum belle was ronge,
> and every man yed to harneys, for at the tyme
> every man was out of ther array, and they joynid
> batayle anon; and it was done with inne half
> houre.[19]

The royal party was suddenly drawn into the fighting and the
fact that both sides were now crammed together in a confined space

---

16   J. Gairdner (ed.), *Gregory's Chronicle, The Historical Collections of a Citizen of London*
     (1876), p. 198.
17   The Great Chronicle of London, ed. A.H. Thomas and I.D. Thornley (1983) p. 187.
18   Phillips Relation in J. Gairdner (ed.), The Paston Letters, Vol. 3 (1904), p. 30.
19   The Paston Letters, Vol. 3 (1904), p. 30.

would have increased the confusion. Battle was joined in the very heart of St Albans and within minutes the marketplace filled with 5,000 fighting men. Several of the royal household, who were trying to protect the king by closing ranks around him, were instantly killed or wounded by Yorkist archers, and King Henry himself was wounded, probably only slightly, in the shoulder or neck by an arrow.[20] The first of the king's household to bear the royal banner was Lord Sudeley, who was hit in the face by an arrow. Subsequently, both James Butler, Earl of Ormond, and Sir Philip Wentworth probably made an effort to recover the fallen banner, but later both were charged with casting it down and fleeing. Although the men of the king's household fought bravely, it was clear that all was lost. Many contemporary chroniclers and sources who seem to have had local eyewitness knowledge give similar accounts: firstly describing the shock of a sudden attack by one of Warwick's men; secondly, the masses of men who suddenly filled the area; and thirdly that the king and his men, unexpectedly drawn into the fight, were completely overwhelmed, having had no time to put on their armour and helmets before battle commenced.

It is likely is that Jasper was one of the noblemen who stood close by the king. However, it is not known what his movements were since his name is not mentioned except to record his presence.[21]

Eventually, many of the king's men were killed and others fled or were driven away, leaving Henry unprotected. According to the most reliable report, from the Dijon Relations:

> At last when they had fought for the space of three hours the king's party seeing themselves to have the worst of it broke on one wing and began to flee and the Duke of Somerset retreated within an inn to save himself and hid. Which things seen by those of the said Duke of York, incontinent beset the said house all about. And there the Duke of York gave orders that the king should be taken and drawn out of the throng and put in the abbey in safety and thus it was done. And in this abbey took refuge also with him the Duke of Buckingham who was very badly

20 The Dijon Relation, Archives de la Cote d'Or, Dijon, B. 11942, no.258. Cited in C.A.J. Armstrong, 'Politics and the Battle of St. Albans, 1455', Bulletin of the Institute of Historical Research, vol. 33, no. 87.

21 The Paston Letters, I. 327.

wounded by three arrows. And incontinent this
done began to fight Somerset and his men who
were in the place within the inn and defended
themselves valiantly. And in the end after the
doors were broken down the Duke of Somerset
seeing that he had no other remedie took council
with his men about coming out and did so, as a
result of which incontinent he and all his people
were surrounded by the Duke of York's men. And
after some were stricken down and the Duke of
Somerset had killed four of them with his own
hand, it is said, he was felled to the ground with
an axe and incontinent being so wounded in
several places that there he ended his life.[22]

York's goal was accomplished. With Somerset's death the first
battle of St Albans was over. York immediately returned to the king,
kneeled before him and asked pardon for himself and his followers.
He had never, he said, had any intention of hurting His Majesty but
only of having Somerset.[23]

Many among the casualties that were killed by the Nevilles were
Percy men, including the 2nd Earl of Northumberland himself. It
seems that York had had no control over his Neville allies, especially at
the beginning of the battle. Only the Nevilles would find satisfaction
in the deaths of Lord Clifford (whose mother was a Percy) and Henry
Percy, Earl of Northumberland. Among the wounded was Somerset's
son Dorset, who had to be carried home in a cart. Also badly injured
was Sir John Wenlock, as were the Duke of Buckingham, who had
been wounded in the face by three arrows, and his son the Earl of
Stafford, injured in the right hand.[24] According to most reports,
around 100 to 200 gentlemen and commoners lost their lives in
the battle, more than forty of them being buried in the abbey or in
St Peter's churchyard. But an unknown number of casualties must
also have died afterwards from wounds inflicted during the fighting.

---

22 Armstrong, 'Politics and the Battle of St Albans, 1455', p. 64.
23 A.B. Hinds (ed.), Calendar of State Papers and Manuscripts existing in the Archives and
    Collections of Milan, Vol. I (1912), p. 17.
24 Stow Relations, in J. Gairdner (ed.), The Paston Letters, Vol. 3 (1904), p. 28.

The first battle of St Albans sealed the fate of the kingdom.[25] The bloodshed on 22 May 1455 signalled the beginning of what would become known as the 'Wars of the Roses'.

Escorted by the victors, the king returned to London the next day, 23 May, with York on his right, Salisbury on his left and preceded by Warwick bearing the Sword of State, to the Palace of Westminster. Settled again in London, the king seemed strong enough to call for a new parliament meeting on 26 May, but after this he appeared to slip slowly back into a depression. For some weeks he travelled from place to place and then required at least two weeks of medical treatment. York was again in the ascendant and was able to take a firm grasp of the government, first creating himself Constable of England and then providing his Neville supporters with great positions and appointing Warwick captain of the Calais garrison, though very few other nobles were rewarded for their service. In order to restore normal political life, York found himself forced to forgive Buckingham, Sir John Wenlock and even Somerset's son the Earl of Dorset for their part in the battle, and they were released from prison. The government was now in York's hands.

The battle of St Albans was Jasper's first taste of warfare and it must have been shocking to him, or at least confusing. While no account suggests that Jasper played any role during the fight, we know that he stood behind his brother the king. However, Jasper's associations with the Duke of York did not end because of the battle of St Albans.

Jasper and Edmund, like the Duke of Buckingham and the 2nd Earl of Shrewsbury, took a middle path between the partisans of the two opposing wings in English politics. Nonetheless, there is no evidence of any close political association between the Tudor brothers and the duke and earl, and no middle party was formed.

On 2 June, the Duke of York assumed the offices, to be held for life, of constable of the castles of Aberystwyth, Carreg Cennen and Carmarthen – ironically possessions formerly held by Somerset. At this time Jasper was still in London and, on 4 June, together with York, Warwick, Bourchier and Fauconberg, he attended a council meeting at St Paul's. Two days later, on 6 June, Buckingham and Shrewsbury, who at first had, like Jasper, taken the middle path, now renewed their associations with York at another council meeting. But Jasper and

25 W. Stubbs, *The Constitutional History of England*, Vol. 3 (1903), p. 176.

Edmund did not. On 9 July, parliament opened at Westminster in the presence of the king. This session was primarily used by York to prove his loyalty to the king once again and the king's speech described how Somerset had used the king's power to extend his feud with York by concealing two letters written by York prior to the battle. Somerset was castigated as a traitor for deliberately misinforming the king by hiding these letters. Parliament then took steps to secure the king's half-brothers' allegiance by safeguarding the estates of Richmond and Pembroke, as they were both extremely valuable, for both the king and the Duke of York.

Edmund was still absent from court on 23 July, when Jasper took the oath of allegiance to King Henry in Westminster's great council chamber. In the presence of the king each of the thirty-three lords spiritual and twenty-seven lords temporal laid his hand upon his breast and, with the other hand taking the king's, swore:

> I promise unto your Highness by the faith and truth that I owe to God, and to you, that I truly and faithfully keep the alliance that I owe unto you my most Sovereign Lord, and to put me in my devoir to do all that that may be to the welfare, honour and safeguard of your most noble person, and royal estate, pre-eminence and prerogative: And I shall at no time will or consent to anything which might be or sound to the hurt or prejudice of your said most noble Person, Dignity, Crown or Estate. And over that, I shall with all my power, resist and withstand all them that wold in any wise presume to attempt the contrary. So God me help and his Saints.[26]

York's need to heal the wounds of St Albans was great and therefore parliamentary proceedings closed on 31 July with a declaration of a general pardon to Egremont and Exeter.

It is difficult to determine whether it was during York's protectorate or whether it was by the queen that the decision was made to send Edmund to Wales. His first presence in Wales is recorded in September 1455, but it is very likely that he was there earlier and this explains his absence from earlier events. Certainly, there could have been no more appropriate choice than a Tudor for a mission to this

---

26   RP, p. 282, Henry VI 1455.

part of the country. Edmund's Welsh bloodline would appeal directly to the hearts of the people of Wales. Edmund never really participated in English politics. Despite being summoned to all meetings of the great council, his attendance is only recorded that once in 1454. In this period Edmund had other matters to occupy him and his presence was very much needed in Wales. That September he resided at the palace of Bishop John de la Bere of St David's at Lamphey, which became one of his favourite lodgings while at work in the South.

His marriage with the by now eleven-year-old Beaufort heiress, Margaret, daughter of the late John Beaufort, 1st Duke of Somerset, and Margaret Beauchamp, took place on 1 November at the bride's birthplace, Bletsoe Castle.

After the wedding, late in 1455, Edmund returned to south-west Wales on the orders of the Duke of York, who had become Lord-Protector once more on 19 November. Both Jasper and Edmund were absent from the parliamentary session between 12 November and 13 December.[27] Edmund was sent for the express purpose of taking a firm grasp of the chaos that was then prevalent there under the lax control of the local rulers. His first confrontation seems to have been with Gruffydd ap Nicholas and his family. Attempts had been made since October 1452 to collect debts owed by Gruffydd and in March 1453 he was forced to surrender himself to the new Earl of Pembroke, Jasper, although Gruffydd was forced to answer to Edmund, as the older brother who was assigned to take control of that area. Attempts had been made since October 1452 to collect debts owed by Gruffydd and in March 1453 he was forced to surrender himself to the new Earl of Pembroke, Jasper. Further efforts were made to curtail Gruffydd's lawlessness and abuse of authority. In May 1454, the king's council, led by the Duke of York, ordered James, Lord Audley, the Bishop of St David's (John de la Bere, who was also the king's chaplain) and John, Lord Beauchamp of Powick, to deprive Gruffydd and his sons of all the offices granted to them. Gruffydd totally ignored all the complaints made and challenged all efforts to reduce his authority. By 30 November, Edmund was still in residence at the tranquil and faraway Lamphey Bishop's Palace, which lay close to Jasper's Pembroke Castle.

---

27 PPC, Henry VI, 279–81.

With the king in better health in February 1456, the queen dismissed York from his short protectorship before 25 February.[28] York's ally Bourchier was replaced as chancellor and treasurer by the Earl of Shrewsbury and Bishop Waynftet of Winchester, and the queen's chancellor Lawrence Booth became keeper of the privy seal. Once again the Yorkist lords were left empty-handed and out in the cold.

On 8 March, Edmund was still lodged at the palace of Lamphey, signing warrants there. He must, however, have interrupted his work to meet his young wife for, in early spring, Edmund made Margaret pregnant – according to tradition, whilst they were staying at Jasper's castle of Caldicot in the Welsh Marches. The newly-weds did not have much time together, for Edmund shortly afterwards returned to his other duties in south-west Wales. There he again encountered Gruffydd ap Nicholas, who was somewhat displeased by Edmund's arrival and clearly considered him as his rival. Whilst Jasper stayed with the king at the royal manor house of Sheen, John Bocking, being at Horsley Down near Guildford, reported, in a letter of 7 June 1456, to John Paston at Norwich 1456 that whilst:

> '[...] th'Erle of Pembroke is with the Kyng an
> noo moo lordis, thÉrl of Richemond and Griffith
> Such ar at were gretely in Wales'.[29]

This skirmish, news of which resounded all the way to Surrey, probably took place in or around Pembrokeshire. Gruffydd and his sons had taken control of the castles of Carreg Cennen, Carmarthen, Aberystwyth and Kidwelly, and by August a victorious Edmund repossessed Carmarthen Castle. Finally, Gruffydd and his sons Thomas and Owen acknowledged Edmund as overlord of the area, and from that time their loyalty to the cause of the Tudor brothers was ensured. Gruffydd and his sons were pardoned by the queen on 26 October that year.[30]

By 15 November, the queen had taken over the government and Jasper and Thomas ap Robert Vaughan of Monmouth, one of his counsellors and future adherent, were jointly granted a house in

28 Huntingdon Herald (Bib. Nat. MS Fr. 18441), fo. 112.
29 N. Davis (ed.), *Paston Letters and Papers of the Fifteenth Century*, Vol. 2, Oxford 1976, p. 148.
30 CPR, Henry VI 1446–1452, p. 326.

Stepney near to London.[31] Besides their main estates, most noblemen in these times had their own residence in town, which they could use when, for instance, attending council meetings and, in Jasper's case, this might have ended the necessity of meeting in inns like the King's Head in Cheapside.[32] While Jasper and Thomas Vaughan together acquired 'le Garlek House' at Brook Street in Stepney[33] (this street covered the far eastern part of Cable Street, approximately from where The Stepney Causeway joins Cable Street today, leading to the southern side of White Horse Road),[34] Edmund was given the fortified town-house of Baynards Castle, 'with all appurtenant gardens and houses', alongside the Thames.[35] Originally a Norman castle but rebuilt several times after destructive fires, including in 1428 when it was the residence of Humphrey, Duke of Gloucester,[36] after Humphrey's death in 1447 Baynards passed to the crown and was granted to Richard, Duke of York. Here was another instance of York losing one of his possessions to the king's brothers, although this does not seem to have decreased their mutual respect and sympathy for each other. This was not the case with relations between York and others – for example, Edmund Beaufort, Duke of Somerset – who had similarly gained possessions and land at York's expense.

As soon as York was once more deprived of the protectorship, matters slowly began to unravel dangerously for Edmund. The Duke of York's prominent retainers in eastern Wales decided to reassert their master's rights over those castles of which he had formerly been constable and, most importantly, to re-establish his authority. Attempts made to discipline Gruffydd ap Nicholas during York's brief protectorate had failed, and when Edmund succeeded in this just four months after York had lost his protectorship for a second time, it caused the duke great embarrassment. The raison d'être of the whole campaign centred on the demoted protector's determination to assert his control over the government by taking action as the legitimate constable of the castles and neutralising potentially dangerous rivals in the region. York's motives for his subsequent actions can only be ascribed to jealousy. By April 1546, York's supporters - Sir Walter

---

31   CPR, Henry VI 1452-1461, p. 359.

32   CPR, Henry VI 1446-1452, p. 51.

33   *DOWB*, p. 1008 – CPR, Henry VI 1452–1461, p. 359.

34   According to City of London Corporation.

35   CPR, Henry VI 1452–1461, p. 79.

36   John Stow, *A survey of London by John Stow* (1598), ed. William J. Thoms, Whittaker & Co. (London 1842)

Devereux and his son-in-law Sir William Herbert - decided to make their move. Having gathered a force of about 2,000 men from around Herefordshire and neighbouring Welsh lordships, they seized the Mayor of Hereford and Herbert attacked the Earl of Wiltshire's property at Orcop. Local skirmishes escalated in June when an attempt was made for an assault on Kenilworth, with the avowed intention of killing the King.

From there William Herbert, Walter Devereux and members of the Vaughan clan joined forces and, turning their focus on asserting York's authority, slowly advanced into West Wales towards Carmarthen Castle, so recently taken by Edmund. They immediately seized the castle and took Edmund prisoner. From there they went on to Glamorgan and Llandaff and, by 25 October, took Aberystwyth Castle as well. Carmarthen Castle was technically still under York's jurisdiction and therefore his authority in West Wales as constable of these castles was re-established. It is not really clear why Herbert switched his allegiance from Edmund and Jasper after York lost his protectorship, for there is reason to believe an early friendship existed between the Herberts and Tudors. For example, on 1 October 1453, Earl Edmund granted Herbert an annuity of £10 per year for life and this gesture was certainly made out of friendship since Herbert held no offices for the earl.[37] In fact, Herbert seems to be one of only two men ever to receive an annuity from either of the Tudor brothers with no office attached. These grants refer, as was usual, to the good services that these men had performed and would do in the future, without placing any obligation on them. Perhaps resentment and jealousy brought about the change. Nonetheless, a contemporary poem testifies to friendship in earlier times:

> [...] He [William] saved the life
> of Matthew Gough for evermore;
> the two of them there [in France] did not withdraw
> from giving battle to men of yore.
> Roland would go to the front line
> with another for St Charlemagne;
> so too would William
> seek the hardest part of the battle.

---

37 CPR, Henry VI 1446-1452, p. 627, (ratified in October 1460); and CPR, Henry VI (1452-1461), P. 215.

> If Jasper was being pounded,
> he'd [= William] pound through a thousand men.
> The nobleman's full of sincerity
> (that will serve him well);
> Gwilym [= William] is true and skilled
> for one God before everything else,
> also for the Crown, kindly eagle,
> and above for the earl of Pembroke and his men.[38]

In the meantime it seems that York requested King James II of Scotland to support his claim to the throne.

Unfortunately, Edmund would not be able to demonstrate further his prowess in Wales, for he died at Carmarthen just two days after his first wedding anniversary, on 3 November 1456. The plague is one suggested possible cause of death. Another possibility, perhaps more likely although there is no specific proof, is that Edmund's sudden death – clearly a great shock to everyone – following so soon after the events of that summer, might have resulted from violence or neglect during his imprisonment, or perhaps from wounds suffered in opposing the force led by agents of the Duke of York.

Attempts to condemn the Devereux-Herbert upheavals were made on 15 February 1457 at a great council, which opened at Coventry and closed some time before 14 March. Devereux was imprisoned until February 1458 while York received a token gesture of reconciliation – on 6 March 1457, he was reappointed as lieutenant of Ireland with effect from 8 December.[39] Unfortunately, there are no surviving contemporary accounts of this council so we have no insight as to what truly happened when Edmund was seized at Carmarthen Castle. But there are reasons to think that the plague was not the cause of death. Even though indictments made of the Herbert and Devereux circle make no direct accusations of York, Herbert and Devereux were called to appear before the oyer and terminer sitting at Hereford from 2 to 7 April and legal proceedings were started against them. But, in the end, it is difficult to see why King Henry responded to these men as he did and to what purpose. It can also be seen in another perspective - that the queen cleverly separated York's English supporters from his Welsh followers by pardoning the latter

---

38 'In praise of William Herbert' (composed in November/December 1452), in
     D. Johnston (ed.), *Gwaith Lewys Glyn Cothi* (Caerdydd, 1995), poem 16, lines 27–42.
39 CPR, Henry VI 1452-1461, p. 341.

(for example, the Vaughans and Herberts) and punishing the English (Devereux, James Baskerville and others).

Something that needs to be clarified is that Herbert was very ambitious and over the years managed to make profits from both parties. Moreover, unlike most nobles, he was able to convince Queen Margaret of his loyalty without forfeiting his ties with York and Warwick. Herbert and his followers received a general pardon on the following 22 May [40] and 7 June [41] 'by reason of a treason adjudged against him in the sessions of oyer and terminer held last at Hereford'. On the same day a large group of men from Hereford, the Marches and Wales also received a general pardon for all offences and penalties committed.[42]

Interestingly, a document of 15 April declares that 'Edmund, late earl of Richmond, was seized during his marriage with Margaret, daughter and heir of John, late Duke of Somerset [...]'[43] This wording also suggests that it was the fact that he was seized that was the cause of Edmund's death, for if this was not the case it could simply have been written that 'he died during his marriage with Margaret'. Another piece of evidence that may testify that Edmund's death was caused by violence is the elegy for Edmund written by the bard Dafydd Nanmor in or after 1461, in which he mentions foul play or at least that Edmund's enemies were happy about his death (see Appendix D).

To so many people Edmund's death came as a big shock. Several Welsh bards, who expressed their emotions and lamented his death through their poetry, transferred their hopes and faith into Jasper and the young Henry. For example, Lewis Glyn Cothi (see Appendix E).

Edmund was buried at the Grey Friars at Carmarthen, just before the main altar. His tomb was removed to St David's Cathedral after the dissolution of the monasteries in 1536, where it can still be seen today. His brass image is visible on top of the tomb and the whole is surrounded by twelve shields with coats of arms connected to Edmund. His own – the Royal Arms (France modern & England quarterly) in a border of blue with golden doves and Fleur-de-Lis, which was given to him by his half-brother Henry VI – is at the south-

---

40 CPR, Henry VI 1452-1461, p. 353.
41 CPR, Henry VI 1452-1461, p. 360.
42 CPR, Henry VI 1452-1461, p. 367.
43 CPR, Henry VI 1452-1461, p. 368.

east corner. At the south-west corner of the tomb is the coat of arms of his father Owen – a silver chevron between three silver helmets on a red field. At the north-west corner the shield of Owen and Katherine de Valois combined – dexter, the chevron and helmets and sinister, three golden Fleur-de-Lis on a blue field. And at the north east corner the combined shields of Edmund and his wife Margaret Beaufort. On the west side of the tomb are the arms of Edmund and on the east side Margaret's. Along the north side are three shields. In the centre is that of John of Gaunt, Duke of Lancaster, on the right his son John Beaufort's arms and on the left the shield of Somerset and Beauchamp, Margaret's parents. On the south side of the tomb are three other shields. In the centre the combined arms of Henry V and Katherine de Valois, on the right France and England and on the left France alone. Finally, in the centre of the west side are the combined arms of Henry VII and Elizabeth of York, sinister, and the shield of the Prince of Wales, standing for the son of Henry VII.[44]

After Edmund's death the income from his property was valued at £600 a year. As he left behind a very young wife who was six months pregnant, all of the earl's properties were transferred to the crown and by 15 April 1457, Lady Margaret retained a reasonable dower of £200 a year.[45] Following his brother's death, Jasper left court and did what duty required of him - to fill Edmund's place in Wales where he could count on much support. There he set about making his earldom a secure base for himself as well as for the house of Lancaster. On a personal level, Jasper extended his care to his vulnerable young sister-in-law, having her to stay with him at Pembroke Castle, both for her own safety and for that of her unborn baby.

44   E. Allen, 'The Tomb of the Earl of Richmond in St David's Cathedral', *Archaeologia Cambrensis*, vol. 13, 5th series (1896), pp. 315–20.
45   CPR, Henry VI 1452–1461, p. 368 – CFR Henry VI 1452–1461, p. 182–3.

Figure 11   Lamphey Bishop's Palace.
                 (© 2015 Debra Bayani)

Figure 12   Tomb of Edmund Tudor in St. David's Cathedral.
                 (© 2015 Debra Bayani)

Figure 13   Detail of the brass image of Edmund Tudor from his tomb
in St. David's Cathedral.
(© 2015 Debra Bayani)

Figure 14   St. David's Cathedral.
                 (© 2015 Debra Bayani)

5
THE LULL BEFORE THE STORM
January 1457 – September 1459

O N A cold winter day early in 1457, thirteen-year-old Margaret underwent a long and exhausting labour. Even by the standards of the time her age was considered as very young, and her youth and small size gave rise to serious doubts as to whether she and her baby would survive their ordeal. It is believed that the childbirth itself did sufficient damage to Margaret to make her unable to bear any more children, and this was commonly attributed to her young age at the time. Eventually, she gave birth to a healthy but, according to Henry's contemporary biographer Bernard Andre, delicate boy. The longed-for son of the deceased Edmund and recently widowed Margaret was born at Pembroke Castle on 28 January 1457 and named Henry, after his uncle the king. Poet and antiquarian John Leland, who has been described as the father of English local history and bibliography, wrote:

> In the outerward I saw the chamber where
> King Henry VII was born in knowledge wherof
> a chimmeney is new made with the arms and
> badges of King Henry.[1]

---

1   *The Itinerary of John Leland*, ed. L. Toulmin Smith, Series 5, vol. 3,
     (London, 1964), p. 116.

The so-called Henry VII Tower at Pembroke Castle is commonly said to be the room where Henry Tudor was born, for there were traces of the coat of arms on the wall above the fireplace. Perhaps it was Margaret's sudden widowhood at six months pregnant and fear of losing her baby because of her difficult labour that caused her to become utterly devoted to her son from the moment she laid eyes on him. The infant son of Edmund and Margaret would spend his first four years at Pembroke Castle under the close guardianship of his beloved uncle Jasper and was, according to the chronicler Elis Gruffydd, called Owen by the Welsh people for many years. This may have been Jasper's choice as a tribute to his father, the boy's grandfather.

> Many of the leaders and common folk of North Wales held their backs straight and foretold and firmly prophesied that he [Henry Tudor] would be king of England. There was still much talk about the king's true name and that some maintained that the name given to him at baptism was Owain, the name which was the name given in the prophecy to the deliverer who would do much good to Wales.[2]

Baby Henry's birth was celebrated by the bards and one year after his birth a prophetic poem was composed by the bard Dafydd Nanmor (see Appendix F).

From the moment Margaret became a widow she sought Jasper's guidance for herself and also for important decisions regarding her son, who needed a strong base. It is often claimed by novelists, and thought by many people, that Jasper and Margaret were in love with each other but as brother-in-law and sister-in-law were forbidden to marry Jasper chose, out of compassion, to take care of her son, his nephew. This is most likely unfounded gossip and there are in fact several reasons which disprove it. If Jasper and Margaret were really in love and wanting to marry they could have easily discussed this with the king, who would have been able to ask the pope for a dispensation. Whether or not the request would have been granted remains open to question, but the fact is that the pope did give his permission in other similar cases: for example, the later marriage of Henry VIII to his widowed sister-in-law Catherine of Aragon. Further, custody of

---

2   *Chronicle of the Six Ages* NLW Manuscript 3054D, Elis Gryffydd.

Margaret was fully in Jasper's hands after Edmund's death,[3] something that would surely have expedited matters if there were any feelings of love between them. On the contrary, Jasper started negotiations with the Duke of Buckingham (with whom he had by now developed a close relationship) for Margaret's marriage to the duke's son, probably just two months after she had given birth. As soon as the young mother was churched in March, Jasper, Margaret and probably baby Henry VIsited the duke at his manor at Greenfield near Newport and it is likely that this was when Margaret's third marriage was arranged with Buckingham's second son Henry Stafford, her second cousin.[4] By this marriage Jasper lost a source of income, but as he made the match himself he must have preferred Margaret and his young nephew's safety and the cementing of this powerful and political alliance above the financial side.

Another counter-indication of a secret love affair between Jasper and Margaret is a tradition that, between 1453 and 1459, Jasper fathered two illegitimate daughters, Joan and Helen or Ellen, by a Welshwoman named Mevanvy ferch Dafydd from Gwynnedd. Both daughters are said to have been born in Snowdonia.[5] Joan (born 1453) is said to have married William ap Yevan (son of Yevan ap William and Margaret Kemoys), by whom she had twin sons called Morgan and John ap William(s) born in Lanishen, Wales, in 1479. It is believed that Joan herself died while giving birth, but Morgan, in 1499, married Thomas Cromwell's sister Katherine Cromwell in Putney Church, Norwell, Nottinghamshire, and so became fourth generation ancestor to Oliver Cromwell. Jasper's alleged second daughter, Helen or Ellen, is said to have been born in 1459 and married, after 1485, William Gardiner (son of Thomas Gardiner and Anna de la Grove), a cloth merchant who became a spearman for the Lancastrians at the Battle of Bosworth.

As a blood relation of the winning side, Sir William's trade as a clothier was much enhanced by the custom of aristocratic and even royal buyers. Ellen and Thomas Gardiner had at least one son, Stephen Gardiner, who became a prominent figure under the Tudor monarchy, especially during Henry VIII's reign. Therefore, it is not known if and

---

3   CPR, Henry VI 1452-1461, p. 504.
4   *The King's Mother: Lady Margaret Beaufort, Countess of Richmond and Derby*, M.K. Jones and M.G. Underwood (Cambridge University Press, 1992)
5   A Weir, *Britain's Royal Families, The Complete Genealogy* (Vintage, 2008), pp. 131–2. William Dugdale, *The Baronage of England*, Vol. 3, pp 241–2.

how long Jasper's relationship with Mevanvy lasted but it is a possibility that she was his mistress until around the early 1460s, since there is no mention of any other children he had with her. In fact, there is no official or contemporary mention at all of his daughters. Not even Jasper's will refers to the girls or Mevanvy and there is no evidence for their existence in any remaining contemporary source. The earliest known source is William Dugdale's Baronage dating to 1676, but this gives only Ellen as Jasper's illegitimate daughter and makes no mention of Mevanvy. Dugdale reports that Jasper 'leaving no other issue than one illegitimate Daughter, called Ellen, who became the Wife of William Gardner, Citizen of London'.[6] At all events, there is no indication that Jasper's association with Margaret was anything more than just friendship or a brother–sister relationship.

Whatever ties Jasper once had with the Duke of York, recent events had broken them entirely. From the beginning of 1457, Jasper became the most determined supporter of the House of Lancaster and, picking up Edmund's task where he had left it at his death, took control of south-west Wales by bringing peace and stability. By 6 March, the queen had found a way to get rid of the Duke of York by re-appointing him as lieutenant of Ireland,[7] and on 21 April Jasper was appointed instead as constable of the Welsh castles of Aberystwyth, Carmarthen and Carreg Cennen. The duke was supposed to receive a modest annuity of £40 by way of compensation,[8] but he never did so.

In those days, assaults and violence against women committed by groups of men was very common. One such occurrence is recorded involving a widow called Alice Veell against whom six men had misbehaved (we can only guess what happened to her as no details of this case survive). These men had been given a court order to appear before the council, but they had refused to do so. By 8 August the king gave instructions to Jasper, the Earl of Wiltshire, Sir Ralph of Sudeley, Sir John Beauchamp of Powick and the Sheriff of Gloucester to arrest this certain group of men. This was also one of Jasper's responsibilities.[9]

It is clear that Jasper's interest in Wales increased and in particular the south, where he felt at home, with his two castles of Pembroke and Tenby, the latter having become his preferred headquarters after the

---

6   Willliam Dugdale, *The Baronage of England*, vol. 3 (London 1676)
7   CPR, Henry VI 1452–1461, p. 341.
8   CPR, Henry VI 1452–1461, p. 340.
9   CPR, Henry VI 1452–1461, p. 370.

birth of his nephew. Jasper encouraged the mayor and burgesses of Tenby to improve the defences of their town and, at a meeting of the hundred court on 3 October, when Thomas White was chosen as mayor by the whole body of the twenty-four burgesses,[10] the townsmen officially proposed to reconstruct the town walls as they were in such a ruinous condition that the town was effectively defenceless. A letter patent of Jasper's dated 1 December 1457 gives details of the measures proposed by Mayor White and the burgesses, and also of the series of grants given by Jasper. According to the letter:

> The town walls needed to be strengthened and to become 6 ft. thick everywhere, providing a continuous platform for the defenders: building to be carried out on any intra-mural property without hindrance, and the town moat should be cleaned and made and maintained 30 ft. wide all round.

Jasper was very dedicated to this town and its people and so he made the unusual arrangement to pay half of the costs of this major task:

> The expenses of the work shall be shared thus: the Moat: half to be borne by the tenants of the extra mural properties bordering the moat, and half by the whole community of the town. The Walls: Where the walls adjoin the properties of the mayor, burgesses and free tenants, they are to bear half the expense and the whole community half. The Earl is requested to meet the expense where the walls adjoin his properties [11] [this eventually extended to half the cost of all the works on the wall].

With this grant Jasper also empowered the mayor and burgesses to carry out the work themselves, additionally instructing them to find carpenters, masons and other workmen anywhere in the county of Pembroke and to pay them the authorised rates. Furthermore, he

10 On borough courts in Pembrokeshire, see P.G. Sudbury, 'The *Medieval Boroughs of Pembrokeshire*', unpublished M.A. thesis, University of Wales, (1947) p. 124.

11 Etchings of Tenby plate no. 3 in the possession of Tenby Corporation, the 1844 edition carries a cover label, ' A Historical Sketch of Tenby and its Neighbourhood, Charles Norris.

gave the walls and moat to the mayor, burgesses and free tenants for ever.

In effect, Jasper made it possible for the people of Tenby to do the improvements by themselves quickly and without the need to request authorisation.

By these grants Jasper introduced a new way of management in Tenby that had not existed before 1457. Hitherto, the hundred court had not possessed this much law-making power, and to allow the board to regulate itself by making bye-laws represented a new approach to municipal self-government for the townsmen. Moreover, archaeological excavations have shown that much more work was carried out at the time than was originally proposed and set out in Jasper's letters patent. It is very reasonable to conclude that the existing towers were also increased in height and the curtain walls increased in length as well as other mural towers.[12] We can be certain that the Square Tower (bastion G), bastion I, Hooper's Cot (bastion N) and the Whitesand Gate were also built on Jasper's orders.[13]

Tenby occupied an ideal position for defence, much more so than other towns in the region. Built for the most part on rocks and with access to the open sea, it also had a well-defended castle of its own, particularly after the additions were made. Tenby was regarded as an important citadel during Jasper's power in South Wales and many of the improvements and reconstructions that Jasper had undertaken are still to be seen. Having secured his earldom of Pembroke as a strong base offering possible connections to England, France, Scotland and Ireland, Jasper would, on more than one future occasion, be able to escape his pursuers and return with support from overseas.

Jasper's prestige and influence flourished rapidly and by November that year he was empowered to cut down and sell 200 acres of wood in Sherwood Forest.[14]

On 3 January 1458, Margaret married Buckingham's son Henry Stafford and from that day she left her nearly one-year-old to the care of his uncle. Five days later, on 8 January 1458, Jasper and Earl John of Shrewsbury officially gained joint custody over young Henry,

---

12   The National Library of Wales Journal XVI, p. 8, R.F. Walker (1969)
13   Archaeologia Cambrensis, 5th Series, Vol. VIII, Notes on the Fortifications of Mediaeval Tenby, p. 177-194, E. Laws, The Bedford Press (1896)
14   CPR, Henry VI 1452-1461, p. 398.

the earldom of Richmond and his estates until he should attain adulthood.[15]

On 27 January, Jasper and the other peers were summoned for a great council meeting at Westminster, where the king, once again, proved himself a weak and unfit leader. Without setting specific and enforceable rules, he proposed reconciliation between the partisans of York and the queen, desiring a 'Love day' to be held on 25 March – which was a useless event. In February, Sir Walter Devereux was given his liberty after a year of imprisonment and York himself was still in Ireland, all this was to keep York and his retainers separate to avoid any likelihood of rebellion.

Following Edmund's death, Jasper had to deal with several legal complications, the chief ones being that his nephew Henry was still an infant in the spring of 1458 and Jasper was not married and had no heir, the escheat of his deceased brother's lands, the Beaufort wardship and the other jointed held estates. Many of the grants made to Jasper were in fee tail, tail male or survivorship, so his failure to marry and father an heir produced legal problems. Some three years earlier the king had made a provision in the Act of Resumption specifically excluding his half-brothers from its scope, but now this act had expired and the chancellor of the exchequer upheld the opinion that Jasper, being unmarried and without a male heir, had no further right to these benefits.[16]

> Provided always and except that this act, or any other act made in this present parliament, shall not extend or be prejudicial to Jasper, earl of Pembroke, or to Henry, earl of Richmond, son and heir of Edmund, late earl of Richmond, with regard to any gift or gifts, grant or grants, made to the said late Edmund and Jasper by us, our letters patents, act or acts of parliament, individually or jointly, by whatever name or names the said Jasper or the said late Edmund, are described, named or called in them.[17]

Despite all the obstacles, Jasper was a very wealthy man as, besides the joint wardship of his nephew, he retained complete control

---

15   CPR, Henry VI 1452-1461, pp. 209, 433.
16   RP, Vol. 5, p. 309.
17   PRO C49/62/45B.

over the estates he and Edmund formerly shared. Jasper's income increased to nearly £1,500 a year.[18] Moreover, he would have obtained full wardship of Margaret Beaufort as well as custody of her dower lands until her marriage.[19] In May, Jasper had to approach the king for clarification of the issue and on 29 May the king sent a writ of the privy seal to the treasurer and barons of the exchequer to lay down the course they should follow:

> Yet now late divers opinions were had and taken by you upon an act of resumpcion (1455) [...] and by cause the words in the said provision be thought opinable obscure and derk, for as moch as the said Jasper Erle of Pembrok hath not as yet issue male of his body begotyn and other causes werefor for the wele and indempnite of oure said brother Jasper we woll and charge you that ye open and plainly declare oure entent and Will and more at large of and in the said provision now that neiyther our will nor purpose was not nor as yet is to have take or resume by force of the said resumption any lands tenements or other thing fro the said Jasper or the said late Erle of Richmond as long as and during the tyme that the same [...] have or either of theym hath or shall have by possibilite issue male of his body lawfully begotten [...] How be hit that he ne had neither shuld have issue male of his body which god defend wherpon we well and charge you that ye in no wyse cantrarie not this oure declaracion and entent neither inquiete trouble nor vex the said Jasper but suffer hym and all other oure officers accomptable to us before you of any of the premises to be quiete allowed and discarged of all things ayenst thaym or any of thaym by force of the said act or provision in demaund the which might growe in hurt or charge to the said Jasper.[20]

---

18 Thomas, p. 141.
19 CPR, Henry VI 1452-1461, p. 504 – Chancery, Inquisitions, series I, 165/1 m.15.
20 Exchequer, K.R., Memoranda Roll 234, Adhuc Communia, Recorda, Trinity, m.7.

The fact that the king defended his half-brother and at the same time did not take steps to arrange a marriage for him, seems to prove that Jasper did not wish to get married and that he asserted his own wishes in this matter. It is probable that the king may have given Jasper advice on the issue, but clearly this did not change the earl's mind. It is, however, unclear why Jasper had so far remained unmarried as, given his situation, it would have been easy for the king to find him a suitable bride, even though there was a shortage of eligible candidates at the time. Perhaps the king's illness hindered this process. Or perhaps Jasper preferred to devote himself to the Lancastrian cause or simply wanted to marry a woman for love or did not fancy a marriage at all. We can only speculate about his reasons, but in any case it seems most likely that Jasper had his own mind in this and simply refused any offers made to him by the king. It would not be until nearly thirty years later that Jasper would take a bride.

It seems to be a fact that Jasper retained his alliance with Gruffydd ap Nicholas for, on 1 March 1459 he, together with his father Owen and the sons of Gruffydd, Thomas and Owen ap Nicholas, was commissioned to arrest, among others, some servants of Sir John Dwnn, the most influential Yorkist in West Wales and also an important poet in his time.[21] The arrest seems very likely to have been an attempt to weaken York's influence in Carmarthenshire, for there had been attacks by York's retainers at the castles of Kidwelly and Carreg Cennen.[22] The Welsh people trusted Jasper because he was one of them and treated 'his people' with respect and listened to them, something they had not seen before from the English government. This made them willing to gather themselves behind Jasper and support the Lancastrian royal house. His diligence in West Wales secured those parts for the Lancastrians but also provided a force that would be a threat to the Yorkists.

Finally, the voice of Wales was to be heard and this was attributable to Jasper's great loyalty and splendid services to king and crown. Jasper was more highly regarded by the court than ever and by the end of April 1459, he was elected as a Knight of the Garter, ostensibly as replacement for the late Alphonso V of Aragon and Naples, who had died on 27 June 1458, but also in recognition of his outstanding abilities.[23] Furthermore, Jasper received, on 21 April 1459, for a term

---

21 CPR, Henry VI 1452-1461, p. 494.
22 Griffiths, Welsh History Review, Vol. 2, p. 227 (1965)
23 Memorials of the most noble order of the Garter, G.E. Beltz, p. 162 (1841)

of ten years, the farm of the manors of Cantref Selyf, Alexanderston
and Llangoed in Breconshire, which lay in the Welsh Marches,[24]
an area then suffering from the continuing effects of many years of
lawlessness, murder and civil disorder. Additionally, on 2 May 1459,
Jasper received a very suitable grant, being the use for his lifetime of
a tower in the Palace of Westminster. This tower, which he could use
for council meetings and other administrative tasks, was described as:

> '[...] a tower in the lower end of the
> great hall within Westminster Palace, for the
> communication and easement of the earl and
> his council, to hold as the Queen holds the other
> tower at the end of the hall at the entry of the
> Exchequer for her and her council.[25]

Jasper already made use of the tower but to be granted a tower
for life in the palace enhanced his status and clearly showed the
king's appreciation of his support. These grants were without doubt
part of Jasper's equipment for the approaching conflicts. There are no
surviving records that tell us exactly what Jasper's actions were during
the summer months of 1459. However, it is very likely that he returned
to Wales to make preparations for the approaching confrontations
in England and to undermine the Yorkist party by preventing any
attempt made by the Duke of York to return to England as an invader
via Denbigh Castle in North Wales. Close to the Welsh Marches,
Denbigh was York's main channel of communication between
Ireland and England. The uneasy peace that had existed between the
opposing factions during the previous four years was now stretched to
the limit and would reach breaking point in that autumn. Both sides
were eager for a fight and, when the conflict did erupt in September
1459, there was no obvious endpoint on the horizon.

---

24   CFR, Henry VI, 1452-1461, p. 231.
25   CPR, Henry VI 1452-1461, pp. 486-7.

Figure 15   The Henry VII Tower at Pembroke Castle.
Traditionally the location of Henry Tudor's birth.
(© 2015 Debra Bayani)

Figure 16   Pembroke Castle exhibition showing Henry Tudor's birth.
            (© 2015 Debra Bayani)

Figure 17   The tower on Tower Hill in Tenby, overlooking the harbour.
              (© 2015 Debra Bayani)

Figure 18   Remains of the original walls built in 1457 on
                   Jasper's orders.
                   (© 2015 Debra Bayani)

Figure 19   Modern depiction of Jasper Tudor in conversation with
                Mayor White in front of the walls of Tenby.
                On display in Tudor' Merchant House in Tenby.
                (© 2015 Debra Bayani)

Figure 20   Tenby in 1586 by Eric Bradforth ARCA.
                 (Courtesy of Tenby Museum & Art Gallery Collection)

6

THE STORM BREAKS
September 1459 – 30 December 1460

THE SUMMONING of parliament was followed by an outbreak of the expected armed conflict. York and the Nevilles had been excluded from the great council meeting the previous June at Coventry, at which they had correctly predicted they would be charged with treason.

By the end of the summer Warwick had returned from Calais, bringing troops from his Calais garrison. On his way to join York, who by 23 September was at Ludlow with his family, Warwick narrowly escaped an ambush by Henry Beaufort, the new young Duke of Somerset. Meanwhile, the Earl of Salisbury had gathered a stalwart group of 2,000 men and marched from Middleham Castle westwards, also intending to join the Duke of York at Ludlow. However, as soon as Queen Margaret heard of this she immediately sent a force of Cheshire men under the command of lords Audley and Dudley ahead of her. Audley, with between 8,000 and 10,000 men, intercepted Salisbury's march at Blore Heath.[1] The fighting lasted for about four hours, from 1pm until 5pm, during which time Lord Audley was killed by Sir Roger Kynaston of Hordeley.[2] In all about 2,000 men were said to have lost their lives, including some

---

1 Benet's Chronicle, p. 224. Reg. Wethemstede, Vol. I, p. 338.
2 Gregory's Chronicle, p. 204.

who had been knighted by Queen Margaret that very day.[3] Among
the Lancastrians who were wounded and captured were Lord Dudley
and fifteen other knights.[4] Salisbury managed to retreat at around five
o'clock, just in time to avoid another encounter with the main royal
army who were about to arrive, and moved towards Worcester to meet
up with York. But Salisbury's two sons were captured at Acton Bridge
by Thomas Harper[5] and imprisoned at Chester Castle.[6] According to
Gregory's Chronicle, Salisbury was pursued by the royal forces until
the early morning.[7]

This battle was a major loss and disappointment for the
Lancastrians. An ambush was planned against Warwick at Coleshill
by way of retaliation, but was mistimed and the earl was able to press
on to Worcester.

The Lancastrian court was in no mood for discussion and the
king's force was now at Nottingham en route to join the queen and
her company. With an army twice the size of the Yorkists' – reputedly
around 50,000 against 25,000 men – the king pursued York and the
Nevilles all the way to Ludlow.[8]

While the king was on his way to parliament at Leominster on
9 October (later known as the 'Parliament of Devils' because of its
attack on the Yorkists), he responded personally to the Yorkists' appeal
with the offer of a pardon. The offer was extended to the Duke of York
and the Earl of Warwick, but not to Salisbury, and only if they
surrendered within six days.[9] These terms were deemed unacceptable
and parliament was again summoned to Coventry for 20 November.
The king's army reached Leominster, ten miles south of Ludlow, by
10 October.[10] Two days later, on 12 October, a cold and extremely
wet autumn day, the Yorkist army had to confront a Lancastrian force
twice their size just outside Ludlow at Ludford Bridge on the River
Teme and just below the hill on which the town and castle stood.
According to Gregory's Chronicle, the royal army numbered around

3   English Chronicle, p. 80. Gregory's Chronicle, p. 204. London Chronicle, p. 169. J.T.
     Driver, Cheshire Men in the Later Middle Ages (Chester, 1971), p. 18.
4   Brut, p. 60. Flenley, p. 147. CPR Henry VI, 1452–1461, p. 595.
5   CPR, Henry VI, 1452–1461, p. 536.
6   English Chronicle, p. 80. Benet's Chronicle, p. 224.
7   Gregory's Chronicle, p. 204.
8   Benet's Chronicle, p. 224. Flenley, p. 147. Chronicle of London, p. 140.
     Gregory's Chronicle, p. 205.
9   Reg. Whethamstede, I, pp. 399–41. RP, Vol. 5, pp. 348–9.
10   Reports from the Lord's committee ... touching the dignity of a peer,
     Vol. 4, p. 940 (1820–29)

12,000. Presumably the Yorkists were disappointed by their numbers. They were led by York and his two eldest sons, March and Rutland, along with the Earl of Salisbury with his retinue and Warwick with his Calais commanders, as well as Clinton, Richard Grey Lord Powis and Walter Devereux Jr (his father, Walter Sr, having died the previous April), who had raised a small force to come to the Yorkists' aid.[11] Part of the shortfall on the Yorkist side can be attributed to the fact that Salisbury's sons John and Thomas could not be present:

> But in the morning [after the Battle of Blore Heath], by-twyne the fylde and Chester, Syr John Dawneys sone that was at home in hys fadyrs place hadde worde that hys fadyr was slayne; a-non he raysyd hys tenantys and toke by-syde a lytyl townei-namyd Torperlay Syr Thomas Nevyle, Syr John Nevyle, and Syr Thomas Haryngdon, and brought hem unto the castelle of Chester, ande there they abode tylle the batayle of Northehampton was done.[12]

According to Gregory's Chronicle, the Duke of York had a great deep ditch dug and fortified it with guns, carts and stakes. Once again the Yorkists would fight a battle against the royal army and, moreover, with the king being present. Even though York had won the first Battle of St Albans, he had been disconcerted by the king's presence there and doubly so that he had been wounded. When the Yorkist Andrew Trollope, a former companion of the Duke of Somerset, received a letter sent by Somerset he immediately defected to the King's party.[13] This was a major blow to the Yorkist force especially since Trollope[14] knew all their plans. Judging their situation to be hopeless, York and his councillors decided to retire during the night like cowards, leaving their unsuspecting followers at their posts so the royal army would not realise until the morning that the birds had flown.[15] Either way, Henry VI's presence with his troops proved decisive. It took the heart out of the rebels, the majority of whom, including Devereux and Lord Powis, defected to the royal party and were mostly pardoned.

11   RP., Vol. 5, 349. Estates and finances of York, pp. 177, 179, 180, 185 and 191.
12   Gregory's Chronicle: 1451–1460, p. 204.
13   Reg. Whethamstede, I, p. 343–4. Benet's Chronicle, p. 224. Great Chronicle, p. 191.
14   Fabyan's Chronicle, p. 634.
15   RP, Vol. 5, pp. 348–9. Brut, pp. 526–7. Great Chronicle, p. 191.

On 30 October, other commissions were issued for the arrest of all who committed treason,[16] and by 20 November, a heavily packed parliament, which would last until 20 December, assembled at Coventry. This parliament strengthened the Lancastrian grip even further, by the Act of Attainder, confiscating all the Yorkists' lands and offices, condemning them as traitors[17] and debarring their heirs from succession.[18] The Yorkist leaders fled abroad: Salisbury, Warwick and York's eldest son Edward returned to Calais, while York himself, his son Rutland and Lord Clinton, pursued by Jasper and his Pembrokeshire men,[19] fled from place to place within Wales, breaking down all bridges behind them to avoid being captured prior to their safe escape to Ireland.[20]

In fact, this victory at Blore Heath was not the major triumph the Lancastrians hoped for. Nevertheless, despite their great disappointment at the escape of the Yorkist leaders, it was at least some kind of a triumph. A triumph they would have to make the best of.

York was further frustrated when he was replaced as lieutenant of Ireland by his enemy James Butler, the Earl of Wiltshire and Ormond. Wiltshire was a staunch Lancastrian supporter and companion to Jasper. But when Wiltshire's agent was sent to Ireland to deliver a warrant for York's arrest, he was promptly seized and executed.[21] York in his turn tried to gather as much support from Ireland and Scotland as possible before attempting a return to England. He managed to enlist to his cause King James II of Scotland, who sent an envoy with a proposal that one of his daughters should marry one of York's sons. At the same time York exerted his influence on the Irish government and the Irish simply ignored the Lancastrian summons to reject York as their lieutenant.

It is uncertain exactly when Jasper's siege of Denbigh Castle began, though it is very likely that if, as is thought, he returned to Wales that previous autumn, he had started some preparations then. We do know that he returned to Coventry, where he arrived a little later

---

16   CPR, Henry VI 1452–1461, p. 557.
17   Benet's Chronicle, p. 224.
18   Somerville, pp. 421, 514.
19   Ludford Bridge & Mortimer's Cross, p. 25.
20   Gregory's Chronicle: 1451–1460, p. 205.
21   CCR, Henry VI 1452–1461, p. 426. English Chronicle, p. 83.

than most nobles, on 6 December, with a large company[22] and swore
his oath of loyalty when parliament reassembled on 11 December. A
formidable gathering of the nobility, this was attended by the dukes
of Exeter, Norfolk and Buckingham, Jasper and the other earls of
Arundel, Northumberland, Shrewsbury and Wiltshire, and viscounts
Beaumont and Bourchier along with two archbishops and sixteen
bishops. All those present swore an oath of loyalty to the king and
his son and heir Prince Edward, and to preserve the queen[23] and,
according to the Paston Letters, Lord Grey of Ruthin and Bishop
Neville of Exeter declared 'them ful worshipfuly to the Kynges grete
plesir'.[24] Naturally, York, Warwick and Salisbury were not among
those summoned. Parliament proceeded to parcel out the confiscated
Yorkist properties amongst the Lancastrian lords[25] but grants were
limited in number and size compared to times past. The king had
learned from previous mistakes and most of the individuals who were
favoured had a special claim on him. Jasper was made one of the new
royal stewards, along with Beaumont, Dudley and some others, all of
them faithful courtiers.

Both Jasper and his father benefited greatly from the ensuing
redistribution of the forfeited Yorkist properties. On 19 December,
Owen was granted for life an annuity of £100 from six forfeited
manors that had belonged to the Yorkist Lord Clinton: Folkstone,
Benstead and Walton in Kent, Blakenham in Sussex, and the lordships
and manors of Shustoke and Bolehall in Warwickshire. He was also
granted the custody of the parks of Moelwick, Caresnodeoke, Kilford,
Baghan and Posty in the lordship of Denbigh, as well as some offices
in Denbigh,[26] King Henry VI declaring that:

> Out of consideration of the good services of
> that beloved squire, our Owinus Tudyr, we for
> the future take him into our special grace, and
> make him park keeper of our parks in Denbigh,
> Wales.[27]

22 CPR, Henry VI 1452–1461, p. 686. CCR, Henry VI 1454–1461, p. 421. *Paston Letters*,
    Davies, Vol. 2, pp. 187–8.
23 RP, Vol 5, pp. 351–2.
24 *The Paston Letters*, Davies, Vol. 2, p. 188.
25 PRO C49/62/12.– PRO C49/31/2–3.
26 CPR, Henry VI 1452–1461, pp. 532–3, 547. CCR, Henry VI 1454–1461, p. 405.
27 Foedera, vol. X, p. 435.

Additionally, Owen was granted the following May, but with effect from the previous 19 December, a lease for seven years of the lordships or manors of Folkstone, Benstead, Huntingdon and Millbroke in Kent, and Hamsey in Surrey, all forfeited properties of Lord Clinton.[28] These appointments were all carefully considered decisions intended to finance the undertaking of a full-scale siege.

Jasper was appointed constable of Denbigh Castle and steward and master forester of the lordship of Denbigh on 5 January 1460,[29] but in order to make these grants effective and eradicate York's power in the lordship, Jasper first had to take possession of the castle and bring York's agents over to his side. To do this he needed extra powers to raise more men and accordingly, in mid-February 1460, he sent his esquire Thomas Wyriot to the king with a petition requesting a commission to him help raise men in Wales for assistance in subjugating the castle of Denbigh. Jasper also asked for the power to pardon those rebels who were prepared to submit, excluding those who were outlawed or brought to justice, and to keep the latter in prison until given sureties of good behaviour. He requested authority to execute rebels at his discretion and also asked for a grant for all moveable goods belonging to those occupying the castle, so that he could reward the men who assisted him. Finally, Jasper asked for a commission to recruit three groups of men, from his own and Prince Edward's territories in the south and east of Wales, whom he could trust and rely on to support his siege of Denbigh Castle. These contained gentry of south-west Wales, including representatives from the county's major families. The first group, to assemble men in Pembrokeshire, would be Sir William Vernon, Sir Robert de Vere (younger brother of the Earl of Oxford), Sir Henry Wogan, Sir Thomas Perrot, Thomas Wyriot and Thomas Wogan. The second group, of men from Carmarthenshire and Cardiganshire – Rhys ap Dafydd ap Thomas, Robert ap Rhys ap Thomas, Ieuan ap Jankyn Llwyd and Peter Baret. The third group, men from Gower and Kidwelly – Philip Mansel, Henry Dwnn Jr., Richard Cradock and Thomas Burghill.[30]

Meanwhile, on 4 February, a powerful commission of oyer and terminer was issued to Prince Edward, Jasper, Buckingham, Beaumont, Shrewsbury and a host of lawyers and gentlemen to

28   CFR, Henry VI 1452–1461, p. 266.
29   CPR, Henry VI 1452–1461, p. 534.
30   PRO C49/32/12A, Jasper's undated petition.

inquire into all offences in the five royal counties of Wales, and in Cheshire and Flint.[31]

Since Jasper's former counsellor Thomas Vaughan was by now declared a rebel, Jasper was fully granted, in tail male, the townhouse Le Garlek in Stepney.[32]

As soon as King Henry received Jasper's request he wrote without delay, on 16 February, to the chancellor, ordering him to act with speed to meet Jasper's requests and saying that he had already warned the treasurer about these procedures.[33] On 22 February 1460, Jasper received a special commission with the extensive powers he had asked for to swiftly bring the town under his control.[34] Then, on 3 March, Jasper and the same group of men were given full authority to pardon any rebels in the Welsh castles, with the exception of those who had been pardoned before.[35] It was their goal to destroy the Yorkist lords and their counsellors but not to alienate the mass of lower men. Denbigh defended itself stubbornly and showed brave resistance to the, eventually, victorious Jasper. On or just before 13 March, the town submitted and Jasper was permitted to hold it 'as of our gift', together with all that was within.

He was able to commandeer all the removable goods belonging to the garrison and to distribute them amongst his soldiers according to his own discretion. On this same day, the earl was granted a sum of £1,000 to cover expenses incurred in reducing the town and other Yorkist castles in Wales, the exact sum to be raised from the Welsh estates of the Duke of York and the Earl of Warwick.[36]

Soon after this event, on 29 March, it appears that Jasper was at Ruthin in Denbighshire when he sent an urgent request for money to Lord Scales.[37] Unfortunately, this letter is severely damaged so that parts of it are illegible and it is not possible to make out why Jasper was in such need of money.

At the same time Warwick, with 500 men and a fleet that included ships captured at Sandwich the previous January, sailed to Ireland to offer York his assistance.[38] Rumours reaching the Lancastrian faction

31 CPR, Henry VI 1452–1461, pp. 564–5.
32 CFR, Henry VI 1452–1461, p. 541.
33 Chancery, Warrants for the Great Seal, 1376–79.
34 CPR, Henry VI 1452–1461, pp. 550, 565.
35 CPR,, Henry VI 1452–1461, p. 578.
36 CPR, Henry VI 1452–1461, p. 574. Foedera, Vol. XI, pp. 444–6.
37 SCAC, 51/86.
38 CPR, Henry VI 1452–1461, p. 554. English Chronicle, pp. 91–4.

of a secret conference at Dublin between the Yorkist leaders suggested the possibility of a Yorkist attack. It was regarded as a matter of utmost importance that such an enterprise should be crushed before it came to fruition. But this appeared to be an almost impossible task.

On 5 May he was given the farm of York's forfeited lordship of Newbury in Berkshire for seven years.[39]

By 25 May, Jasper was certainly at Pembroke Castle when he wrote from there to John Hall, informing him that he had sent instructions to John White to hand over a Tenby ship called Le Mary to his adherent Thomas Wogan, enabling him to attack an unwelcome vessel belonging to the king's enemies that had entered Milford Sound.[40] Milford Sound, with its many inlets, would be an ideal landing place for the Yorkist leaders, who were now trying to return from Ireland.

Even though Jasper made it impossible for them to land at this location, they would surely try elsewhere before long. The Lancastrian position would remain insecure as long as York and his followers were beyond the king's reach. Meanwhile, the Earl of Wiltshire, together with the lords Scales and Hungerford, had terrorised the town of Newbury to punish the Yorkists. By 21 June, there was a major development. March, Warwick and Salisbury (York and Rutland were still in Ireland and would follow later), having managed to land at Sandwich, seized the town and, after a triumphant march through Kent, reached London on 2 July. As soon as Wiltshire heard of the Yorkists' arrival, he fled to the Low Countries, and Scales and Hungerford were commissioned to hold London for King Henry. Scales and Hungerford seem to have tried unsuccessfully to secure the support of the citizens of London, but as soon as Warwick left his father and Lord Cobham in London to reinforce the Tower, both men were forced to take refuge inside it. Scales and his supporters fought vigorously from the walls of the Tower to prevent its capture by Salisbury, but by 18 July they were almost starved and found themselves forced to surrender. Out in the open Scales tried to find sanctuary, but was soon murdered.

Warwick, March, Fauconberg and their numerous followers swiftly headed north with the intention of confronting the King. Henry, who had been at Coventry until he heard news of the

39 CFR, Henry VI 1452–1461, p. 267.
40 Cardiff CL. 42/1094.

approaching Yorkists, moved his court to Northampton before he had
time to muster his army in full strength. At Northampton the royal
army encamped in the fields south of the town, close to Delapre Abbey.
On the morning of 10 July, the Yorkists arrived with an enormous
army of around 60,000 men. According to Gregory's Chronicle, a
scout called Sir William Lucy heard gun shots whereupon he tried
to warn the royal party of the approaching Yorkists as quickly as he
could but before he could reach the king 'one of the Staffordys was
ware of hys comynge, and lovyd that knyghtys wyffe and hatyd hym,
and a-non causyd hys dethe'.[41]

The Yorkists found King Henry VI in a strongly fortified
position defended by cannons. Negotiations, led by the Archbishop
of Canterbury, for the earls of March and Warwick, who had come
to the king's presence, failed immediately. The Duke of Buckingham
refused them any access to the king, saying, 'The earl of Warwick shall
not come to the King's presence, and if he come he shall die.'[42] Battle
was now inevitable. The royal party was clearly taken by surprise and,
probably, due to heavy rain, their guns were unusable and 'paralyzed',
which was to York's advantage. It is said the Duke of Buckingham
was still standing at his tent when he was killed along with the Earl of
Shrewsbury, Viscount Beaumont and Lord Egremont, and, according
to the English Chronicle, 'many men were drownyd by syde the
fylde in the revyr at a mylle.'[43] Aided by the traitor Lord Grey of
Ruthin, who had fought on the Lancastrian side at Ludford Bridge,
the Yorkists easily overcame the royal party and the king was seized
but unharmed.

The Yorkist leaders brought the king back to London. It was
impossible that the new Yorkist government would accept the
Lancastrian dominance on the country's west side and, on 9 August,
Jasper and Roger Puleston were ordered to surrender Denbigh Castle
to Edward Bourchier, the son of Viscount Bourchier.[44] Similar orders
were sent to the constables of the other Lancastrian strongholds in
Wales, at Beaumaris, Conway, Flint, Ruthin, Montgomery, Holt and
Hawarden. Inevitably, these orders were ignored and, on 17 August,

---

41 Gregory's Chronicle, p. 207.
42 English Chronicle, pp. 95–7.
43 English Chronicle, pp. 95–7.
44 DWB, p. 816.

Devereux, Herbert and Roger Vaughan were empowered to take all these castles by force.[45]

As soon as York returned from Ireland in September, he made it clear he had every intention of taking the crown for himself and he arrived in London with great pomp. According to the English Chronicle, York was so confident of success that he even arranged for his coronation to take place on 1 November.[46]

Most of the other Yorkist leaders were uncomfortable with the idea of deposing their anointed king. The fact that York had remained in Ireland for so long, leaving it to others to do the dirty work for him, and probably also because they knew the other peers would be reluctant to abjure their oaths of alliance to King Henry, meant that York had to settle for less support than he had expected to receive. The disinheriting of the king's son, Prince Edward of Lancaster, would have to suffice for the time-being. But the prospect that York himself would succeed to the throne gives grounds for suspicion, for he was ten years older than the king and must have had some plan in mind to accomplish this.

According to Gregory's Chronicle, York came to the Palace of Westminster in great triumph over the weak-willed King Henry and forced him to acknowledge York as his heir; and the king, fearful for his life, was compelled to agree and thereby to disinherit his own son:

> And so he [York] come to Habyngdon, and
> there he sende for trompeters and claryners to
> bring hym to London, and there he gave them
> baners with the hole armys of Inglonde with owte
> any dyversyte, and commaundyd hys swerde
> to ben borne upperyghte be-fore hym; and soo
> he rode forthe unto Lundon tylle he come to
> Westemyster to Kyng Harrys palys, ande there he
> claymyde the crowne of Inglonde. Ande he kepte
> Kynge Harry there by fors and strengythe, tylle
> at the laste the kynge for fere of dethe grauntyd
> hym [th]e crowne, for a man that hathe by lytylle
> wytte wylle sone be a feryd of dethe.

---

45 PPC, vol.6, pp. 304–5 .
46 English Chronicle, p. 100. Waurin, Vol. 5, pp. 315–17.

> And that same nyght the kynge remevyde
> unto London a-gayne hys wylle, to the
> byschoppeys palys of London, and the Duke of
> Yorke com unto hym that same nyght by the
> torchelyght and toke a-pon hym as kyng, and
> sayde in many placys that thys ys owrys by very
> right.[47]

It seems clear that Henry VI was now more of a puppet-king than ever before. Queen Margaret, who had been waiting for the king at Coventry, was taken by surprise by the swift victory of the Yorkists and fled with her seven-year-old son to seek refuge in Jasper's Wales.[48] From the Lancastrian stronghold of Harlech the queen and Prince Edward were escorted, in disguise, to the safety of their brother-in-law and uncle Jasper. Queen Margaret, quite justifiably, feared for her own life, but even more for her son's life. If York ever managed to seize the prince all would be lost.

By 31 October, an agreement was reached, the king being quite unable to do anything else. Under its terms York was declared heir apparent and a great sum of money was assigned to him and his two eldest sons, while Prince Edward of Lancaster was stripped of his inheritance as well as his status. All the assembled lords swore an oath to accept York as heir to the kingdom, and York was to acknowledge King Henry VI as king for life.[49] During mid-October, Queen Margaret and Prince Edward were still in Wales. They moved to Jasper's headquarters at Pembroke and Tenby Castle. From South Wales, Margaret sailed to Scotland to appeal to her fellow queen, Mary of Guelders, who had been regent for her son since the death of her husband King James II the previous August. Queen Margaret felt she had to act quickly in order to save her husband and protect the rights of her son. Before her departure for Scotland, she sent urgent messages to the Earl of Devon, the Duke of Somerset and Andrew Trollope to join forces as soon as possible, and with as many men as they could muster, with their tenants in the North, where the Percys and the lords Neville, Dacre, Clifford and Roos were ready and loyal to their king. Jasper remained in Wales where he retained control over the strongholds that were still loyal to Lancaster. These threats

---

47 Gregory's Chronicle, p. 208.
48 C.L. Scofield, *The Life and Reign of Edward IV*, Vol.1 (London, 1923).
    Letters of Queen Margaret of Anjou ..., Camden Society, 1st series (1863)
49 Benet's Chronicle, p. 228.

motivated York, Salisbury and Rutland to lead an army of between 6,000 and 12,000 men northwards to one of York's own strongholds, Sandal Castle, in early December. The combined Lancastrian force was approximately twice the size of York's.[50] York and Salisbury had probably miscalculated the level of support they could expect to receive from their own lands and might have assumed that a northern Lancastrian army would not be able to recruit so many men. In any case, when the Duke of York arrived at Sandal Castle between 21 and 24 December, it became clear to him that his position was much more difficult than first thought. The queen persuaded the political community of the North to reject the Duke of York's control over the area and sent her men out to meet him. York and Salisbury found their properties in the area destroyed, Somerset had garrisoned Pontefract Castle, and the Earl of Devon had occupied the town of York.

By 28 December, a Lancastrian force including the dukes of Somerset and Exeter, the earls of Devon, Wiltshire and Northumberland, and the lords Neville, Dacre and Clifford, together with Andrew Trollope and thousands of soldiers, marched towards Sandal Castle.[51] York, who had used violence so often to solve his political problems in the past, was now confronted by the younger generation of the same dukes and earls, the sons whose fathers he had butchered in previous years, who were now eager for revenge. On their arrival the Lancastrians tried to lure York out of the castle, but without immediate effect. However, after waiting for two more days, during which time York might have expected his son March to arrive and come to his aid, the Lancastrians were successful. There are two suggestions as to why York decided to come out of the castle on 30 December. One is that, while a number of his men were away in search of food and supplies, York made the most unwise decision to leave Sandal Castle to attack the approaching rival faction who was disturbing the Christmastide truce. But another and probably more convincing suggestion is that York was taunted to draw him out of his stronghold when he thought he had gathered enough men to win this fight.[52] It is claimed that Sir Thomas Neville, cousin of York's wife Cecily, had led him to think that he would come to his assistance and as soon as Neville's force of around 8,000 men appeared, York left the

---

50 Flenley, pp. 151–2. Stevenson, Vol.2, p. 775. Benet's Chronicle, p. 228.
51 C.R. Markham, *The Battle of Wakefield*, Vol. 9 (1886), pp. 112–13.
    Hall's Chronicle, pp. 249–50.
52 E.A. Freeman, *The Battles of Wakefield* (1894), p. 228.

safety of the castle.[53] The opposite turned out to be true. Neville was on the Lancastrian side. York had been drawn into a trap and, after fighting bravely, was killed by the squire James Luttrell or Lotrell,[54] in front of the castle of Sandal in Wakefield, along with many men. His son, the seventeen-year-old Edmund Earl of Rutland, was also killed, either when he tried to escape[55] or, as it has also been claimed that Rutland was well-versed in the use of arms, while fighting his way to the location where he was slain,[56] very likely by Lord Clifford.[57] During the night or the next day the Earl of Salisbury was captured, along with some others, and taken to Pontefract Castle and while it seems that the Lancastrians – or Somerset in particular[58] – would have allowed Salisbury to ransom himself, the earl was beheaded the next day, either by the commons of Pontefract Castle who 'loved him not'[59] or by Robert Holland, the Bastard of Exeter.[60]

The heads of several Yorkist leaders were placed on the Micklegate Bar of the city of York. Among them was the Duke of York's own, adorned in mockery with a crown of paper and straw.[61]

The Battle of Wakefield had, in a single meeting, killed two of the Lancastrians' arch-enemies, three if we include Rutland. However, it could not be accounted a turning point in the 'Wars of the Roses'. The king was still in the hands of Warwick and, by the Westminster accord of the previous 30 October, York's son, Edward Earl of March, was still the king's next heir.

---

53 Waurin, pp. 325–6.
54 CPR, Henry VI (1467–1477) p. 522.
55 Leland, Vol. 1, p. 43.
56 Gregory's Chronicle.
57 Hall's Chronicle, pp. 250–51.Worcestre Itineraries, p. 485.
58 English Chronicle, p. 107.
59 Annales, p. 413.
60 Worcestre Itineraries, p. 485.
61 Hall's Chronicle, p. 251. Stow Relation, p. 684. Worcestre Itineraries, p. 485. Vergil, p. 108.

Figure 21   Denbigh Castle and St. Hillary's Tower.
                   (© 2015 Debra Bayani)

7

UNEXPECTED LOSS AT MORTIMER'S CROSS
January 1461 – February 1461

A FEW weeks prior to the Battle of Wakefield, while the Duke of York had been in the North, Edward of March was in Wales with a view to preventing Jasper and his troops from making an attempt to free his unfortunate half-brother the king from Warwick's firm grasp at Westminster. March celebrated Christmas at Gloucester accompanied by Devereux, William and Richard Herbert, the Dwnns of Kidwelly, Roger Vaughan, the young Lord Audley and Humphrey Stafford (who had both been captured in Calais after Ludfordbridge).[1] It seems Edward had toured through his father's and Warwick's lordships to recruit men to take to his father's aid. It is very likely that he had been keeping a close watch on Jasper, who had been the greatest immediate threat to the Yorkists. After the news of his father's death at Wakefield was brought to him, Edward prepared himself to return to London and may have increased his recruitment drive as the queen was known to be moving south from Scotland. From his castle at Wigmore, Edward was informed that Jasper was also advancing southwards, from Denbigh towards Hereford, and it was the Yorkists' top priority to prevent Jasper from joining forces with the queen.[2]

---

1   Worcestre Itineraries, pp. 203-5, Harvey.
2   Brut's Chronicle.

Jasper had recruited troops from Wales. With him were his father Owen; Sir Thomas Perot of Haverfordwest; Owen and Thomas, the two sons of Gruffydd ap Nicholas, and various other esquires from Gower and Carmarthen; Sir John and Sir William Scudamore and Sir John's son Henry, with some thirty retainers; Lewis Powys of Powyland; Hopkyn Rheinallt Gwenedd of Harlech; Lewis ap Rhys of Carmarthen; the Herefordshire lawyer Thomas Fitzharry; and the Englishman John Throckmorton of Shrewsbury. Jasper's march did not go entirely as planned. He had to wait for James Butler, Earl of Wiltshire and Ormond, to arrive from Ireland with his foreign contingents at Pembroke or Milford Haven. When they finally landed, the combined army of Welsh, Irish, Bretons and Frenchmen,[3] marched from Pembroke, either through Brecon towards Wigmore or to the Valley of Towy via Radnorshire. Having reached Presteigne, they followed the Valley of the Lugg in the direction of Leominster where the two forces met. Whichever route they took, unlike their enemy who had advanced to be on their own territory, Jasper, Wiltshire and their men had marched in the winter cold for more than 100 miles and through a country totally strange to many of them. Without wasting any time, Edward gathered an army of around 2,000 men, among them the Dwnns, William Herbert, Roger Vaughan, Richard Croft, Walter Mytton, John Lingen and Reginald, Lord Grey of Wilton (Jasper's brother-in-law, married to his supposed sister Tacina), and men from Herefordshire.

On 2 February, at a place called Mortimer's Cross, in the county of Herefordshire on the border of Wales and England, and just four miles south of Edward's Wigmore Castle, the Lancastrian army clashed with supporters of the furious eighteen-year-old son of the slain Duke of York. The descriptions of the battle are contradictory but what is certain is that on that morning the weather was very cold for, just before fighting began, a parthelion (sometimes referred to as 'three suns') occurred. Another certainty is that the Earl of Wilshire maintained his reputation for being a coward, as he had done previously at the first Battle of St Albans, by fleeing the field before battle had actually started. Many of the remaining Lancastrians were driven into the River Lugg and were slaughtered or drowned. Jasper's army did not stand a chance against Edward, Earl of March, who was determined to avenge his father's death. Within a short time

---

3   Great Chronicle, p. 193. London Chronicle, p. 172. Brut's Chronicle, p. 531.

the Lancastrians were completely overwhelmed by the Yorkists, and Jasper and Sir Thomas Perrot, who shared command over the defeated army, were forced to flee. While both escaped successfully from the field, it is likely that Sir Thomas was wounded during the battle. Although he got away to Bristol afterwards, he died on 10 April that year.[4] Unfortunately, Jasper's father Owen was not able to do the same as his son. He may have refused to abandon the field even though defeated, or perhaps he was simply unable to make good his escape. Captured by the Yorkists, he was led to the block in Hereford's market place, either that same day or within the next few days, by Roger Vaughan of Tretower, together with at least two of 'his kinsmen and comrades', Henry Scudamore (son of Sir John Scudamore) and John Throckmorton, and many other Welshmen. Owen, as the first person on whom the Earl of March could avenge the deaths of his brother Rutland and his father, was the first to die. It is said that Owen presumed he would be spared because of his relationship with the former royal family – being the widower of Queen Katherine de Valois made him King Henry VI's stepfather. According to Gregory's Chronicle, which very likely derives from an eyewitness account, the elderly Owen (he was in his early sixties) apparently remained unconvinced of his approaching death until the red velvet collar was ripped off his doublet by the executioner and 'he fully meekly took his end'. Owen's final words were: 'That hede shalle ly on the stocke that was wonte to ly on Quene Kateryns lappe'.[5]

It is said that after the execution Owen's head was taken by a woman who combed his hair and washed his face and surrounded it by a hundred candles: 'hys hedde sette a-pone the hyghesyeste gryce of the market crosse, and a madde woman kembyd hys here and wysche a way the blode of hys face'.[6] Jasper's father was buried in Hereford's Greyfriars church.[7]

Contemporary verses (see Appendix G) give an idea of the hopes the Welsh people had in the Tudors, who they believed had the Welsh interests at heart. Those Welsh hopes and faith now focused on Jasper and his nephew Henry Tudor.

In another elegy by the famous Robin Ddu, a great admirer of Owen, the bard takes some satisfaction in the thought that, 'although

---

4   Turvey,, 240-41, correcting the report of William Worcester (Oxford, 1969), p. 339.
5   Gregory's Chronicle, p. 211.
6   Gregory's Chronicle, p. 211.
7   Gregory's Chronicle, p. 211.

[Owen] the swallow's head was hewn', Jasper, "the Great Eagle", remained at large (see Appendix H).

Not only was Owen forced to leave behind his son Jasper and grandson Henry, he had also fathered another son from an unknown woman about two years earlier in 1459. This now fatherless toddler, half-brother to Jasper, was named David Owen. Born in Pembroke,[8] probably in Pembroke Castle, David was very likely taken under Jasper's wing after their father's execution.[9] With this in mind, it is also likely that Jasper's nephew Henry Tudor and his young half-brother David spent their early years in each other's company while living at Pembroke Castle until the autumn of 1461.

Jasper had to live with the fact that he had managed to withdraw from the battlefield but had not been able to save his father's life. Probably encouraged by the fact that Queen Margaret, with her army of Scots, Welsh and Northern men, had successfully defeated Warwick by 17 February 1461 at the second Battle of St Albans, Jasper wrote, on 25 February, a letter from his headquarters at Tenby to his servants and kinsmen at Denbigh, Roger Puleston and John Eyton. Jasper and Roger Puleston shared a great-grandfather, Tudur ap Goronwy (c. 1300–67) (also called ap Grono), and were third cousins. Puleston had been a loyal servant to the Tudors for years. For instance, on 10 September 1456, Edmund granted him £10 in recognition of good services. This was at the time Edmund was controlling the rebellion in South Wales and Puleston seems to have aided him with weapons.[10] Further, both John Eyton and Roger Puleston helped Jasper in besieging Denbigh the year before. In this letter Jasper urged them to stay faithful and reminded them of the great dishonour March, Herbert and the Dwnn's had done them. He expressed his trust in them and exhorted them to stay loyal to the

---

8   Vitellius B. XII, p. 124, MSS, British Museum.
9   *Sussex Archaeological Collections, Illustrating the History and Antiquities of the County,* vol. 7, ed. John Russell Smith (London 1849), pp. 22-43.
10 'Edmund comes Richmondiae oibz ad quos pntes Ire puen't saitm. Sciat quod nos consideracoe boni et laudabit suic' dilect' nobis Rogero Pylston armiger', nob impenso, et imposteru impendend', dedim et concessim eidm Rogo, quadm annuitate siue anual reddit', decem marcar', legal' monet' Anglie, pcipiend anuatim p & [in] annuitatem siue anualem reddit' decem marcar' infra dominiu nrm de Kyallayt Oweyn, in ptibz Northwallie, p man recept' nri ibm, p tempe existent', a die dat' pntiu qua diu nob placuerit. Dat' sub sigitt n[ost]ro, decimo die mens' Septembr', Anno Regni Henric[us] sext[us] post conquests, tricessimo quarto. E RYCHMOND': *Archeaology Camb..* I. i. pp. 146–7.

Lancastrian cause. But most of all Jasper swore to avenge his father's death:

> To the right-trusty and well-beloved Roger
> à Puleston, and to John Eyton, and to either of
> them.

> Right-trusty and well-beloved Cousins and
> frinds, we grete you well. And suppose that yee
> have well in yor remembrance the great dishonor
> and rebuke that we and yee now late have by
> traytors Marche, Harbert, and Dunns, with their
> affinityes, as well in letting us of our Journey to
> the Kinge, as in putting my father yor Kinsman
> to the death, and their trayterously demeaning,
> we purpose with the might of our Lord, and
> assistance of you and other our kinsmen &
> frinds, within short time to avenge. Trusting
> verily that yee will be well-willed and put your
> hands unto the same, and of your disposicon,
> with your good advice therein we pray you to
> ascertayne us in all hast possible, as our especiall
> trust is in you. Written at our towne of Tenbye
> the xxvth of ffeu'r.

> J. PEMBROKE[11]

In another letter, written in a similar context to Roger Puleston on 24 July, it appears that Denbigh Castle was still under the control of the Lancastrians:

> To our Right trusty and well-beloved Roger
> Puleston, Esq., Keeper of the Castle of Denbigh

> Right trusty and well-beloved – We greete
> you well, letting you witt that we have received
> yor letters by Hugh, and understand the matter
> comprised therein; and as touching the keeping
> of the Castle of Denbigh, we pray you that you
> will do your faithful dilligence for the safeguard

---

11   John Williams, *Ancient and Modern Denbigh: A Descriptive History Of The Castle, Borough, and Liberties* (Denbigh, 1850), p. 86.

of hit, as far as in you is, taking the revenue of
the lordship there for the vittaling of the same,
by the hands of Griffith Vychan, receyvor there
– we have written unto him that he should
make p'veyaunce therefore – and that yee will
understand the goodwill and dispossicon of the
people, and that countrey, towards my Lord
Prynce [Edward, Prince of Wales, son of King
Henry VI] and us, and to send us word as soone
as you may, as our trust is in you. Written at my
towne of Tenbye, the xxiiij of July.

J. PEMBROKE.[12]

From the summer of 1461, Jasper was about to begin the life
of a constant adventurer, determined to survive and restore the
Lancastrians to the throne as the most loyal supporter and champion
of his half-brother King Henry VI and the house of Lancaster.

---

12 Williams, *Ancient and Modern Denbigh: A Descriptive History Of The Castle, Borough,
    and Liberties* (Denbigh, 1850) p. 87.

8
FIRST YEARS IN EXILE
February 1461 – September 1467

WITH THE king now back in her possession, it seemed that all Margaret had to do to take control of the country was to march into London. Instead, the city refused her entry and she withdrew her army northwards to Dunstable. This proved a disastrous decision. When news reached Edward, Earl of March, at Ludlow, he immediately moved his troops south-eastwards to Gloucester and from there to the border of Oxfordshire, where he met Warwick on 22 February. Together they planned a new attack and were soon ready to move on. By 26 February 1461, their combined forces reached London, where they were welcomed with open arms by its citizens.[1] New dynastic problems arose for the Yorkists in that they now held the capital with its financial power and department of state to control the kingdom, but could no longer claim to act on the authority of King Henry VI, as they had previously done. Their solution was to create a king of their own. On 3 March, the Yorkist leaders, Archbishop Bourchier of Salisbury, Walter Devereux, Sir John Ratcliffe, William Herbert, the Duke of Norfolk and the Earl of Warwick, met at Baynards Castle. There, on the next day, 4 March, they formally offered Edward the crown and the chancellor proclaimed him King Edward IV. An official coronation would have to wait. Edward, the usurper king, hurried north to confront Queen Margaret.

---

1   Scofield, vol. 1, pp. 141–52.

Meanwhile, more citizens of London had joined Edward's army under the leadership of the newly appointed chancellor, George Neville, youngest brother to the Earl of Warwick. Their force grew to enormous proportions, numbering between 20,000 and 30,000 soldiers. By 27 March, Edward and his troops reached Pontefract, ready for battle. Margaret of Anjou and her Lancastrian troops retreated towards York, where she began to re-group, sending for reinforcements from Scotland and Wales. Soon her force grew to an estimated 30,000 soldiers. The Lancastrians maintained the widely held support of the nobility, having the assistance of nineteen peers against eight for Edward. The two armies now numbered around 50,000 men, the largest force Great Britain had ever witnessed. Battle came on a snowy Palm Sunday, 29 March 1461, at Towton. The Lancastrians, who found themselves facing into the wind, were blinded by snow as arrows rained down on them and were completely overwhelmed. At the end of ten hours of fighting, many were drowned in the river as they fled in great panic from the battlefield. Warwick's brother George Neville wrote: 'So many dead bodies were seen [...] as to cover an area of 6 miles long by 3 broad.'[2] In all, 28,000 men lost their lives in the bloodiest battle in British history, including six Lancastrian noblemen and forty-two knights, who were killed or captured and later executed. Most notable among them were Henry Percy, 3rd Earl of Northumberland; Thomas Courtenay, 6th Earl of Devon (beheaded after the battle on 4 April); Sir Andrew Trollope and Lord Dacre.[3] Those Lancastrian lords that did survive were forced to make peace with the usurper king. King Henry VI, the queen and their son, together with the Duke of Somerset, Exeter and Lord Roos, made speed to cross the border to Scotland where, arriving safely at Edinburgh, they found shelter at the Scottish court. [4]

These events combined to leave Jasper unsupported and vulnerable in Wales. After Towton it became clear that the very few Lancastrian nobles who had survived the previous battles were less committed and many of them made terms with Edward. Margaret Beaufort's husband, Henry Stafford, had fought for Lancaster at Towton but now turned his coat and received a pardon for himself and his wife. In contrast, Jasper remained faithful to his half-brother and to his own moral code, maintaining the kind of loyalty that seemed to be

2   Croyland Chronicle, p. 425.
3   *Paston Letters*, ed. Gairdner, vol. 3, 451. Gregory's Chronicle, pp. 217–118.
4   *Paston Letters*, ed. Gairdner, vol. 3, 450.

discarded by most men if it could be traded for safety, wealth and power.

In order to deal with his lack of authority in Wales, on 8 May Edward appointed his loyal supporter William Herbert chamberlain of South Wales and steward of Carmarthenshire and Cardiganshire.[5] It was very clear that the new king's intentions were to replace Jasper as the premier nobleman and effective leader of Wales. On 26 July 1461, William Herbert was created Lord Herbert of Raglan, Gower and Chepstow, thus becoming the first ever full-blooded Welshman to be advanced to the peerage. At the same time, Herbert's brother-in-law – and another enemy of Jasper's – Walter Devereux, was created Lord Ferrers of Chartley.[6] Furthermore, it was not just at a political level that Jasper was to be replaced by Herbert. He would also be pushed aside by his Yorkist rival at a more personal level.

By August, Herbert and his attendants were back in Wales to take control of what were now his possessions, including Jasper's castle at Pembroke. Even though Jasper had given instructions to its constable, Sir John Skydmore, and his servants, and made sure the castle was well-prepared, provisioned and manned for a potential siege, Pembroke Castle surrendered without any resistance on 30 September.[7] Once inside, Herbert was no doubt pleased to find the four-year-old Earl of Richmond, Jasper's nephew Henry Tudor. Herbert took the boy to his home at Raglan Castle and reserved Henry's wardship for himself, intending to marry him to his eldest daughter Maud. Although a prisoner, Henry was well looked after and treated as a member of the family by Herbert's wife Anne Devereux. Henry's nurse was the wife of Philip ap Howell of Carmarthen, and it is said that she taught her charge to speak Welsh.[8]

Jasper was not present at the time of Pembroke's surrender. Confident that the castle could withstand an attack – or perhaps the attack itself took him by surprise – Jasper may have suspected that his enemies knew he was elsewhere and would not come for his nephew. Jasper's doings in the spring and summer of 1461 are not recorded, although it has been suggested by some that during this time he was at his headquarters at Tenby. Despite all the care and money he had bestowed upon the town and its defences, Tenby, like Pembroke,

---

5   CPR, 1461–1467, pp. 7, 30.
6   Thomas, *Herberts of Raglan*, p. 61.
7   RP, vol. 6, p. 29.
8   Polydore Virgil, pp. 134–5.

offered no resistance to the Yorkists and submitted to them. If Jasper was there, he was able to break out and avoid capture. Another theory is that Jasper was already in North Wales, with the intention of raising resistance in that area. Certainly, on 16 October, assisted by Henry Holland, Duke of Exeter, and Thomas Fitzhenry, he caused a disturbance at Twt Hill, just outside the north wall of Caernarvon, threatening the loyal forces within the town:

> As moch also as Henry Duc of Excestre, Jasper Erle of Pembroke, and Thomas Fitz Herry Late of Herford Squier, at a place called Tutehill, besid the Toune of Carnarvan in Wales, on Friday next after the fest of Translacion of Seint Edward last past, rered werr ayenst the same oure Soverayne Lord, puposyng then and there to have proceded to his destruction, of fals and cruell violence, ayenst their faith and Liegeaunce.[9]

This was an act of desperation and led to nothing. But, even though the Yorkists triumphed once more, Jasper again found a way to escape his pursuers and fled to Ireland. From there, he could stir up some resistance and prepare for a new confrontation during the winter. The Paston letters report that 'these three weeks neither ship nor boat came out of Ireland, and so it seems there is a lot to do with the earl of Pembroke'.[10] Jasper left Ireland for Scotland, where he joined the royal family and the Scottish court, and some time before February 1462 he travelled from there to Brittany.

Meanwhile, the Yorkist parliament had met on 4 November 1461, when it immediately attainted and confiscated the estates of the Lancastrian supporters. According to the Act of Attainder:

> Margarete, and also Henry Duc of Excester, Henry Duc of Somerset, Jasper Erle of Pembroke, James late Erle of Wiltshire, Robert Lord Hungerford, Thomas Mannyng Clerk, John Lax, late Parsoune of Walton in the shire of Somerset Clerk, Henry Lewis Knyght, Robert Whityngham Knight, John Ormond otherwise called John Botillier Knight, Frere Robert Gasley, of the ordre of the Freres Precours, and

9   RP, vol. 5, p. 478.
10   *The Paston Letters*, ed. Gairdner, vol. 1, p. 266.

Thomas Cornewayle Squier have ayenst their faith and Liegeaunce, divers times sith the fourth day of Marche last past stirred, laboured and provoked the ennemyes of our said Soverayne Lord Kyng Edward the Fourthn of outeward lands to entire into his seid reame with grete bataille, to rere were ayenst his astate within the seid reame with grete bataille, to rere were ayenst his Astate within this seid Reame, to conquere the same from his possession and obeysaunce, to depose hym of roiall Astate, Corounes and Dignite, and to destroy his moost noble persone and subgects.[11]

In the same act Jasper, along with others, was stripped of his lands and title.[12] This was only a formality, confirmation of what Jasper must have expected. He believed that Edward was a usurper and his government illegal, and that the only true and anointed king was King Henry. While in exile at the Scottish court Jasper had much to reflect upon – his brother and father both killed by the Yorkists and the only son of his dead brother now fallen into the hands of that same enemy who had been responsible for Edmund's death. Despite the fact that all seemed hopeless, Jasper remained fearless and determined. He continued to direct all his efforts towards the restoration of the Lancastrian monarchy.

Over the following months plans were undoubtedly made. The capture in mid-February 1462 of a Lancastrian scout, who was thought to be carrying letters from the Earl of Oxford to Queen Margaret, uncovered a possible plot. Many different stories have appeared about the plot, some more plausible than others. The most fantastical is probably that of John Stowe, who wrote, in the *Three Fifteenth Century Chronicles*, of the plot as being international and of incredible proportions and that an enormous invasion was planned to take back the kingdom. The architects behind it were supposed to be John de Vere, 12th Earl of Oxford, and his son Aubrey, Lord Audley, with many other Lancastrians also involved. Jasper, accompanied by Henry Holland, Earl of Exeter, and John Ayne, Baron of Burford, was to land at Beaumaris in Anglesey on receiving the appointed sign

11 RP, vol. 5, p. 478.
12 RP, vol. 5, pp. 478–81.

from the captain of the Duke of Burgundy, Robert Gold. In addition, the Duke of Somerset, Lord Hungerford, Dr John Morton and the Duke of Calabria, Queen Margaret's brother, would land in Norfolk and Suffolk with a force of 60,000 Spaniards, while another army under Sir John Fortescue and others would land on the Kentish coast. A further invasion by nearly 250,000 men commanded by the kings of Portugal, Denmark, Aragon and France, and Margaret's father Rene of Anjou would soon follow.[13]

Another more logical and reliable account came from Antonio della Torre, envoy from Milan to King Edward, who wrote to Francesco di Coppino, Bishop of Terni, on 25 March 1462 from London:

> Their plan was as follows: to follow the king as his servants towards the North, as his Majesty was not going to take more than a thousand horse and their two thousand or more, and once among the enemy they were to attack the king and murder him and all his followers. In the mean time the Duke of Somerset, who was at Bruges and is still there, was to descend upon England, and King Henry was also to come with the Scots, and the Earl of Pembroke from Brittany. Some priests and others also have been taken, because so they say, they wrote some notices over the doors of the churches in which they stated that the supreme pontiff had revoked all that your lordship had done in this kingdom, that he gave plenary absolution to all those who would be with King Henry and excommunicated those who were with our king. I believe they will be punished as they deserve.[14]

As fantastical as Stowe's plan may seem, there must be some basis of truth in it. For example, in February 1462, John de Vere, Earl of Oxford, and his eldest son Aubrey, Lord Audley, were captured in Essex by John Tiptoft, Earl of Worcester, and the lords Herbert and Ferrers, and executed for high treason.[15] Moreover, a poem written by

---

13 *15th Century Chronicles*, p. 158.
14 CSP Milan, pp. 106–8.
15 Benet's Chronicle, p. 232.

the bard Dafydd Nanmor suggests that Jasper was the leader of a big international invasion (see Appendix I).

Whatever the true situation may have been, Edward IV attacked with decision, defusing the proposed coup and destroying the scheme before it could mature to be a real threat. Queen Margaret was left with no other choice than to seek the help of Louis XI of France, who had inherited the throne following the sudden death of his father Charles VII in 1461. Louis, known for his shrewdness and conspiracies, and with an eye to the diplomatic advantages that might be gained, was more than willing to shelter her. Margaret arrived in Brittany on 16 April, then journeyed south-eastwards to Angers, where she waited with her father for King Louis' arrival from further south. Finally, on 5 June, Queen Margaret met Louis XI at his magnificent castle at Chinon, on the River La Vienne in Touraine, some further fifty miles south-east from Angers.[16] Negotiations at Chinon began, aimed at securing French support for the Lancastrian cause and a new invasion of England. When exactly Jasper arrived is unknown. However, we do know that he had, in the meantime, paid a short visit to his half-brother Henry VI at Edinburgh, for Jasper and Henry VI's chancellor, Sir John Fortescue, arrived together in Flanders and reached Rouen in Normandy on 13 June, carrying letters of credibility from Henry VI to Louis XI. In Rouen they discovered that a licence to travel freely in his lands, which Louis had earlier granted to all supporters of Henry VI, had now been repealed and safe-conducts were necessary from all travellers who desired to enter France. Luckily, the Count of Charolais, Charles the Bold, and the future Duke of Burgundy (who would marry Edward IV's sister Margaret in 1468), was sympathetic towards the Lancastrian travellers' request for help and provided Jasper and Fortescue with letters for King Louis' officers which allowed them to continue their journey to France.[17]

For unknown reasons, Jasper arrived at the French court without Fortescue. There he learned that an agreement between Margaret and the French king had been concluded by 24 June. Further negotiations moved to the city of Tours, where Jasper arrived at the end of the month. When negotiations between the French King and Margaret

---

16 Scofield, vol 1, p. 250. Haut-Jussé, pp. 49–50.
17 B.N., fonds Francais 4054, f. 177, printed in *The Works of Sir John Fortescue* (1869), ed. Lord Clermont, pp. 29–30 (which dates the event, probably wrongly, to 1465). Scofield, vol. 1, pp. 250–51. Calmette and Perinelle, p. 36 (which dates the event, also wrongly, to 1463)

resulted in the Treaty of Tours, signed on 28 June, Jasper was present and signed the treaty.[18]

A hundred-year truce was agreed between Louis XI and Henry VI with both sides pledging not to aid each other's enemies. On 24 June, Margaret and Louis XI had also come to the agreement in which Louis would lend Margaret a great sum of money, 20,000 livres tournois, with a further promise of 40,000 crowns. This loan came, however, at a heavy price, being granted on condition that if Henry VI were restored to the throne, then either Jasper or another Lancastrian supporter, probably Jean de Foix, Earl of Kendal, was to be made Captain of Calais. The new captain would then have to swear an oath to hand over Calais to the French within a year or otherwise repay the loan at once. If Calais were handed over, the further 40,000 crowns would be forthcoming.[19] It is no surprise that the Lancastrians wanted to keep this treaty as secret as possible. Calais was England's last foothold in France, territory that had been won by Edward III in 1347. The fact that the Lancastrians were prepared to countenance such a universally unpopular decision reveals just how desperate they were to seek military and diplomatic support against the Yorkists. Like Queen Margaret, Jasper must have also been very pleased with the outcome. It now appeared that the Lancastrians enjoyed the complete support of England's biggest neighbour and attempts could be made once again to overcome and remove the Yorkist government.

But very soon Louis XI discovered an obstacle in the conspiracy. In order to reach Calais, his troops would need to cross Burgundian soil, something Duke Philip of Burgundy would certainly refuse. Louis realised the treaty was worthless and cancelled it.

Whether Margaret and Jasper repaid Louis XI the first loan of 20,000 livres is unknown. Either way, before Margaret landed in Northumberland on 25 October, Jasper had already left France in time to take charge of Bamburgh Castle. Bamburgh had been left in the hands of Henry VI's chamberlain Sir Richard Tunstall's brother William, who readily handed the castle over to the Lancastrians. Jasper, together with Henry Beaufort, 2nd Duke of Somerset, Lord Roos and Ralph Percy had a company of 300 men to defend the fortress against the earls of Worcester and Arundel. Margaret, having

---

18 Calmette and Perinelle, pp. 19–21. Scofield, vol. 1, pp. 251–3.
19 Archives Nationales Paris, j648 piece 2, pp. 283–4, cited in Calmette and Perinelle, p. 20 note 5.

been joined by 800 men, sailed to pick up Henry VI in Scotland.[20] The small fleet sailed down to Bamburgh Castle and continued their journey to Alnwick, where they besieged the castle. However, the approach of a large Yorkist force, led by the Earl of Warwick, brought an end to the siege. Upon which the queen and her party decided to return to Scotland. As the royal fleet sailed northwards it was struck by a heavy storm and four ships were wrecked. Somehow Margaret and Henry managed to reach Berwick in a rowing boat and were able to reach Scotland, but many of their soldiers were stranded.[21]

Abandoned by their king and queen, Jasper and Somerset, along with Lord Roos and Percy, again found themselves in a vulnerable situation. Isolated and exposed at Bamburgh Castle, in the cold winter weather and with supplies running out, it is said that Jasper, Somerset and their companions were left nothing else to eat other than their own horses. Their only hope lay in reinforcements being sent from Scotland, but that hope was in vain. On 24 December,[22] they were forced to surrender to the Yorkists. Somerset and Percy accepted a pardon and swore an oath of loyalty to Edward IV, lured by the reinstatement of all their lands and titles. Jasper and Lord Roos refused to do this. Somehow they obtained a safe conduct to Scotland where they joined the king and queen in exile at the Scottish court.[23] Alnwick fell a week or so later in early January 1463. Only Harlech Castle remained in Lancastrian hands.

The queen's mission had ended in failure yet she remained convinced that the success of her cause lay in persuading Louis XI to grant further assistance, or at least preventing him from coming to terms with Edward IV. For this reason, somewhere between mid-April and early May 1463, Jasper again set sail from Scotland, together with the Duke of Exeter and some other Lancastrians, and travelled to Sluys in the Low Countries. There the Duke of Burgundy, Philip the Good, and his son, the Count of Charolais, gave permission to Jasper and his companions to travel to Lille and Tournai, from where they passed to France to seek an audience with Louis.[24] Not realising she would never see her husband again, Margaret followed with her

20 Warkworth's Chronicle, p. 2.
21 15th Century Chronicles, p. 158. Scofield, vol. 1, pp. 261–5.
22 15th Century Chronicles, p. 158.
23 Worcester, Annals, pp. 780–81. Stowe, Annales, p. 417.
24 Marie-Rose Thielemans, Bourgogne et L'Angleterre – relations politiques et economiques entre Pay-Bas Bourguignons et L'Angleterre (1435–1467) (Brussels, 1966), p. 395 note 160.

son Prince Edward in July, hoping that her heir's attendance would help persuade the French king that there was still a future for the Lancastrian cause.[25]

Yet again, on 8 October, their hopes were shattered when Louis signed a united treaty with Edward IV and the dukes of Burgundy and Brittany, pledging not to aid each other's enemies.[26] Margaret was running out of options. Her overriding concern was to keep her ten-year-old son as safe as possible and she therefore decided to travel to the safety of her father's residence in Lorraine, where she and her son would stay for the next seven years.[27]

Jasper remained in France for another two months. He was granted 500 livre tournois to return and left in December, probably for Scotland.[28] The Scots, for their part, realised the problems they incurred by supporting the Lancastrians. Louis XI's new treaty with England had set aside the traditional alliance between France and Scotland and because of this the Scottish government had no other choice than to open negotiations with England, now the England of Edward IV. On 9 December a truce was agreed between the Scots and Edward IV. It included the crucial promise Edward must have wanted so badly – that the Scots would no longer give support to the Lancastrian cause. Henry VI was told to leave the country.

The Lancastrians continued to work for the overthrow of Edward and towards the breaking of the Anglo-French treaty. Somerset and Ralph Percy's treachery towards Edward IV earlier that year gave new hope to the Lancastrians when handing over Bamburgh and Dunstable castles. Henry departed from St Andrews, on the south-east coast, and sailed for Bamburgh. At Christmas 1463, Somerset and Percy arrived at Bamburgh all set to serve their former master, King Henry VI.

While a Lancastrian alliance with France was now out of the question, Jasper refused to give up the seemingly lost field. Strengthened by Somerset's defection he saw a possibility of new opportunities. This came from Jasper's second cousin, Duke Francis II of Brittany, whose grandfather, Louis I de Valois, Duke of Orleans, was a younger brother to King Charles VI of France, the father of Katherine de Valois, Jasper's mother. By the end of the year Duke

25 Scofield, vol 1, p. 301.
26 Scofield, vol.1, pp. 301–8, Calmette et Perinelle, pp. 42–45.
27 B.N. fonds Francais 6970, f. 501v.
28 B.N. fonds Français 6970, f. 501v.

Francis sent an envoy, Guillaume Causinot, to meet King Henry and Somerset at Bamburgh Castle. Causinot spent Christmas with the Lancastrian king and returned to Brittany on 22 February 1464 with letters from Henry VI to his queen, Margaret of Anjou, her parents and Duke Francis II. Once he was back the envoy reported to Duke Francis that Henry VI was in danger and had great need of men, food and materials, and requested the duke send the aid asked for, either direct to him or to Jasper in Wales.[29] Furthermore, in the letter, Henry VI assured Francis confidently that once he received enough support from abroad the Lancastrian king would be restored to his rights. Soon afterwards Jasper travelled to France and then to Brittany to receive the requested supplies. He arrived in March, carrying letters from King Louis XI to Duke Francis II. In one letter, Louis requests Duke Francis to aid Jasper by assisting his return to Wales. This, Francis agreed to and, on 26 March, ordered a fleet from St Malo, led by Vice-Admiral Alain de la Motte, to provide support to Jasper on his mission.[30]

In the meantime, Lancastrian loyalists in England and Wales had been equally active but, on the whole, largely unsuccessful. Somerset led the rebellion in the northern counties of England and Jasper's loyal supporters and kinsmen Roger Puleston and John Hanmer were entrusted with the leadership of North Wales, while in Carmarthenshire Jasper's supporters Philip Mansel of Gower and Hopkyn ap Rhys of Llangyfelach were ringleaders in a minor insurrection in the Towy Valley. But again the Lancastrians were unable to take things further. John Dwnn, sheriff of the Welsh counties Gwynnedd and Ceredigion and captain of Carmarthen and Aberystwyth, along with Roger Vaughan, crushed the rising at Drystwyn in the Valley of Towy, between Carmarthen and Llandeilo.[31] (Philip Mansel, who was brother-in-law to Thomas and Owen ap Gruffydd ap Nicholas, had been a close ally to Jasper and the Lancastrian cause and this link evidently remained unbroken after Edward's usurpation.) Roger Puleston and others were hunted down by the Duke of Norfolk but were soon pardoned by Edward IV.[32] Roger remained secretly loyal to Jasper and the Lancastrian Both Mansel's and Hopkyn ap Rhys's lands were forfeited and

---

29 Scofield, vol. 1, pp. 315–18. Haut Jussé, pp. 74–5.
30 Haut-Jussé, p. 75. Scofield, vol. 1, pp. 329–30, 333–4.
31 The *Paston Letters*, vol 2, pp. 151–2. RP Vol 5, pp. 511–12.
32 The *Paston Letters*, vol 2, pp. 151–2.

granted to Roger Vaughan.[33] Edward knew he needed to take control and suppress the remaining Lancastrian resistance as soon as possible, and began to muster a huge army. On 25 April 1464, a battle took place at Hedgeley Moor and another at Hexham on 15 May, both resulting in Yorkist victories. Many Lancastrians were either killed or captured and executed afterwards, including the Duke of Somerset and his stepbrother Lord Roos. This was followed by the bombarding of the king's refuge at Bamburgh, which became the first castle in the kingdom to be overcome by artillery. Henry VI was once again forced to flee. He was eventually captured in July 1465 and taken to the Tower.

There is no record of when Jasper actually arrived in Wales from Brittany in 1464, or indeed of any of his activities at that time. It seems likely, however, that he remained in Brittany during the rebellion of the first half of 1464 for on 7 June, Louis XI, who was known for good reason as 'the Universal Spider', had suddenly changed his mind once again. Spinning a new web of trickery and deceit, Louis XI wrote another letter in which he criticised Francis for his support of Jasper, whereupon Duke Francis replied with surprise that he thought he was only carrying out the French king's wishes.[34]

At last, after five years bearing the weight of the crown, Edward IV had finally succeeded in eliminating the last remnants of Lancastrian resistance and achieving control of his kingdom. The only stronghold in Lancastrian hands that would prove itself as steady as a rock remained Harlech Castle, which was held by David ap Eynon. Clearly this situation appeared of minor importance to Edward, who did not take steps to resolve it at this point. Probably because of the remoteness of Snowdonia and because winter was now approaching, he disregarded the possibility that in the future Harlech could be very useful for the Lancastrians.

Jasper's whereabouts during the next three-and-a-half years are unknown, but it is certain that he did not sit on his hands. He 'remained at large', embarking on raids across North Wales, where his reputation for annoying the Yorkists was celebrated by Welsh poets who wrote of his capability to command raiding parties from the Dyfi Estuary. There are two poems written by a great admirer of Jasper, the

---

33 Worcestre Itineraries, p. 203.
34 Paul Raymond, *Correspondence inedite de Louis XI avec le duc de Bretagne, 1463–1464.*
    Annuaire-Bulletin de la Societe de L'historire de France, vol 2, pp. 179–80 (1867), J.
    Vaessen. *Lettres de Louis XI, roi de France*, vol 2 (Paris, 1883–1909), p. 196.

bard Tudur Penllyn, in praise of Jasper and his supporter Gruffydd Fychan of Corsygedol (see Appendix J). The latter's residence at Barmouth, a fifteenth-century house called Ty Gwyn, was mentioned as being the location Jasper used as his headquarters and from where he sailed, probably to Brittany, during these years. Another poem by the same bard confirms the location (see Appendix K).

After years of ceaseless effort, determination and unselfish loyalty, Fortune's wheel was about to turn again to Jasper's advantage. His continued support of a cause now so weakened could not hope to change the situation without considerable backing from a foreign power in the form of both money and men. Only then might Jasper offer a significant threat to Edward IV. So far the tide of diplomacy had run in Edward's favour, but largely because of Jasper's endless determination this would soon change.

Figure 22   Raglan Castle.
            (© 2015 Debra Bayani)

Figure 23   Harlech Castle.
            (© 2015 Debra Bayani)

Figure 24   Ty Gwyn
                (© 2015 Debra Bayani)

Figure 25   Harlech Castle's Gatehouse Inner Façade.
                (© 2015 Debra Bayani)

9

'THE BLACK EAGLE OF WALES'

September 1467 – May 1470

B Y THE end of the summer of 1467, there was considerable discontent in England and, according to the Milanese ambassador in Paris, who reported on 12 September 1467 that the Welsh had taken up arms, Jasper travelled to Wales with supporters sent by Queen Margaret.[1]

William Herbert again received a royal mandate to apprehend all rebels within Merionethshire and to capture Harlech Castle. Despite Herbert having been made constable of Harlech the previous year, it was still in Lancastrian hands and stubbornly refused to surrender. David ap Eynon, Captain of Harlech Castle, who was accorded only the highest praise in both contemporary Welsh literature and the official records, was determined to keep this large stronghold for the Lancastrian cause and held Harlech safe for Jasper and his Lancastrian supporters.[2]

Having been courted by Jasper and Margaret of Anjou, Louis XI agreed on 1 June 1468 to authorise his treasurer of war, Antoine Roguier, to provide Jasper with three ships (one of them would be captured by Herbert on its return journey to Normandy[3]), and with

---

1   CSP Milan, I, 121. CSP Venice, I, 408.
2   *Archeaologia Cambrensis*, (1848), p. 69. Dafydd Llwyd, Cardiff MSS.
3   Worcestre, Annales, p.791.

£293 5s. 5d. in livres tournois to enable him to travel back to Wales.[4]
In reality, Louis probably saw this as a way to aggravate Edward IV for
comparatively little cost, and Jasper was just a convenient pawn in this
game of thrones.[5] A chess piece or not, Jasper was determined to make
the most of the opportunity that was offered to him. Having landed
in the Dyfi estuary on 24 June, close to Harlech Castle, with 'fifty
men and a few pence',[6] he set out across Wales and marched towards
Denbigh. The Welsh poet Dafydd Llwyd, who was well aware of
Jasper's invasion, wrote in an ode to David ap Eynon: 'The brave,
long haired invader will come with a fleet, and will hover around the
North Wales coast after the Feast [Feast of Saint John the Baptist,
i.e. 24 June]'.[7] The town of Denbigh that Jasper had successfully
besieged in 1460 now favoured Edward IV[8] and William Herbert had
been granted the office of chief justice of the area the previous year.[9]
Jasper knew that Denbigh had to be secured as soon as possible. As he
marched towards it his force swelled to 2.000 men along the way.[10] At
the same time Jasper held official court sessions in the name of King
Henry VI – 'The olde Lorde Jesper and sum tyme Erle of Pembroke
[...] roode ovyr the contraye and helde many cessions and cysys in
Kyng Harrys name'[11] – a clear demonstration that he still considered
Henry VI the true and lawful king of the realm.

There are scant records of this second siege by Jasper of the town
of Denbigh. However, the sixteenth-century antiquarian Sir John
Wynn of Gwydir reports that his own great-great-grandfather, Ieuan
ap Robert ap Maredudd of Eifionydd, and all of his kinsmen were
Lancastrian supporters, and that Ieuan was one of Jasper's captains at
the besieging and sacking of Denbigh.[12] Jasper and his men managed
to capture Denbigh but, probably because 'the new toune', the segment
of the town that had been rebuilt after Jasper's siege in 1460, resisted
and was burned down and left 'clere defaced with fier by hostilitie'.[13]

4   Bibliotheque Nationale de France, Fonds Francais 6970 fo. 50IV and 20,496 fo. 91.
     Scofield, vol. 1, p. 458.
5   Scofield, vol. 1, pp. 522–3.
6   Worcestre, Annales, p.791.
7   Dafydd Llwyd, Cardiff MSS.
8   N.L.W. MS. 3054d (Mostyn 158), ff. 328–29,
     Welsh chronicler Elis Gruffydd (1468–69)
9   CPR 1467–1477, pp. 41, 136.
10   Worcestre, Annales, p. 791.
11   Gregory's Chronicle, Gairdner, p. 237.
12   Gwydir Family, p. 29.
13   John Leland, *The Itinerary in Wales*, ed. L.T. Smith (1906), p. 97.

It was not only Denbigh that suffered. After being raided by Jasper, the adjoining county of Flintshire, which favoured Edward IV's cause, was unable to pay Edward a promised contribution of 1,000 marks.[14] According to Wynn: 'He also wasted with fire and sword all Nanconwy and the whole country lying between Conway and Dovi'.[15] News spread across the courts of Europe. Giovanni Pietro Panicharolla, the Milanese ambassador at the French court, described on 2 July to his master the Duke of Milan how:

> My Lord of Pembroke, brother of the deposed King Henry of England, with some armed ships has entered the country of Wales, which has always been well affected towards him, and in large part up to the present, always submissive. There is news that when he entered he had some 4,000 English put to death, and he is devoting himself to gathering as many of his partisans there as he can, in order to set himself forward.[16]

The Milanese ambassador also reported that, as a response to Jasper's uprising, Margaret of Anjou, who was at that time in Lorraine, was soon to visit Louis XI in order to appeal for further aid.

By now Edward IV had realised the supreme importance of Harlech Castle and how imperative it was to attack this mighty fortress, described as 'so stronge that men sayde that hyt was inpossybylle unto any man to gete hyt'.[17] Its status as a safe haven of refuge for the Lancastrians had to end; yet, except for the issue of a number of proclamations calling for its garrison to surrender, nothing else had been done. By 3 July Edward ordered Herbert and his brother-in-law Lord Ferrers to raise an army of men from the Welsh Marches, Gloucestershire, Shropshire and Herefordshire, against Queen Margaret, Jasper and other rebels in order to suppress the upheavals.[18] The time had come for the two rival armies to come to blows. Herbert's amassed strength of between 7,000 and 10,000

---

14 D.K.R., XXXVII, pt. II, 285, Chester Recognisance Rolls (1876).
15 Gwydir Family, p. 57.
16 CSP Milan, I (1385–1618), 125.
17 Gregory's Chronicle, Gairdner, p. 237.
18 CPR, 1467–1477, 103.

men[19] was divided into two, possibly three, invading forces. One wing moved northwards from Pembroke and the other moved into the Conwy Valley, so as to converge upon Harlech Castle from the south and east. Richard Herbert, William Herbert's brother, who approached Harlech from the North Welsh coast, met Jasper's force somewhere between the town of Denbigh and the Conway Valley. According to Gregory's Chronicle:

> [...] a lytylle before the sege of that castelle, the olde Lorde Jesper and sum tyme Erle of Pembroke was in Walys; and he roode ovyr the contraye and helde many cessyons and cysys in Kyng Harrys name. But men wene that he was not owte of Walys whenn that the Lord Herberde come with hys oste; but favyrat sum tyme dothe grete ese, as hit ys prevyd by the hydynge of that lorde sum tyme Erle of Penbroke.[20]

In the aftermath, a number of prisoners were taken from Jasper's army and several put to death. A hurricane of slaughter and violence must have swept across the area, for a century later it had still not recovered. Sir John Wynn (1553-1627) wrote in his chronicle of the Gwydir family: 'the print is yet extant, the very stones of manie habitations in and along my demaynes carrying yet the colour of the fire'.[21]

While Richard Herbert dealt with Jasper's force, William Herbert's army came from Pembroke and advanced northwards to Harlech along the old Roman road, Sarn Helen. After many years of holding out strongly against the Yorkist regime, the fortress yielded with only minor resistance and fell into their hands on 14 August, although one of Herbert's men, the experienced soldier Philip Vaughan of Hay, is said to have been killed during the siege.[22] Fifty men from Harlech were taken prisoner and conveyed to the Tower in London. Among them were Sir Richard Tunstall, who had also held Alnwick Castle for the Lancastrians in 1463, Sir William Stoke and Sir Henry Bellingham. According to the Brief Latin Chronicle,

---

19 Worcestre, Annales, p. 791. Several poems estimate Herbert's force at between 7,000 and 9,000 men (see, for example, Gutor Glyn in Records of Denbigh and also the bard Hywel Dafydd ap Ieuan ap Rhys)
20 Gregory's Chronicle, Gairdner, p. 237.
21 Gwydir Family, pp. 49–50.
22 Worcestre, Itinerarium, p. 328. Guto'r Glyn in Records of Denbigh, pp. 202–3.

Tunstall was pardoned by Edward IV,[23] but this sounds unlikely for he had already received a pardon from Edward once before, and that very pardon had given him the opportunity to hand over Alnwick Castle to the Lancastrians in 1463. Worcester's report that Tunstall was executed seems more likely to be correct.[24] Two other captains were captured and executed, John Troublote and Thomas Elwick.[25] Surprisingly, David ap Eynon, Harlech's Captain and Constable, who was also one of the fifty prisoners taken to London, was not executed. Instead, probably due to Herbert's influence, Eynon was pardoned and, some years later, actually received some sort of grant.[26] Many other strong supporters of Jasper, such as Gruffydd Fychan, Roger Puleston and Ievan ap Robert ap Meredith of Caernarvonshire, were all granted a general pardon on 1 September by Edward IV. From one point of view the decision not to punish these men can be seen as very shrewd. Although many of them had made life extremely difficult for those in North Wales who had yielded to Edward, it was now of utmost importance for him to win as much of their loyalty as possible.

Although the Yorkists had triumphed once more, Jasper was yet again too quick and too cunning for them and found a way to escape his pursuers. One story relates that Jasper was hidden by a gentleman, possibly his kinsman Hywel ab Ieuan Fychan of Pengwern and Mostyn, and, disguised by carrying a bundle of peas pods on his back 'for fear that someone should spot him – for there were plenty to spy on him on those parts', fled to Brittany.[27] According to the Welsh chronicler Elis Gruffydd, Jasper managed to escape and commandeer a small boat from a gentleman who lived at Mostyn, at a place called Picton Pool. Once on board, Jasper managed to sail to Brittany, thanks, it is said, 'more to the craft of the Earl than the craft of the boatmen of Picton'.[28] Jasper was enormously lucky to have made a safe escape, but in spite of his safety it was a devastating setback for the Lancastrians to have lost Harlech, their last firm foothold in the kingdom.

Jasper's humiliation was complete when, on 8 September, Edward IV rewarded Herbert for putting down the rebellion and

23 Brief Latin Chronicle, p. 182.
24 Worcestre Annales, p. 791.
25 Gregory's Chronicle, p. 237.
26 Historical MSS Commission; Puleston MSS, p. 150, Archaeologia Cambrensis (1880)
27 History of the Family of Mostyn of Mostyn, London (1925), pp. 57–8.
28 N.L.W. MS. 3054d (Mostyn 158), f. 323 b.

the capture of Harlech, by bestowing on him Jasper's earldom of Pembroke.[29]

When, in the spring of 1468, Edward IV had turned his attention to formalising new alliances with Brittany and Burgundy, this had not met with the favour of his powerful councillor, the Earl of Warwick. In doing so, Edward estranged himself from Louis XI, which made matters rather convenient for the French king who now felt justified in taking up his cousin Jasper's cause again.

Jasper was not the only one dismayed by Herbert's elevation to the earldom. The Earl of Warwick, who himself came from a family of earls and dukes and had worked hard to better his own position, considered Herbert, now elevated to his equal in rank, to be an upstart of lower birth plucked from relative obscurity. In 1464, Warwick entered into negotiations for a marriage between Edward and the French king's sister-in-law, Bona of Savoy, a match that would have secured a long-lasting peace between England and France. Instead Edward had secretly married Elizabeth Woodville, who was not only a commoner and came from a Lancastrian family, but also a widow whose husband, Sir John Grey of Groby, had actually fought for Lancaster and had been killed at the 2nd Battle of St Albans in 1461. Furthermore, John of Lancaster, the first husband of Elizabeth's mother Jaquetta, was the younger brother of King Henry V and thus uncle to King Henry VI. When King Edward IV and his new queen provided her Woodville relations with very successful marriages at the expense of the Earl of Warwick and his family, Warwick realised that his position as premier earl was in danger and it became inevitable that he would take measures to protect it. From 1464 many disagreements occurred between Edward IV, his brother George, Duke of Clarence, and the Earl of Warwick, and by 1467 the earl had had enough of it. Lacking a male heir, Warwick hoped to marry his two daughters to the king's younger brothers, George and Richard, Duke of Gloucester, but Edward had other plans and suggested that George should instead marry Duke Philip of Burgundy's daughter Mary. The jealous and ambitious heir presumptive George now also turned against his brother and conspired with Warwick that he should marry Warwick's daughter Isabel and put himself on the throne.

Jasper's whereabouts from August or September 1468, when he fled from Wales to Brittany, until October 1469, are obscure. It is

29   Worcestre, Annales, p. 791.

known that he was certainly at Louis XI's court from October 1469 until September 1470, where the French king paid him, in four quarterly payments – on 24 January, 20 March, 3 May and 13 August 1470 – a pension of 100 livres tournois a month.[30] However, it was reported in May 1470 by 'A knight who was on his way to Jerusalem' that 'a brother of King Henry has gone to Arcis in Champagne, on behalf of the mother, who is going to the King of France'.[31] But how and why Jasper fled to Brittany a year later and again ended up in France is something we can only guess at.

At the English court rumours circulated that some sort of plot was being planned between the Lancastrians, Warwick and Clarence. By the end of 1468 a man named John Cornelius confessed in the Tower that several Lancastrians – among them Warwick's friend Lord Wenlock, and Warwick's brother–in–law John de Vere, 13th Earl of Oxford – had been conspiring with Margaret of Anjou. Although Oxford was committed to the Tower, he was able to convince Edward of his innocence and was fortunate enough to escape with his life. Some others, however, were not so lucky. Thomas Hungerford and Henry Courtenay, heir to the Earl of Devon, were both found guilty of treason and on 12 January 1469 had to endure the terror of the traitor's death – execution by hanging, drawing and quartering. Warwick and Clarence even started to circulate the rumour that Edward was a bastard and Clarence should be the rightful king. Edward was reluctant to believe that Warwick and his brother could do these things to him and still did not punish them. In June, when Edward was on pilgrimage in East Anglia, he was interrupted by news of fresh disturbances in Yorkshire, instigated by Robin of Redesdale and Robin of Holderness, two shadowy figures who were the leaders of local riots, and calmly took measures to suppress them.

On 9 July further rumours of Warwick and Clarence's treachery were brought to Edward's attention. Even though he was still reluctant to believe these rumours, the king wrote them a letter, calling on them to show they were not 'of such disposition towards us, as the rumour here runs'. The next day Edward learned the truth. Six days earlier, on 4 July 1469, Warwick, his daughter Isabel, Clarence and Oxford had crossed the Channel to Calais. There, on 11 July, Isabel and Clarence were married by Archbishop Neville, despite

---

30   Comtes de la Chambre aux Deniers, A.N., KK62, f.51v.
      Archives Nationales KK 62 fo. 5lv.
31   CSP Milan, pp. 134–45, no. 185.

being outside his jurisdiction. The next day they explicitly invoked rebellion and issued a manifesto, deploring the exclusion of the true nobility from Edward's secret council in favour of certain 'seditious persons', naming the Woodvilles, Herbert, Devon, Lord Audley and Sir John Fogge.[32] Upon their return to England on 16 July, Warwick and Clarence called on their supporters to join them at Canterbury and from there they marched to London, where they were reluctantly allowed in by the City Fathers. From London Warwick and Clarence set out for Coventry, probably hoping to join Robin of Redesdale. Edward, for his part, retreated to Nottingham, where presumably he hoped to join forces with Herbert and Devon, but was outflanked by Redesdale's army who hastened southwards to meet Warwick and Clarence. But on 26 July, at Edgecote, Redesdale's army encountered those of Herbert and Devon.[33] Completely taken by surprise, Herbert and Devon and their loyalist forces somehow became separated and Herbert's force was forced to face Redesdale's army alone. It is said that Herbert's forces fought very hard and that Herbert proved himself as a true knight with a great sense of duty and courage,[34] while Herbert's brother Richard, who was well-skilled with the poleaxe, passed through the battle twice without a mortal wound. Herbert initially held the winning hand but later in the day an additional force sent by Warwick came to Redesdale's aid and Herbert's men were outnumbered and completely overwhelmed. William Herbert and his brother were both captured and beheaded two days later in Northampton.[35] Many other prominent Welshmen, including John and Henry Wogan, Henry and John Dwnn, and Thomas and William Lewis,[36] died along with the Herberts. Given the total list of Welsh gentry who died in this single event, it is easy to understand why this defeat was regarded by the Welsh as a national disaster. For example, the bard Guto'r Glyn lamented, 'Let us hasten to the north to evenge our country. My nation is destroyed, now that the earl [Herbert] is slain,'[37] and Lewis Glyn Cothi wrote, 'This greatest of battles was lost by treachery; at Banbury dire vengeance fell upon Wales.'[38]

---

32 Warkworth's Chronicle, pp. 46–9.
33 Warkworth's Chronicle, pp. 6–7. Chronicles of the White Rose of York, p. 24.
34 Hall's Chronicle, p. 274.
35 Croyland Chronicle, p. 446.
36 Worcestre, *Itineraries*, p. 119. CPR, p. 29.
37 Guto'r Glyn; Cein. Llen. Gymreig, pp. 192–3.
38 Lewis Glyn Cothi, I., 17.

A few days later, on 29 July, totally unaware of what had happened to his supporters, King Edward IV was taken captive at Olney in Buckinghamshire by Warwick's brother, Archbishop Neville, and escorted to Warwick Castle. Apparently, Warwick knelt before Edward, just as Edward had done before Henry VI, and pledged his loyalty. Strangely, Edward appears to have accepted his constricted role – for now.

With the king in his hands, it was easy for Warwick to eliminate the 'seditious persons' on his list. He published a manifesto in which he specifically cited the exclusion of the true nobility from Edward's council and the elevation of the queen's father, Richard Woodville, Earl Rivers and her brother John, as his reason for supporting Clarence against the king. The publication of this manifesto was considered by Warwick as legitimising the execution of both men. The earl and his son were captured by Warwick's men and taken to Coventry, where they were beheaded on 12 August and their heads displayed above the gates of the city. The Earl of Devon suffered the same fate when he was lynched by a mob at Bridgewater.

For a few months Warwick ruled in Edward's name but things did not go as easily as Warwick had expected, and several Lancastrian rebels, among them Sir Humphrey Neville and his brother Charles, created disorder in the name of King Henry VI. Men summoned to join the royal army refused to do so and would not obey orders given by Warwick until these were confirmed as actually coming from Edward IV himself. Warwick was therefore forced to let Edward IV appear in public. And as soon as Edward saw a chance to regain control he seized it. An army to crush the rebels was quickly gathered and Edward sent word to his brother Richard and to other nobles, who came quickly to his side. For a while there seemed to be a stand-off between Warwick, Clarence and Edward IV, during which Edward even forgave both men officially in parliament.[39] But these words from the Croyland Chronicler perhaps best described the true situation at court:

'Still, however, there probably remained, on the one side, deeply seated in his mind, the injuries he had received and the contempt which had been shown to majesty, and on the other – A mind too conscious of a daring deed.'[40]

39 Croyland Chronicle, p. 117.
40 Croyland Chronicle, p. 117.

After Herbert's death, the now twelve-year-old Henry Tudor, who had been a witness to the horrible scene at Edgecote, found himself in an extremely dangerous situation. Fortunately for Henry, in the panic of defeat he was rescued from the battlefield by Sir Richard Corbet, a gentleman who was married to the niece of Herbert's wife Anne Devereux, and taken to the home of Anne's brother, Lord Ferrers, at Weobley in Herefordshire. As Corbet later described in his petition to Henry as Henry VII:

> Pleaseth your Grace to call to your remembraunce the first service, that after the death of Lord Herbert after the field of Banbury, hee [Corbet] was one of them that brought your grace out of danger of your enemys, and conveyed your grace unto your towne of Hereford, and there delivered you in safety to your greate Uncle now Duke of Bedford.[41]

A soon as she heard of Herbert's defeat, Margaret Beaufort started looking for her son. She sent one of her servants to Worcester, who in turn passed on a message to John Bray, who rode to Raglan, only to find that Henry was not there. Bray then travelled to Weobley where, some days later, he found Henry accompanied by Anne Devereux. After finding her son, Margaret's next concern was for Henry's lands and earldom of Richmond, both of which were in the Duke of Clarence's hands. For Margaret, Herbert's death came at a convenient time as it threw her son's future wide open. Henry Tudor had been in Herbert's care for nearly eight years and the earl's death now gave Margaret the opportunity to take control of the boy's future. On 24 August, while Edward IV was still a prisoner, Margaret and her husband Henry Stafford arrived at Clarence's residence in London.[42] This was a risky step to take, but Margaret hoped it would be possible to reach an agreement by which the Richmond lands might be restored to her son.

On 21 October, Margaret and Stafford dined with Lord Ferrers and Anne Devereux's council at the Bell Inn in Fleet Street in London to discuss Henry's wardship.[43] The meeting seems to have

---

41   Owen and Blakeway, Shrewsbury, I. p. 248. Hall's Chronicle, pp. 285–7.
     Vergil, pp. 134–5.
42   WAM 5472 fos. 45v–47r.
43   WAM 5472 fos. 45v–47r.

been a success, for in the following days Margaret paid for several letters to be written and for searches to be made concerning her son's lands, wardship and marriage. Margaret's intended swift resolution of her son's position ended prematurely when Edward IV returned to the capital. Margaret and Stafford's negotiations with Clarence had naturally offended the king, which presumably explains why there was no peerage for Stafford when Edward set about rewarding his most loyal supporters. In contrast, Henry Stafford's younger brother, John, was created Earl of Wiltshire.

In early 1470, there were serious disturbances in Lincolnshire. It is not certain that these were caused by Warwick and Clarence but it does appear that when this rebellion was suppressed Edward IV was not as forgiving towards them as he had been in the past. Another rising in Yorkshire followed in mid-March and this time there was no doubt that Warwick and Clarence were responsible. When Edward reached Newark with his army, he received messages from the earl and his brother, who were in arms and not far away, requesting an audience with guaranteed safe conduct for all. These terms were unacceptable to Edward, as agreeing to such demands would show a dangerous weakness. Warwick and Clarence were informed they would have to submit on Edward's terms or else they would be pursued and destroyed – whereupon they decided to run. Their supporters fell away and eventually they found themselves forced to flee the country. By the end of April 1470, pursued by Edward IV, Warwick and Clarence managed to gather their families, including Clarence's pregnant wife Isabel, assembled a fleet and, taking ship at Dartmouth, sailed for Calais. But, arriving at Calais, the rebels found no sanctuary there either and the town opened fire on their ships.[44] Unable to land and forced to stay at sea in a storm, Isabel went into what seems to have been a premature labour and gave birth to a stillborn son.

The Duke of Burgundy too refused to permit Warwick's fleet to land at any port in the Low Countries. Running out of options, they sailed further down the French coastline. On their way, the rebels even attacked merchant ships to obtain supplies. But now Edward's naval commanders Earl Rivers and Sir John Howard were also at sea and relentless in their pursuit. It is said that Warwick lost fourteen

---

44 Commynes, p. 183.

ships and 500 sailors to Rivers in just one encounter.[45] After being at sea for so long, Warwick and Clarence needed to find shelter as quickly as possible and they finally took refuge in the Seine Estuary near Honfleur in May.

Without knowing it, by leaving England Warwick had opened the door to new opportunities for the Lancastrians and there was no way of turning back the tide.

45 Hicks, Warwick, p. 287.

10

THE WHEEL OF FORTUNE KEEPS ON TURNING
May 1470 – June 1471

O N HEARING of Warwick and Clarence's arrival at Honfleur, King Louis XI was at first rather displeased at Warwick's presence, urging him to leave as soon as possible. The Milanese ambassador, Sforza de Bettini of Florence, reported:

> 'from what I gather, he [Louis XI] is urging him [Warwick], by every means in his power, to get him to return to England, and has sent to offer him ships and troops to fight, advising him to return to the enterprise of England.'[1]

Soon, however, the Universal Spider realised his chance had come. Louis XI had been waiting for such an opportunity for months – already in March the Milanese ambassador had reported Warwick and Clarence's falling out with Edward IV: 'The king here is greatly rejoiced about it, considering it good news, and he is devoting himself more than ever to preparations for war'.[2]

---

1   CSP Milan, pp. 134–45, No.184.
2   CSP Milan, pp. 134–45, No. 182.

If the improbable alliance between the Lancastrians and Warwick was successful with his assistance, Louis would be able to overrule the previous treaties between England and Brittany and, especially, Burgundy and perhaps realise his ambition to establish an Anglo-French military alliance. And now he grasped his opportunity with both hands. On 2 June, the French king left for Denguin, a place close to Torsi in Aquitaine, where he would meet Warwick and Clarence. It was already at this point that the arrangement of a marriage between Warwick's daughter and the Prince of Wales was considered. It was also expected that Warwick would take Prince Edward along with him on his return to England.[3] Louis XI returned to his Chateau of Amboise where, on 8 June, 'in the most honourable and distinguished manner imaginable', he received Warwick and Clarence:

> His Majesty, all the principal lords who happened to be at the Court, three or four leagues to meet them, and he himself went some distance out from the castle on foot to receive them, embracing them in the most friendly way. He also made her Majesty the queen come to the door of the castle to receive them and be kissed, according to the custom here. His Majesty then took them to their chambers in the castle and remained with their lordships two long hours most privately and with great familiarity. And so every day his Majesty has gone to visit them in their rooms and has remained with them in long discussions.[4]

Warwick and Clarence were treated by Louis as his dearest friends, honoured by him most lavishly with feasts, dancing and tournaments. The French king had clearly sent word to Margaret of Anjou of Warwick's arrival, for it was reported on 12 June that she was to arrive in about a week at the French court. While Queen Margaret and Prince Edward were on their way from Lorraine, a journey of around 340 miles south-westwards to Amboise or Tours, Clarence left for Normandy to be with his wife, and mother- and sister-in-law, and Warwick left for Denguin and Vendôme:

3   CSP Milan, pp. 134–45, No. 186.
4   CSP Milan, pp. 134–45, No. 188.

> [...] passing the time without taking any further steps, until the arrival of the queen, wife of King Henry, and the Prince of Wales, her son. The Earl of Warwick does not want to be here when that queen first arrives, but wishes to allow his Majesty to shape matters a little with her and induce her to agree to an alliance between the prince, her son, and a daughter of Warwick, and to put aside all past injuries and enmities. That done, Warwick will return here to give the finishing touches to everything.[5]

After that, Warwick followed Clarence to Normandy to raise his troops.

On 25 June, Margaret and her son arrived at the Chateau of Amboise in the Loire Valley to meet King Louis XI. While Margaret and Prince Edward were graciously received, Louis immediately started to negotiate:

> His Majesty has spent and still spends every day in long discussions with that queen to induce her to make the alliance with Warwick and to let the prince, her son, go with the earl to the enterprise of England. Up to the present the queen has shown herself very hard and difficult, and although his Majesty offers her many assurances, it seems that on no account whatever will she agree to send her son with Warwick, as she mistrusts him.[6]

Naturally Margaret was more than a little resistant to the idea of negotiating with Warwick, the man who had done everything in his power to destroy her and her family. Eventually it took Louis XI a month to get both parties to an agreement.[7] Margaret and Warwick met in Angers on 22 July, where Warwick 'with great reverence' asked on his knees for Margaret's forgiveness 'for the injuries and wrongs done to her in the past'.

Tradition has it that this was a humiliating ceremony for Warwick and that Margaret left the earl kneeling for at least fifteen minutes.

---

5 CSP Milan, pp. 134–45, No. 188.
6 CSP Milan, pp. 134–45, No. 189.
7 Calmette et Perinelle, pp. 110–14. Scofield, vol. I, pp. 527–33.

But, according to the Milanese ambassador, Margaret forgave Warwick graciously.[8] Finally terms were agreed for a remarkable alliance – one as unpleasant to both sides as was necessary – with both parties committing themselves to an alliance with Louis XI as its mediator. If all went as intended, Warwick was also to aid Louis in a planned war against Burgundy. Warwick's demand to take Prince Edward to England was not met, Margaret adamantly refusing to release her precious son before success was assured. Instead, the young man's uncle, Jasper, was to go in his place to conquer the kingdom for the Lancastrians.[9] Queen Margaret and the seventeen-year-old Prince Edward, who was said to be anxious to reclaim his lost inheritance,[10] gave permission that, if King Henry VI was not fit to govern the country, then Jasper and Warwick should do so until Prince Edward matured and was capable of ruling the realm himself. This would have only been a matter of months. According to the Milanese ambassador in France, Giovanni Pietro Panicharolla, who wrote to the Duke and Duchess of Milan some years earlier about a dinner conversation between King Louis XI and Margaret of Anjou's brother, John Duke of Calabria:

> As the King [Louis XI] persisted in his praise of the Earl of Warwick, the duke said that as he was so fond of him he ought to try and restore his sister in that kingdom, when he would make sure of it as much as he was sure at present and even more so. The King asked what security they would give or if they would offer the queen's son as a hostage. This boy, though only thirteen years of age, already talks of nothing but of cutting off heads or making war, as if he had everything in his hands or was the god of battles or the peaceful occupant of that throne [...] [11]

According to the Burgundian chronicler Jean de Wavrin, when the prince was asked by his mother what should be done with some particular Yorkist captives after the Lancastrian victory at Wakefield in 1460, he cold-bloodedly replied that they should be beheaded.

---

8   CSP Milan, pp. 134–45, No. 191.
9   CSP Milan, pp. 134–45, No. 190.
10   Warkworth's Chronicle, p. 12. Vergil, pp. 131–2.
11   CSP Milan, p. 117.

Edward's character is often judged as vicious and heartless but if one considers what this young prince had gone through that does not seem particularly surprising. Edward's father the king was a prisoner in the Tower and Edward himself had, from a very early age, been almost constantly in exile and facing a doubtful future. Moreover, if Edward did talk of cutting off heads and call for the execution of the Yorkists, he was most likely giving the reaction that the adults around him expected of him.

The agreement, which was announced by the newly arrived King Rene of Anjou, Margaret's father, was sealed by the betrothal of Warwick's youngest daughter Anne Neville and Prince Edward on 25 July.[12] (The actual marriage would not take place until December that year, although a papal dispensation, necessary because the young couple shared a common great-grandfather in John of Gaunt, was issued on 17 August 1470.) Five days after the betrothal, on 30 July, an agreement was reached about the way to restore Henry VI.[13] All Warwick had to do now was remove one final obstacle, restoring Henry VI to the throne.

Preparations were being made to return to England and depose Edward IV. Louis XI provided Jasper and Warwick with weapons, ships and men for the purpose. Queen Margaret and the prince would remain in France for their safety until Henry VI was freed from the Tower and restored to his throne, and then they would return to England.[14] On 31 July, the Lancastrian party left for Normandy to celebrate 'the nuptial of their children',[15] and on 7 August, the Milanese ambassador reported that Jasper and Warwick left the French court in preparation for their journey to England.[16]

On 9 September they were ready to embark from Saint-Vaast-la-Hougue in Normandy with a fleet of sixty French ships under the command of the French admiral and set out for England. In the meantime, the Duke of Burgundy, incensed at this alliance, had sent a fleet of many ships to the coast of Normandy to intercept Jasper and Warwick's convoy. Despite this, the Lancastrians' journey was unobstructed and four days later, on 13 September, they disembarked

---

12 Scofield, vol. 1, p. 530.
13 Scofield, vol. 1, pp. 527–33. Calmette et Perinelle, pp. 110–14.
14 Scofield, vol. 1, pp. 527–33. Calmette et Perinelle, pp. 110–14.
15 CSP Milan, pp.134–45, No. 193.
16 CSP Milan, pp. 134–45, Nos 192, 194.

safely after nightfall at Dartmouth and Plymouth on the south coast.[17]
As no one was better qualified than Jasper to secure the Lancastrian
position in Wales, he immediately headed westwards – to see what was
left of his properties, to find his nephew and to raise troops for what
was about to come. While the rest of Warwick's army moved north-
eastwards, Warwick's brother, John Neville, Marquess of Montagu,
who had hitherto supported King Edward through and through,
even against his own brother, now defected to Warwick's side and
was ready to capture Edward. At this point Edward, who had only
a small force at his disposal, recognised that it would be impossible
for him to prevail – and that he would certainly not be spared if he
were to be captured again. Edward had no other option but to flee the
country, together with his youngest brother Richard, his brother-in-
law Anthony, the new Earl Rivers, and Lord Hastings, to seek safety
and help from his brother-in-law, Charles Duke of Burgundy, in the
Low Countries.

Edward's flight cleared Warwick's way to march on to London
and led Henry VI to be freed, on 6 October, from the Tower[18]
where he had been 'not so cleanly kept as should be such a prince'
for the past two years. The years of captivity had taken their toll on
the unfortunate king, whose mental state was extremely weak and
unstable. He was most probably unaware of what was happening to
him when, after ten years of alternating captivity and exile, Warwick
carried his train through the streets to St Paul's Cathedral and the
crown was once again ceremonially placed upon his head. It could not
have been clearer to everyone who it was who pulled the strings, and it
was the earl who issued an official proclamation declaring Henry VI's
'readeption to royal power'. Warwick's powerbase now rested on just
a few noblemen – Clarence, Jasper, Oxford and Warwick's brother
Montagu.

As soon as the Lancastrian fleet landed on British soil, Jasper
turned his attention to his nephew to ensure that he was well-provided
for by the new government. During the negotiations of Henry Tudor's
wardship, the boy had remained at Weobley with Countess Anne
Devereux. Some time in the first half of October Jasper travelled to
Hereford where Richard Corbet handed over the thirteen-year-old
Henry. According to Vergil, 'Jaspar tooke the boy Henry from the

---

17   Scofield, vol. 1, p. 536.
18   Scofield, vol. 1, pp. 539–40.

wife of the lord Harbert, and browght him with himself a little after whan he cam to London'. Finally nephew and uncle were reunited after more than nine years of separation, it must have been an overwhelming and emotional moment for both of them.

Jasper and Henry spent some weeks in one another's company and after that they moved to London, where Jasper reunited Henry with his mother Margaret Beaufort on 28 October at Stafford's house. Henry and his mother had seen each other on several occasions when Margaret and her husband had visited him at the Herberts' at Raglan Castle. That night Jasper dined and slept at Margaret and Stafford's house, and there can be no doubt that he and Stafford discussed the new situation. Also, on this occasion, Jasper temporarily relinquished his nephew's custody to the boy's mother. Margaret was fiercely determined that her son's rightful inheritance would be restored to him, something for which she had fanatically striven since Herbert's death the year before. To achieve this, the king's own authority was necessary and it was decided that Henry should meet with his uncle the king, in the hope of persuading him of the necessity of restoring his young nephew to his entitled lands. On 27 October, Henry was rowed from London to Westminster for an audience with Henry VI. Tradition has it that it was Jasper or Margaret who took Henry to meet his royal uncle. It may well have been Jasper who presented the boy at court – and Polydore Virgil confirms that it was Jasper who 'browght him with himself a little after whan he cam to London unto King Henry'. But because Jasper had just given Henry's custody temporarily back to Margaret, it seems most likely that the boy's mother arranged this meeting.

We cannot know what conversation took place between the thirteen-year-old Henry Tudor and the almost fifty-year-old innocent King Henry. Henry Tudor's first biographer, Bernard Andre, wrote that Henry VI, when enjoying a 'lavish banquet', had washed his hands and sent for young Henry, and 'forecast that someday he would assume the helm of state, and was destined to hold everything in his grasp'. Apparently the king also warned Henry to flee the kingdom, 'to evade the cruel hands of his enemies'. Several years later, Polydore Vergil, who had obviously been influenced by Andre's words, wrote a similar account in his *Anglia Historia*. Whether any part of this event is true will probably never be known. What is clear is that at this point the Lancastrian cause was anything but dead. All Lancastrian hopes now centred on Henry VI and his son, the Prince of Wales, who was yet to arrive from France.

The records do reveal that Henry, Margaret and Stafford remained in each other's company for two weeks, buying new horse equipment for Henry and visiting Guildford, Maidenhead, Windsor and Henley-on-Thames.

On 11 November, Henry was returned to Jasper's custody and together they travelled towards South Wales in the first half of November.[19]

While Jasper was busy in the Marches, parliament was summoned and sat from 26 November until Christmas. After all the sacrifices he had made and the years in exile, Jasper naturally expected his forfeited lands and titles to be returned to him. Given that William Herbert had held the earldom of Pembroke during the Yorkist rule, and his son, also William, had inherited the title after Herbert's execution in 1469. Technically there were now two earls of Pembroke, though Jasper had the stronger claim.[20] As well as having his former estates restored to him, Jasper was richly rewarded with new lands. On 14 November he received the farm of the estates in Wales and the Marches of the late William Herbert, to hold for seven years at a rent to be agreed with the exchequer.[21] On 7 December Jasper was granted 'at his free deposition the advowson of the Parish Church of Meyvode [Meifod]' in the diocese of St Asaph, Powys, as soon as it became vacant.[22] Jasper may have taken young Henry to Pembroke, considering it the safest possible place for the boy to stay, and then immediately travelled back to the Marches where he had other issues to deal with. The southern border counties were obviously of greater concern to the newly restored government. It was probably felt that Wales itself could be relied upon to align itself behind Jasper, whereas Herefordshire and Gloucestershire, controlling as they did the southern route from London to Wales, were sufficiently unsafe to warrant special attention for the preservation of order. Hitherto, this area had been powerfully influenced by the Herberts, the Devereux family and the Vaughans; but now Jasper was active in the Marches. He made a stopover in Monmouth where, on 16 December, the earl wrote a letter, as Locum Tenens for Prince Edward, to his loyal

19 Exchequer, Warrants for Issues, 71/6/12, 13. Vergil, pp. 134–35.
20 Ellis, pp. 192–3.
21 CFR, 1461–1471, pp. 283–4.
22 CPR, 1467–1477, p. 233.

adherent John Puleston, rewarding him 'for his good services', clearly for his loyal services to Henry VI and Jasper, as Sheriff of Flint.[23] On 20 December, Jasper was appointed Justice of the Peace for Hereford- and Gloucestershire.[24] On 16 January 1471, Jasper was appointed to lead a commission of oyer and terminer in the county of Gloucestershire along with Sir William Berkeley, Thomas Fitzharry and a number of other knights and squires.[25] Further, on 30 January, Clarence, Jasper and Warwick received a commission of Array in the county of Hereford for defence against Edward IV 'the usurper and his adherents'.[26]

The entirety of Jasper's activities during these weeks of re-establishing control in the area is not known, for the records of parliament have not all survived. It is, however, clear that Jasper's greatest windfall came on 14 February when he was granted the former lands of Richard Grey, Lord Grey of Powys, the wardship of the properties of John Grey, minor son of Richard, Lord Powys, during his minority and also the boy's wardship and marriage. These lands comprised Welshpool, the castle there and the manors of Pontesbury and Charlton in Shropshire, Whissendine in Rutland, Deeping in Lincolnshire, and Layham and Kersey in Suffolk.[27] On the same day Jasper was granted for life the office of constable of Gloucester Castle with a meadow called Kyngesmede, which was situated near to the castle, and in addition a 'profit' called Castelcoule.[28] Another grant, awarded jointly to Jasper and to Warwick, was the castle and town of Bronllys, the lordships of Pencelli and Cantref Selyf, the manors of Llangoed and Alexanderston, and also a third part of the barony of Pencelli, all in Breconshire and all farmed by Jasper in the past. They were to hold these lands and properties so long as they were in the king's hands and at a farm to be agreed with the exchequer.[29] Finally, as another joint grant, Jasper and Warwick were leased the castles and lordships of Brecon, Huntingdon and Hay, which were in the king's hands because of the death of the late Duke of Buckingham, Humphrey Stafford, and the minority of his grandson, Henry, who was his heir. The earls were to hold these estates and properties

---

23 *Archeologie Cambrensis*, I. i. pp. 146–7.
24 CPR, 1467–1477, pp. 615–16.
25 CPR, 1467–1477, p. 251.
26 CPR, 1467–1477, p. 252.
27 SF, vol. II, p. 701. G.E.C., VI, pp. 139–40.
28 Foedera, XI, pp. 680–81 CPR, 1467–1477, p. 236.
29 CFR, 1461–1471, p. 293.

during the minority of Henry Stafford at a farm to be agreed with the exchequer by midsummer.[30] Together with the restoration of his former lands, Jasper's wealth and power increased greatly. After all the years of danger, perseverance, exile and dependence on other people's generosity, success and victory must have felt rewarding.

Now that the Marches appeared to be largely under control again, it is very likely that Jasper returned to Wales where he may have brought Henry to Pembroke Castle and then, in expectation of Edward IV's return, he set about doing what he was best at: recruiting a large Welsh army.

On 19 February 1471, Edward's preparations to return to England, aided by his brother-in-law Charles, were complete and his fleet of thirty-six ships was ready to depart from Vlissingen (Flushing), some five miles north-east from Brugge (Bruges).

Early in March, Edward returned to England and landed at Ravenspur in Yorkshire. He prevailed on the citizens of York to receive him, not as king but as a loyal subject of King Henry VI. He then passed on to London, which he reached on 11 April. Meanwhile, his brother George once again turned his coat and came over to Edward's side.

Three days later, on 14 April, between four and five o'clock in the morning of Easter Day, Edward and Warwick met at Barnet. Earlier during the night Warwick had given orders to his artillery to fire at Edward's camp. But, much to Edward's relief, Warwick's guns overshot their target, and soon the Yorkist king realized that Warwick had no idea of his enemies' location. The constant bombardment of Warwick's guns produced a large cloud of smoke that blended with the already thickening mist. Edward, now determined to strike first, advanced into the mist. The two forces almost immediately fell into hand-to-hand combat. Soon it became clear that Edward's left flank was outnumbered by the Lancastrians' right flank under the command of Oxford. Within a short period of time the Yorkist flank broke and many took to flight with Oxford in pursuit of them. Edward continued and was able to push Warwick's flank back. Slowly the Yorkists gained the advantage. When Oxford's men returned to the battlefield thinking they had already won, they were surprised to discover that the fighting had not yet ended. Oxford immediately regrouped his force in the dense fog, unaware that the

---

30 CFR, 1461–1471, p. 293.

battle had swung around so that he would be charging into his own side. Warwick's men, mistaking the Oxford livery badge of a star for the Yorkist badge of a sun, started to fight Oxford's men. The latter soon began to cry 'treason, treason', but it was too late. In the panic and confusion Oxford's men fled the field, leaving Warwick and his troops to face the combined forces of Edward and his younger brother Richard. The remaining Lancastrian soldiers abandoned the field altogether, ignoring Warwick's plea to stay and withstand a final charge. Soon Warwick joined them, but found no chance to escape. Edward prevailed and Warwick was killed, beaten to death. Also dead were his younger brother John, Marquess of Montagu, and around a thousand Lancastrians, along with 500 Yorkists. It was barely dawn and the battle had lasted for around three hours. The rest of the Lancastrians had been able to flee, including the Earl of Oxford, who was able to escape northwards to Scotland.

Believing it to be safe, Margaret of Anjou and her son had already crossed the Channel. That same afternoon, while Edward marched in triumph back to London with the young Earl of Pembroke, William Herbert, at his side[31] and rapidly secured Henry VI's custody, the queen's party landed at Weymouth, where they soon learned of Warwick's defeat and the crushing blow to the Lancastrian cause. Prince Edward had been appointed Lieutenant of the Realm of England on 27 March that year and in this office he immediately started to send letters to potential supporters, asking them to fight against Edward.[32] At Cerne Abbey Margaret took council with Somerset and several other Lancastrian leaders. Although her chances of success were now not as strong as they were with the Earl of Warwick at her side, she also had reason for optimism, for without Warwick she was no longer forced to stick to an agreement she had only entered with reluctance. Margaret's chances completely depended on whether Jasper and his force were able to unite with her own. Jasper had travelled westwards to South Wales, where he had begun to recruit a large Welsh army. Margaret set about gathering forces in Exeter and then marched northwards to Bristol and the Severn Valley towards the Welsh border where she intended to try to connect with Jasper.

Realising the seriousness of the situation, Edward IV issued orders to fifteen counties to assemble soldiers, and quickly began his

---

31 *Political Songs and Poems*, p. 280.
32 Hammond, p. 81.

march westwards to intercept Margaret and Somerset's forces before they could join up with Jasper. Practically this meant that Edward had to prevent Margaret from crossing the Severn by any means. Not knowing Margaret's exact location, Edward moved cautiously at first. He reached Cirencester, less than a day's march from the Severn crossing at Gloucester, on 29 April. The race for the Severn was now on. Everything would depend on whether Margaret was able to reach Gloucester before Edward IV, then cross the river and reach Jasper, who was waiting for her on the far side of it at or near Chepstow.

Outflanked, Edward had no chance to catch up with the Lancastrians before they reached Gloucester. Instead he sent messages to its governor, ordering him to hold the town whatever it cost. Edward's plan worked, when Margaret and Somerset reached Gloucester at ten o'clock on the evening of Friday 3 May, the town gates were closed. Somerset threatened to storm the walls, but it was an idle threat. During the night the Lancastrian force had already marched an astonishing thirty-six miles across rough terrain without any proper refreshment.[33] Now, despite their exhaustion, they had no option but to continue north for another twenty-four miles to the next crossing at Tewkesbury. In the previous three days the Lancastrians had covered around sixty miles, an extraordinary achievement, especially for the foot soldiers. By the end of the day, Edward's army, whose marching conditions had been much better than that of the Lancastrians, managed to make great speed and reached Cheltenham that afternoon. There Edward learned that the Lancastrians had reached Tewkesbury and decided, after allowing his troops a brief rest and to refresh themselves, to press on further, finally stopping at just three miles' distance from the Lancastrians. Whether Margaret and Somerset were aware of Edward's advance is unknown. However, both sides must surely have known that, for whichever of them lost on this occasion, defeat would be total.

At daybreak it became clear that the Lancastrians had chosen a strong defensive position, on higher ground to the south of Tewkesbury, with in front of them 'foul lanes and deep dykes, and many hedges with hills and valleys'.[34] This made it extremely difficult for the Yorkists to attack them. But Edward was determined. Drawing up his forces in three divisions, he placed his brother Richard in

---

33 The Arrivall, p. 27.
34 The Arrivall, p. 29.

charge of the vanguard on his left and Lord Hastings on his right, while he himself remained in the centre.

On the Lancastrian side, Somerset chose to command the right flank, while Prince Edward was in nominal command of the centre, aided by the elderly but experienced Lord John Wenlock and Sir John Langstrother.[35] Sir John Courtenay, Earl of Devon, commanded their left. Also among the leaders was Somerset's younger brother John Beaufort, Marquess of Dorset. Edward made his first move by ordering his trumpeters to sound the advance and, almost simultaneously, the archers and gunners to open fire. The Lancastrian attempt to return fire failed due to the Yorkist arrows that rained upon them. Somerset had underestimated the strength of the Yorkist vanguard and soon found himself being attacked from both sides by Edward and Richard's forces in ferocious close combat. For some reason Lord Wenlock and his men had not moved from their position and Somerset's force was slowly driven back up the slope. It was now all a matter of moments before Edward performed a master stroke, ordering his 200 hidden spearmen to launch a surprise attack from the woods against the flank side of Somerset's beleaguered troops. Somerset's men scattered, flying in different directions. Most of them would suffer the fate of being cut down and killed in the rout. According to *Hall's Chronicle*, which was published in 1542, Somerset himself returned to the motionless troops of Lord Wenlock and, in outrage at Wenlock's behaviour, called him a traitor and took his battle-axe and beat the old man's brains out.[36] Very soon most of the Lancastrians had to flee for their lives, again. Many were cut down and others drowned in the rivers Avon, Severn and Swilgate as they attempted to cross. The battlefield had become a death-trap. Many of Somerset's men were caught and killed in a narrow field, still known as Bloody Meadow. Some other Lancastrians managed to flee to Didbrook, but were killed in the church there where they had sought sanctuary.[37]

Worst of all, the Lancastrians' greatest fear had become reality – Prince Edward had been killed amidst the crush of defeat. According to several sources, the prince was first captured and questioned by Edward IV[38] and when he defiantly replied that 'he had come to claim his ancestral realm' he was promptly killed by the dukes of

35 Hammond, p. 94.
36 Hall's Chronicle, p. 300.
37 Hammond, p. 99.
38 Hammond, pp. 124–5.

Clarence and Gloucester and Lord Hastings.[39] Several other sources add Thomas Grey, the future Marquess of Dorset, to the murderers.[40]

Despite these more colourful later sources, other plausible explanations of Prince Edward's death can be that he was slain after the rout while 'fleeing to the town wards',[41] or that he simply fell in battle. In any case, once he fell into Yorkist hands his fate was sealed. Prince Edward of Lancaster was buried in Tewkesbury Abbey.

The whole purpose of the Lancastrian cause was gone, having died along with the Lancastrian prince. Of those Lancastrians that were not killed during their flight, many managed to reach Tewkesbury Abbey where they sought refuge thinking the holy right of sanctuary would afford them temporary protection. In the aftermath of the battle Edward pursued the exhausted fugitives into the abbey and then came a difficult stand-off between the abbey and the crown. Edward wanted his prisoners but, on the other hand, the sanctity of the church had to be respected. The Abbot of Tewkesbury Abbey, Abbot Strensham, faced a dilemma but clearly recognised that Edward was now the undisputed king. The abbey survived by noble patronage and he knew that his interests would not be advanced by crossing the king. A compromise was agreed. The abbot accepted that the abbey did not have the freedom to grant sanctuary to the king's traitors and the king in turn 'agreed to their pardon'. This was just a ruse, the rights and freedoms of the church that were protected by Rome, were disgracefully misused here. According to *The Arrivall*:

> [...] he [Edward IV] gave them all his free pardon, albeit, that there never was, never had not at any time been granted, any franchise to that place for any offenders against their prince having recourde thither, but that it had been lawful to the King to have commanded them to have been drawn out of the church, and have done them to be executed as his traitors [...][42]

The nobles were immediately arrested and most of the common soldiers were released and sent home. Two days later Somerset, Sir John Langstrother, treasurer to King Henry VI and prior of the Order of

---

39 Vergil, p. 152.
40 Hall's Chronicle, p. 301.
41 Bruce, p. 30.
42 The Arrivall, p. 31.

St John of Jerusalem, and others were tried, with Gloucester acting as judge and Norfolk as Marshal. Predictably they were all found guilty and were publicly beheaded in Tewkesbury's marketplace. Other notable Lancastrian deaths at or shortly after the battle included those of Dorset, Devon, Sir John Lewkenor of West Grinstead, Hugh Courtenay and Sir Edward Hampden of Beckley.

This was a truly shattering defeat for the Lancastrians – with Henry VI in captivity and Prince Edward killed, the house of Lancaster was leaderless and Edward IV's solid position as good as unbeatable. During or soon after the battle, Queen Margaret fled to a religious house, probably in Malvern, where she was captured three days later and taken to London.[43]

Meanwhile Jasper had been unable to reach Queen Margaret in time from South Wales to prevent the defeat. He had been safely behind the defensive walls of Chepstow, high upon the Welsh bank of the River Wye, when he heard the news of the catastrophe, and he remained there while he sought advice from friends as to his next move. Edward IV knew that Jasper was still at large and also where he was staying for the moment and sent Sir Roger Vaughan, maternal half-brother to the late Yorkist Earl of Pembroke, William Herbert, and 'a very valiant man', to eliminate this final pocket of rebellion.

According to Hall, 'King Edward at this season, not beynge out of feare for the erle of Penbroke, sent prively in too Wales, Roger Vaughan, a man there bothe stronge of people and of frendes, to the entent of some gyle or sodaynly to trap and surprise the erle.' But Jasper, it is said, through the help of his friends in Chepstow, was able to turn the tables so that 'he having intelligence of certayne frendes, how that watche was privilie leyed for him, sodainly in the towne [Chepstow] toke Roger Vaughan'.[44] It was allegedly the Bishop of Llandaff, John Hunden, who gave Jasper timely warning of Vaughan's approach. This was the same Sir Roger Vaughan of Tretower who had been responsible for the death of Jasper's father, Owen, after Mortimer's Cross ten years earlier. Aware of who this man was, Jasper swiftly arrested Vaughan within the town walls and when Vaughan begged Jasper to spare his life, the earl answered: 'that he should have such favour as he shewid to Owene his Father'[45]and immediately executed him by beheading.

---

43 The Arrivall, p. 31.
44 Vergil, pp. 154–155. Hall's Chronicle, p. 302.
45 Leland, p. 66.

To express his gratitude to the bishop, in 1485 Jasper paid for the building of the north-west tower, the bell tower, of Llandaff Cathedral in Cardiff, which was named after him, 'The Jasper Tower'.

Margaret of Anjou, now a broken woman who was no longer a queen but a bereaved mother, was brought to the Tower of London on 21 May and would remain a prisoner for the next four years until she was ransomed to King Louis XI. That very same night, while Margaret was close at hand – and ironically precisely sixteen years since the first battle of the Wars of the Roses was fought – her husband King Henry VI was cold-bloodedly murdered in the Tower of London. According to Philippe de Commynes, a contemporary politician, writer and diplomat at the Burgundian and French courts, 'If what was told me was true, after the battle was over, the Duke of Gloucester slew this poor King Henry with his own hand, or caused him to be carried to some private place, and stood by himself, while he was killed.'[46] According to John Warkworth, who wrote his chronicle around 1480, Henry was murdered 'between eleven and twelve of the clock, being at the Tower the Duke of Gloucester and many others'.[47] According to Sforza di Bettini of Florence, Milanese Ambassador at the French Court to Galeazzo Maria Sforza, Duke of Milan: 'King Edward had chosen not to have the custody of King Henry any longer. He has, in short, chosen to crush the seed.'[48]

The next evening Henry VI's body was taken to St Paul's Cathedral, where it was displayed in an open coffin. The following morning the body was escorted to Chertsey Abbey for burial.[49]

After his act of personal revenge at Chepstow, Jasper realised that all was lost and that it would just be a matter of time before Edward sent someone else to carry out Vaughan's errand. It is unknown whether Jasper had yet heard about his royal half-brother's death in the Tower. Warwick's death at Barnet and the outcome at Tewkesbury had radically altered the position of his own family, while the death of his nephew Prince Edward had effectively destroyed the Lancastrian claim to the throne. Aside from the Duke of Exeter, Henry Holland, who was one of the closest claimants, the next royal heir appeared to be Jasper's nephew, Henry Tudor. With Henry's mother Margaret Beaufort obliged, because of her husband's connections with the

46 Commynes, vol. 1, p. 280.
47 Great Chronicle, p. 220. Warkworth's Chronicle, p.18.
48 CSP Milan, pp. 145–62.
49 Great Chronicle, p. 220.

House of York, to submit herself to Edward IV and make peace with the Yorkist regime, Jasper understood that the boy's welfare was in his hands alone.

Events left Jasper with no other choice than to leave Chepstow immediately and withdraw to his home at Pembroke Castle. He arrived there only just in time to secure Henry's safety inside, for as soon as Edward IV heard of Roger Vaughan's execution he had sent others in pursuit. At Pembroke Jasper was besieged by Morgan ap Thomas, a grandson of the famous Gruffydd ap Nicholas. This was somewhat unexpected as Morgan and his family had been supporters of the Tudor brothers and of the house of Lancaster after Edmund had suppressed Gruffydd ap Nicholas' disorder in Wales in 1456, and Gruffydd himself is said to have died alongside Owen Tudor at Mortimer's Cross for the same cause. Which makes it even more surprising why Morgan should have turned against Jasper. It is very likely that his reason was a personal one: Morgan happened to be married to Catherine Vaughan, daughter of Sir Roger Vaughan, and it seems that family loyalties superseded the previous alliance. There was very little chance that Morgan would be able to gain access to this mighty fortress, but instead he decided to encircle the castle by digging trenches and ditches around it, so there was no possibility of escape. By preventing all communication from outside, Morgan intended to starve Jasper and Henry out of hiding. Relief came only eight days later – again surprisingly – with Morgan's own younger brother, Dafydd ap Thomas, who arrived at Pembroke with a force of 2,000 men and began to attack his brother's siege 'with hooks, prongs and glaives, and other rustic weapons'.[50] Soon Dafydd was able to free Jasper and Henry, and convey them to Tenby. It would not be the last time members of Gruffydd ap Nicholas's family would give both Tudors reason to feel indebted.

Knowing that this situation had been life-threatening and that next time they might not be as lucky, Jasper decided that, in order to preserve both the life of his young nephew and his own, the time had come to flee the country once again. It was with the help of the White family of Tenby – in particular, Mayor Thomas White and/or one of his sons John or Jenkyn – that uncle and nephew could make a safe escape.[51] Thomas White, a wine merchant, had been mayor of the

50 Vergil, p. 155. Hall's Chronicle, p. 302.
51 Richard Fenton, *A Historical Tour through Pembrokeshire* (London, 1811), p. 462.

town of Tenby several times between 1457 and 1472 and became close to Jasper when he became Earl of Pembroke and started to strengthen the town reconstructions back in 1457. Tradition has it that Jasper and Henry hid in the cellar of White's house in Tenby High Street (where Boots the Chemist now stands), for approximately four days. Accordingly, years later when 'the good prince' (i.e. Jasper) returned to the realm he 'not forgettinge at his comeinge to the crowne rewarded Mr. White, with a lease of all the kings lands aboute the saied Towne of Tenby a good recompence done to one man, for a goode deede to the whole Realme'.[52]

White hastily prepared their safe escape from the cellar underneath his house through a tunnel that led to the seashore and from there, on 2 June 1471, Jasper, Henry and several of the earl's friends and servants took White's boat with the intention of sailing to France, to, once again, seek refuge at the court of King Louis XI.

---

52 George Owen, *Description of Pembrokeshire*, ed. Henry Owen (London, 1892), p. 462. *Church Book of St Mary the Virgin, Tenby* (Tenby, 1907), pp. 13–14.

Figure 26   Chepstow Castle. The place where Jasper executed Sir Roger
Vaughan of Tretower, the executioner of his father Owen.
(© 2015 Debra Bayani)

Figure 27   Location where
tradition suggests
Henry VI died
on the night of
21/22 May 1471.
(© 2015 Debra Bayani)

Figure 28   The Jasper Tower of Llandaff Cathedral in Cardiff.
               (© 1999 John Ball)

Figure 29   Plaque on a house in Crackwell Street Tenby
              (© 2015 Debra Bayani)

Figure 30   The tomb of Mayors Thomas and his son John White in
              St. Mary's Church in Tenby.
              (© 2015 Debra Bayani)

Figure 31   Cellar in Tenby where Jasper and Henry Tudor hid prior to
               their flight to Brittany in the spring of 1471.
               (© 2015 Debra Bayani)

11
EXILE IN BRITTANY
June 1471 – November 1483

A FTER THE Lancastrian refugees had sailed through the Celtic
Sea and into the English Channel, Jasper, Henry and their
entourage were almost certainly seized by the Bretons. Unlike France,
Brittany had not made a truce with Henry VI's new government the
previous year and still continued to detain English travellers during
this period. Accounts differ about the exact location and even about
what really happened. Some suggest that the Lancastrians' ship was
caught in a storm and blown off course so that instead of landing on
French soil as they had intended to do, they may have called in at Jersey
and then disembarked in Brittany. But another far more plausible
possibility is that, perhaps as the result of a storm, they were captured
and brought ashore at Camaret or Le Conquet. This may be confirmed
by a passage in the memoir of Philippe de Commynes when he writes
with displeasure that Jasper, Earl of Pembroke, first cousin to King
Louis XI and a pensioner at his court, and his nephew, the Earl of
Richmond, were travelling to France with the intention of coming to
the French king but that near Brest both earls, with their servants and
personal belongings, were seized by the Bretons.[1]According to some
accounts, Jasper and Henry were taken captive at St Malo, which
strategically makes their supposed brief stay at Jersey a possibility.
Camaret has also been suggested but is not located particularly near

---

1   *Memoires de Messire Philippe de Comines* (1747), p. 138.

Brest (as in Commynes's account), which makes Le Conquet, at a distance of around fourteen miles, most likely. A further fact that supports the idea of their landing at Le Conquet is that Oliviér de Coëtivy, chamberlain of the late King Charles VII of France, and his wife Marie de Valois, an illegitimate daughter of the said king from his liaison with Agnes Sorel, had friends who owned a house overlooking the harbour of Le Conquet. Marie de Valois was Jasper's half-cousin and one of many who lived in this part of Brittany.

In any case soon after landing, Jasper and Henry made their way to the court of Duke Francis II of Brittany. This may have happened with the assistance of an escort sent by the duke. The party made a stopover in Nantes, the capital of Brittany, where they were welcomed, before travelling on to the duke's court at Chateau de l'Hermine in Vannes. There Jasper submitted himself and his nephew to the duke and asked for asylum. Duke Francis welcomed his distant cousins with open arms and treated his guests with every courtesy, giving them the honours appropriate to their status as English noblemen of royal blood. Duke Francis's speech of welcome, which is said to have been delivered to the earls, was turned into verse and published in 1562. The earls were assured they could move freely within the duke's domain.[2]

King Edward IV learned about Jasper and Henry's safe escape and their arrival in Brittany at least before 28 September, when John Paston reported 'men saye that the Kynge schall have delyvere off hym hastely, and som seye that the Kynge of France woll se hym saffe, and schall sett hym at lyberte ageyn'.[3] Edward also discovered that the two men were treated kindly and upon this sent secret messengers to Brittany to negotiate with Duke Francis in an attempt to persuade him to surrender Jasper and Henry to his messengers. Duke Francis realised what a valuable catch both men were and told Edward's envoys there was no way he could hand them over, for he had given his promise to protect them and could not possibly break his word. Instead Francis told the envoys that 'he wold for his cause kepe them so sure as ther should be none occasion for him to suspect that they should ever procure his harme any manner of way'.[4]

Edward was clearly not completely satisfied with the duke's answer but was determined to keep him to his promise and replied

2   Allanic, p. 13. Vergil, p. 155. Commynes, vol 2, p. 234.
3   *The Paston Letters*, Vol. 5, pp. 112–13. Hall's Chronicle, p. 302. Vergil, pp. 158–9.
4   Vergil, p. 158.

in turn that he would give Francis pledges for money, generous gifts and aid if Francis kept his word.[5] Realising the huge advantage the Tudor earls had brought him and that he should do everything to prevent their possible escape, Duke Francis was determined to keep them both in Brittany. He saw to it that Jasper and Henry's servants were replaced by his own men who would keep a close eye on them.

On 27 August 1471, Lord Ferrers and the newly created Earl of Pembroke, Lord Herbert, were authorised to pardon all rebels, except for Thomas Fitzharry, John Owen, Henry Holland, Duke of Exeter, Hugh Mulle and Jasper.[6]

Henry Tudor's stepfather and Margaret's husband, Henry Stafford, died on 4 October that year, probably as a result of severe wounds he had received at the Battle of Barnet. The death of her beloved husband so soon after her only child had once again been forced to go far away, and with no means of knowing when she could embrace her son again, must have been devastating for Margaret. Moreover, as a woman on her own, she was now also very vulnerable and would need to remarry quickly for her own protection. Six months later Margaret secured that protection when she married Lord Thomas Stanley in June 1472, a marriage that seemed more like a business arrangement. Although Stanley had a strong Yorkist pedigree, he had managed to keep himself out of the war. Despite being ordered on several occasions to muster a force and join the royal army, he had always found an excuse to bail out.

By April 1472 Edward had sent his brother-in-law, Anthony Woodville, Earl Rivers, together with a troop of soldiers, to join Duke Francis's service. He had done something similar in the previous September, when negotiating a treaty at Chateaugiron, as confirmation of both sides' wish for a joint Anglo-Breton invasion of France. In November, Breton envoys led by Guillaume Guillemet had arrived in England to negotiate for further military aid. It seemed as if an agreement could be reached by which the earls might be handed over to Edward in exchange for military assistance. Still Francis insisted that, in light of his earlier promise to protect Jasper and Henry, he could not break his word to them. This may have been a genuine insistence on the chivalric code but it could also have been just a very convenient excuse. However, Francis did agree to restrict

5   Vergil, pp. 158–59.
6   Foedera, XI, p. 719.

the Tudors' movements further, something that Edward was pleased enough about to pledge more money and aid to Brittany.

As a result, by October 1472 both earls were moved fifteen miles south to the thirteenth-century fortified residence, the Chateau of Suscinio, near Sarzeau and St Gildas Abbey on the Gulf of Morbihan. Built around 1230 by Due de Roux, in the Middle Ages the château was surrounded by a deep forest, rivers, lakes and streams. It was mainly used by the dukes of Brittany in the summer as a hunting residence and was both luxurious and secluded, with large round towers surrounding a courtyard. The keeper of the castle was the Admiral of Brittany, Jean de Quelennec, Vicomte de Faou and Francis's trusted and well-respected councillor, who was sympathetic towards Jasper and Henry, in particular when rumours started to spread that English agents had been ordered to kill them if they were not able to remove them alive from Duke Francis's safekeeping.[7]

Located less than half a mile from the sea and a flat sandy beach, it soon became apparent that the Chateau of Suscinio would be too vulnerable to an attack or any attempt to seize Henry and Jasper by ships landing close by. It was therefore decided they should return to the ducal court.[8] By late 1473, both Jasper and Henry were at Nantes, but in the absence of any further information it must be assumed that both men accompanied Duke Francis's court as it moved between Vannes, Nantes and Rennes, and the duke's favourite countryside manor houses at Bernon, Plessis and Suscinio.

Francis's determination to keep both earls close to him was influenced by the fact that it was not just Edward who wanted to get his hands on Jasper and Henry. The Tudors had initially intended to travel to the court of the French king, who had previously given refuge and an annual pension to Jasper. For his part, Louis XI took steps as though they were both members of his household who he wished to have returned to his court – which had been their intended destination. In 1474, Louis decided to send a series of detailed instructions to Guillaume Compaing, the dean of the church of St Pierre en Pont in Orleans and the French envoy of Francis's court. Compaing was ordered to seek a meeting with the duke, requesting that both Jasper and Henry be set at liberty. First Compaing should explain the background behind their arrival in Brittany, when their

---

7   Allanic, p. 15.
8   Allanic, pp. 16–17.

intended destination had been France all along. In letters to Duke Francis, Louis writes affectionately with regard to Jasper, saying that he considered the Earl of Pembroke his cousin – which, of course, he was – and that he had received him in the past with good intentions and, wishing him well, had kept him in his household and in his service and had given him a pension. Jasper had stayed in King Louis' estates and travelled with the king to serve and accompany him. Louis also wrote that Jasper had the promise of the French king that, from then on, the Earl of Richmond, his nephew, had a safe place to stay also. Louis digs further back by telling Francis more about Jasper's stay during his exile, including the support he had given Jasper in 1470 to sail back to Wales to regain King Henry VI's crown and to recover his lands. As the fortunes of war had it, Jasper and Henry met their enemies in Wales and were unprepared and in great danger. Therefore:

> Pembroke and Richmond were advised to go to the King as their lord and single refuge, and it would be his pleasure to welcome them as humble servants [...] As god had wished, they had great torments at seas and wind, that they were forced into landing on the coast of Brittany, and came under great danger to the haven of Conquet [...]

> Having been alerted that a subject of the Duke of Brittany had detained Jasper and Henry, Louis informed Francis that, as there was no war between France and Brittany, and neither of them had been done any harm by Pembroke and Richmond, he thought it very strange that Francis had been advised to seize the earls. Furthermore, Louis stated that there had been rumours at the French court that Francis had already freed Jasper and Henry. Louis, doubting this was true, wished Compaing to pray for their immediate release – 'the King would find great pleasure in this and be indebted to him' Compaing wrote. The French king had already written a reply for Compaing, in which he had carefully considered in advance every argument Duke Francis could

employ to justify the keeping of the Tudors. Louis went out of his way in persuading Francis to surrender Jasper and Henry, even going so far as to say that, given that he considered Jasper and Henry his servants, if his servants and people of the king's household were to be detained, it would appear that the Duke of Brittany wished to start a war against him. However, he did not think this was Francis's primary intention, and neither was it his. Louis' meaning could not have been clearer. He concluded the letter by demanding that Jasper and Henry be released immediately and sent to the French court.

Nevertheless, for all his bravado, Louis must have realised that Francis was unlikely to give in to his wishes and that it would be wise to make compromises.

If Francis did refuse all Louis' demands, Louis would go along with the idea that at least Francis would keep them safe at the Breton court and request a written promise to that effect: 'so that good faith be on paper, and so that the King can think of what can be done'. Even though the French king was often seen as a shrewd monarch and a crafty negotiator, his behaviour on this occasion demonstrates sincere concern for his cousins. This tug-of-war game between himself, Edward IV and Louis XI was the main reason for Francis's next step.[9] Because of the possible danger of kidnap, or of plotting by the earls, both Jasper and Henry were moved again by 1474, but this time they were not only moved but also separated from one another. By doing so, the duke made it difficult for both earls to be captured and he ensured that he would at least hold on to one of them. One can only imagine the anxiety of the seventeen-year-old Henry Tudor when he heard he was to be separated from the uncle, who had been his constant adviser throughout most of his adolescence.[10] Both Jasper and Henry must have felt desperate in this situation, not knowing what it would lead to. Jasper was taken about twenty-five miles north-east of Vannes, to the Chateau de Josselin.[11]

---

9   Dom H. Morice, Memoire pour servir de preuves a l'histoire ecclesiastique et civile de
     Bretagne, Vol. 3, cols. 266–70 (Paris, 1742–46). Allanic, p. 17.
10 Allanic, p. 19.
11 Allanic, p. 17.

The castle, which still dominates the valley of the River Oust and the small town of Josselin, had been partly rebuilt in the late fourteenth century and again in the late fifteenth century and had a large keep that was used as prison tower. It was in this tower, which can still be seen today in its original state, that Jasper was probably housed for at least a year. With its three powerful towers built along the river and connected by a strong curtain wall, the Chateau de Josselin makes a most impressive sight. These three towers, along with Jasper's Prison Tower, are the only parts of the castle that remain as they were when Jasper was accommodated there.

Meanwhile, Henry was moved ten miles south-east of Vannes, to the Chateau de Largoët, a fortress hidden deep in the woods, the home of Jean IV de Rieux, Marshal of Brittany and his first wife Françoise Raguenel. There he was lodged in the Tour d'Elven, a huge seven-storey octagonal keep or donjon, built by Rieux's father-in-law, Baron Jean II Raguenel Malestroit, in around 1463, and so still quite new. Financial accounts from January 1475 record Henry as being a prisoner at Largoët but as it was the residence of Jean IV de Rieux, who had himself offered to take the young earl into his home, and treated him with respect and care, it is thought the conditions in which Henry was kept at Largoët were by no means harsh.[12] Rieux was only ten years older than Henry and his only child by his first wife, a daughter named Françoise, was some years younger than Henry and may have been company for him during his stay. There is no doubt that Henry continued his studies at this time and became fluent in Latin and French.

No further information concerning Jasper's imprisonment in Josselin remains and of Henry's at Largoët only fragments. These, however, can still provide brief insights into Henry's isolated years. Preserved in Duke Francis's wardrobe accounts is this record from the spring of 1472:

> To my lord of Richmond for a long robe by gift of my said lord [the Duke], seven ells of fine black velour, costing 4 royals a ell: 35,– for lining the upper arms, half a third of black, cost 23d. And for the lining four ells of changeable taffeta at 2 royals an ell, costing 10,–: and the making of each, sum 45, – 13s. To him for a short robe, an

12 Allanic, pp. 18, 22.

ell and a half of black damask at 4,– an ell, and
padding, 1 ecu, total 7,– 2s 10d.[13]

Another glimpse of Henry is given by the chronicler Philippe de
Commynes, who spoke with him while he was at the Breton court.
Henry told Commynes that 'since the age of five he had been guarded
like a fugitive or kept in prison'.

There also remains a sixteenth-century drawing of a young
Henry Tudor, likely based on an earlier portrait. The drawing is one
of a series drawn by Jacques le Boucq and is preserved in the city
library at Arras.

In the meantime, Edward finally succeeded in winning the
support of his brother-in-law Charles the Bold, the Duke of Burgundy,
for his plans to conquer France. But when Edward invaded France with
a huge army in July 1475, Burgundy was so slow in bringing forward
his forces that Edward was left with no other option than to open
negotiations with the French king in Piquigny, a town in the region
of Amiens.[14] There the English were lavishly entertained. In the result
the Treaty of Piquigny was signed by both Edward IV and Louis XI on
29 August. Louis XI agreed to pay Edward 75,000, crowns along with
an annual pension – or tribute, as the English called it – of 50,000
crowns as recompense for the military expenditure he had made.
Furthermore, the treaty contained a seven-year period of peace and
mutual good will, as well as a framework for negotiating the English
claim to the French throne, a promise that France would not engage in
war with the Duke of Brittany (this because Edward intended to stay
on peaceful terms with Duke Francis), and also a private arrangement
that Louis' eldest son, the Dauphin, would marry Edward's eldest
daughter Elizabeth. This may have given the appearance of, as the
Croyland Chronicler puts it, an 'honourable peace',[15] but to many of
the English nobility it was anything but honourable.[16] Most of those
who had accompanied Edward had done so in expectation of military
glory. Peace was not what they had crossed the Channel for.

Another problem that could now be solved was what was to be
done with Margaret of Anjou, who had been imprisoned in the Tower
since 1471. She was handed over to Louis upon payment of a ransom

---

13 Les Archives départementales (AD) Loire-Atlantique, Serie B, Parchemins non classés,
    dossier Francois II.
14 Vergil, pp. 162–3.
15 Croyland Chronicle, pp. 136–7.
16 Commynes, pp. 378–9.

and on condition that she renounced her claim to both the English crown and her English lands. The unfortunate former queen would also suffer the humiliation of being forced by Louis to give up all she had inherited from her father, Rene of Anjou. Margaret would linger on for another six years, living out her days in poverty, a shadow of the powerful woman she once was.

By now Edward had managed to eliminate nearly every man with royal Lancastrian blood in his veins. Among them was the Duke of Exeter, Henry Holland, who had previously been married to Edward's sister Anne (they were divorced in 1472). Being the grandson of King Henry IV's elder sister Elizabeth of Lancaster, Exeter was a Lancastrian at heart and fought for Henry VI at Wakefield, St Albans, Towton and Barnet. After 1471 he found himself forced to support the Yorkist cause and joined Edward's expedition to France where the Treaty of Piquigny was signed. On the return journey he 'fell' overboard and drowned, leaving no male heir.[17]

On 13 October 1472, there was a parliament session at Westminster that Edward IV used to sell off the confiscated properties of his opponents, new taxes were introduced to fill the empty treasury and old feuds were resolved between the nobles. Edward IV was established as king.

Now that Edward IV had most domestic affairs under control, he was called upon by Duke Charles of Burgundy, his brother-in-law, to intervene in Burgundy's war with Louis XI. Edward could not reject this request for alliance because, quite apart from their family ties, Charles had received him very kindly when Edward was exiled to Flanders the previous year. Moreover, King Louis XI had aggrieved him terribly by providing considerable assistance to Warwick, Jasper and Queen Margaret in their schemes to attack him.

Despite Vergil's description of Henry Tudor as 'the only ympe now left of King Henry the 6ths bloode',[18] there were others who could make a stronger claim to the throne. Nevertheless, both Vergil and Commynes, among other historians, have suggested that Henry Tudor's mere existence might be supposed to fill Edward with fear that his own dynasty might one day be challenged by this Welshman. Of course, as an heir of the house of Lancaster he could be a threat if he was able to unite with several other Lancastrians, but for the

17 Vergil, p. 163.
18 Vergil, p. 164.

time-being it seemed young Henry did not even have the ambition to seize Edward's usurped crown. However, that did not set Edward's mind at rest. The terms of the Treaty of Piquigny included Louis XI's promise to refrain from attacking Brittany. With return of gratitude in mind, Edward once more raised the issue of Henry Tudor's exile in Brittany,[19] in the hope that Duke Francis would now be thankful enough to hand over Henry Tudor – and without his uncle Jasper around to prevent this. At the beginning of 1476 Edward again sent messengers to Duke Francis, partly to negotiate the renewal of the Anglo-Breton treaty, but additionally to deal with the difficult problem of Jasper and Henry Tudor. The negotiations dragged on until the autumn, when King Edward despatched an embassy to Duke Francis at Nantes led by Robert Stillington, Bishop of Bath and Wells, and Thomas Whiting, the Chester herald, equipped with a generous sum of gold to ease negotiations.[20] Duke Francis again repeated his well-worn arguments that he had given his word to his captives to keep them safe and thus he 'might not lawfully' release Jasper and Henry. Edward felt that he had been waiting long enough and now changed tactics, suggesting that Henry should be returned to England and marry one of his own daughters,[21] thereby uniting the houses of York and Lancaster. He requested that Henry should travel back to England in the company of the ambassadors.

At first, Duke Francis was not taken by this highly unlikely suggestion. However, the ambassadors persisted, pressing Francis with an even greater sum of money. Eventually, 'weryed with prayer and vanquisshed with pryce', he eventually gave in and 'delyveryd therle to thambassadors'. In the autumn of 1476, the young earl was taken from Largoët, where he had resided for the last two years, and Edward's ambassadors cheerfully set out for St Malo with Henry Tudor in their company.[22] There a ship was waiting for them to embark for the journey to England. Now that he was in the hands of Edward's ambassadors, Henry's return to an uncertain fate seemed inevitable and sealed. Henry seems to have understood very well what it would mean for him if he actually set foot on that ship and it was either due to 'the agony of mind', or maybe simple deception, that

19 Vergil, p. 164. Scofield, vol. 2, p. 173.
20 Scofield, vol. 2, pp. 166, 172–3.
21 Vergil, p. 165.
22 Vergil, p. 164.

he 'fell into a fever', which postponed their departure.[23] This would prove to be crucial, allowing just enough time for Duke Francis to change his mind. It seems that his decision to allow Henry's return to England had been made without consultation with his councillors and when news of his capitulation reached the Breton court, many of them were shocked. In particular, Jean de Quelennec now rushed to the Breton court and tried everything in his power to prevail upon the duke.[24] Francis was eventually persuaded to reverse his previous decision, but three days had already passed since Henry had left the court and there was no time to lose.

Immediately, Francis sent his treasurer Pierre Landais to prevent the ship from sailing. Fortunately, when Landais arrived at St Malo Henry's ship was still there and he was able to delay its departure. Finding that Henry was gravely ill, Landais arranged for him to be secretly conveyed to secure sanctuary in one of the chapels within the town. As soon as the English ambassadors discovered what had happened they were furious. Desperate to prevent Henry's escape, they went to the chapel and tried to lure him out of sanctuary. Unfortunately for them they met with a hostile reception from townsmen who had surrounded the chapel, determined to keep Henry safe inside. In further negotiations, Landais claimed that it was thanks to the ambassadors' own laxity that Henry had managed to enter sanctuary and now promised either to keep Henry in sanctuary or to ensure the young earl was returned to the custody of Duke Francis. Henry returned to the Breton court, his illness miraculously cured.[25]

When Edward IV's ambassadors returned with news of Henry's near capture, Edward was very 'sorry' but was soothed by the promise that the fugitive would remain under close surveillance.[26] Possession of Henry would be a valuable asset for Edward as it would mean Henry was no longer a threat and could perhaps even be married to one of Edward's daughters. The French king also continued to pressure Francis for the release of both earls, possibly with a view to using Henry as a chess piece to provoke war between England and France or England and Brittany, as well as because of the previous friendly relations between himself and Jasper and Henry. When Louis XI

23 Vergil, pp. 164–5.
24 Vergil, p. 166.
25 Vergil, pp. 164–7, 197. Allanic, pp. 30–35.
26 Vergil, p. 167.

heard Henry had escaped by only a hair's breadth, he was disturbed enough to send a new mission to Francis. This was led by Guillaume de Souplainville, Admiral of Guinne, who Louis dispatched to Nantes just before Christmas 1476 with orders to demand that Francis hand over both Henry and Jasper. This Francis flatly refused to do and Souplainville returned to the French court empty-handed in early 1477.

In the meantime, Henry was escorted back to the ducal court in Vannes at Chateau l'Hermine and soon afterwards Jasper also left Josselin to join his nephew there again. It is certain that during October and November in 1476, both he and Jasper were kept as prisoners at Vannes, Jasper in the custody of Bertrand du Parc and Henry in that of Vincent de la Landette.[27]

Except for just one record that tells us that Jasper and Henry were still at Vannes between 1481 and 1482, where Henry's custodians, Jean Guillemet and Louis de Kermené, were paid expenses of 2,000 livres tournois and Jasper's custodian du Parc was given £607 10s. tournois, there are no sources that specify their exact location. [28] It can, however, be assumed that they spent much time in Vannes and were kept close to Duke Francis until news arrived of Edward IV's sudden death on 3 April 1483. An event that would set in a motion of events and change everything.

Francis had faithfully kept his word to guard Jasper and Henry but now, with Edward dead, the duke was free to release both men. It is certain that at the time of Buckingham's Rebellion, late in 1483, both Tudors were at liberty.[29] From here the tables turned very rapidly and the Yorkist regime began to tear itself apart. Upon Edward's death, noblemen hurried towards the capital expecting the late king's eldest son and heir, the twelve-year old Prince Edward, would shortly be crowned Edward V. For the time being the boy's maternal uncle, Anthony Woodville, was his protector. During Edward IV's lifetime there had been no love between Gloucester and the Woodvilles, the queen's family, but now this rift widened even further. On 30 April, whilst travelling from Ludlow to London, Prince Edward and his party were intercepted at Stony Stratford by Richard, Duke of Gloucester. The prince's protector and uncle Earl Rivers, the prince's half-brother,

---

27   B.N. fonds francais 6982, f. 326v, cited by Haute-Jusse, p. 180. Scofield, vol. 2, p. 173.
28   Archives de la Loire Atlantique, Nantes, E212 cassette 93, Account of 1482–1483, f. 4v, cited by Haute-Jusse, p. 248.
29   Vergil, p. 192.

Richard Grey and Sir Thomas Vaughan, his chief chamberlain, were taken into custody on Gloucester's orders, and escorted to Pontefract Castle.[30] Richard declared his loyalty to Prince Edward and escorted him back to London. There Richard was proclaimed his nephew's new protector during his minority by the royal council. No one knew yet what was about to come, that it was only a matter of weeks before Richard, Duke of Gloucester, would do the unimaginable.

Meanwhile, Richard promptly ordered the execution of Lord Hastings, Edward IV's dearest friend.[31] He would quickly go on to remove other obstacles in his way, among them Anthony Woodville, Richard Grey and Sir Thomas Vaughan.[32] Richard's position was reinforced by Buckingham's supporters, and Buckingham led the investigations into the activities of Bishop Morton, Archbishop Rotherham and Lord Hastings. John Morton, Bishop of Ely, was sent to prison in Buckingham's Brecon Castle to remain in his custody. Throughout the first part of Edward IV's reign Morton had remained loyal to Henry VI and been forced into exile in Scotland and France. John Morton and Jasper must have known each other very well, for after the Battle of Tewkesbury in 1471, Jasper and Morton were in exile together in France.[33] It is, however, unclear what connections he may have maintained with Jasper after 1471, and on Edward IV's recapturing of the throne Morton turned his coat for York.

By the end of April Queen Elizabeth Woodville, naturally and instinctively fearful of danger, took her nine-year-old younger son Richard, Duke of York, together with her daughters and some other relatives, and fled to sanctuary at Westminster Abbey. After some weeks Gloucester somehow managed to persuade Queen Elizabeth to give up Richard to join his brother and to let him leave for Westminster Hall, where Buckingham received the boy and handed him over to Gloucester. The young Duke of York was reunited with his brother, the crown prince, at the Bishop of London's house and after this both boys were taken to the Tower.[34]

Meanwhile, Buckingham received grants of high positions in Wales and the constableships of all the castles in Wales and the border

---

30 Vergil, p. 175. Croyland Chronicle, p. 486.
31 Vergil, p. 181.
32 Vergil, p. 182.
33 DNB, Vol. 39, pp. 151–3. Emden, Oxford, pp. 1318–20. Cambridge, pp. 412–14.
34 Vergil, p. 178.

counties.[35] The Duke of Gloucester met with him at Northampton, and the two men had a long conversation. It is alleged that there Richard told Buckingham he was after the crown, and thereafter many things changed rapidly.[36] Richard successfully plotted to seize the throne by proclaiming the illegitimacy of Edward IV's children and secured his own claim as king. Buckingham was closely involved with every step of the process. A ceremony was held at St Paul's, where Dr Shaw preached a sermon setting out the justification for Gloucester to become king – principally on the grounds that, as Edward IV had previously been betrothed to another woman named Eleanor Talbot, his marriage to Elizabeth Woodville was invalid and their children illegitimate. Buckingham did the same to persuade others at the London Guildhall, where he invited Richard the protector to become Richard the King. Naturally, Richard accepted this persuasive request and was proclaimed King Richard III on 26 June. Now Buckingham received favour after favour – he became Great Chamberlain and Constable of England and, on 6 July 1483, he bore his master's train from the palace to Westminster Abbey for the coronation when he was crowned King Richard III. Richard, Duke of Gloucester, had usurped the crown from his young nephew, his brother's son to whom he had pledged his loyalty. Not long before or afterwards, most probably at the new king's behest, Edward IV's two sons – Edward V and his younger brother Richard, Duke of York – apparently disappeared from the Tower and were never seen again. Within a few weeks rumours of their death were spreading widely.[37]

Now Jasper and Henry's continuing freedom was as big a concern to Richard III as it had been to his brother. If the Tudors and the opposition of England were to unite, the new king's throne would be in great danger. Just a week after Richard's coronation, on 13 July, an eminent cleric, Dr Thomas Hutton, was sent to Brittany to propose a meeting with Duke Francis about commercial affairs between England and Brittany and also to 'enserche and know if there be intended any enterprise out of land upon any part of this realm'. It is clear that the main reason for the discussions was in fact the fates of Jasper and Henry.[38] Dr Hutton returned to England at the end of August and, in turn, Duke Francis sent an envoy, Georges de

35 Foedera, XII, p. 180.
36 Vergil, p. 174.
37 Great Chronicle, pp. 234, 236–7. Chronicles of London, p. 191.
38 Vergil, p. 191. Letters of Richard III, Vol. 1, pp. 22–3.

Mainbier, to Richard in order to discuss his concerns further. The conditions Duke Francis placed on handover of Jasper and Henry to Richard were, to say the least, excessive. Cunning and shrewd, Francis II demonstrated his friendship and loyalty towards Richard III in conventional diplomatic language. According to Francis, Louis XI of France had requested the surrender of Henry Tudor several times since Edward IV's death and was currently threatening the duke with war unless he submitted. It was alleged that Brittany could not hold out long against Louis XI without English support. The duke might be forced to hand Henry over to the French king. Francis's demands to be bought-off were such that it was impossible for Richard to meet them – Richard must provide Francis with 4,000 archers at his own expense within one month and, if necessary, a further 2,000 to 3,000 men at the duke's expense.[39] The real underlying reason for all this was that the duke was seeking to buy some more time for the Tudors and their supporters to get themselves fully prepared for returning to England as invaders, while the Duke of Buckingham was waiting for them.

In the meantime Margaret Beaufort did everything in her power to recruit whoever she possibly could to the service of her exiled son. She was able to communicate with Elizabeth Woodville through the mathematician and astronomer Dr Lewis of Caerleon, a Welshman who was the personal physician to both ladies.[40] Through Dr Lewis, Margaret reiterated to Elizabeth Woodville the earlier idea of uniting the houses of Lancaster and York by a marriage between her son Henry and Elizabeth's eldest daughter Elizabeth of York or, if the latter died, her younger daughter Cecily.[41] With the aid of the extended Woodville family and their supporters Henry would be able to overthrow Richard III and become king himself.

At the same time, Margaret and Buckingham were able to exchange information by means of a retainer called Reginald Bray, long known to both of them as receiver general of the estates of Margaret's late husband Henry Stafford, uncle of the Duke of Buckingham. One of King Edward's former servants, Hugh Conway, who was also a kinsman of Margaret's current husband, also became Margaret's confidential messenger. He was sent to Jasper and Henry in Brittany with a large sum of money as well as news of the situation in England

39 Letters and papers, Vol. I, pp. 37–43.
40 Vergil, pp. 194–5.
41 Vergil, p. 196.

and instructions to urge Henry to return to England but to land first in Wales, where substantial aid from the Duke of Buckingham could be expected.[42]

On 19 July, Richard III set out for Windsor on the first stage of his royal progress. He made his way through the Midlands and at the end of the month reached Gloucester where, apparently, Buckingham took his final leave of him before travelling via Stafford to his castle at Brecon. John Morton was still at Brecon following his arrest earlier that year and, according to Thomas More, it was at this point that plans for dethroning Richard emerged between Buckingham and the bishop.[43] Tradition has it that John Morton persuaded the duke into taking the lead in kindling revolt but since another conspiracy existed between Margaret and Buckingham, it is not clear whether their plans were for Buckingham himself to replace Richard III or to put Henry Tudor on the throne. It is said that when Margaret heard that Buckingham was on the road between Worcester and Bridgnorth she rode on horseback to meet him,[44] and this led to an agreement that, if the rebellion was successful, Buckingham would support Henry Tudor's claim to the throne.[45]

Exactly a fortnight later, Richard, still at York, wrote to his Chancellor in London for the Great Seal. A postscript, in the king's own hand, included these lines:

> Here, loved be God, all is well and truly determined for to resist the malice of him that had best cause to be true, the duke of Buckingham, the most untrue creature living; whom, with God's grace, we shall not be long till that we will be in that parts and subdue his malice. We assure you there never was falser traitor purveyed for [...][46]

The homecoming of Jasper and Henry Tudor was probably not as easy as they had imagined. Essentially, much of it depended on sheer good luck whereby everything had to happen at the right place and the right time. Whatever Henry's precise hopes may have been – and their

---

42 Vergil, p. 197.
43 The History of King Richard III, in *The Complete Works of Thomas More*, Vol. II, ed. Richard S. Sylvester (New Haven and London, 1963), pp. 91–3. Vergil, pp. 194–5.
44 Hall's Chronicle, p. 389.
45 Vergil, p. 198.
46 The National Archives C81/1392/6.

relationship to Buckingham's plans – the rising presented him with an opportunity to return home after twelve years of exile. Through Pierre Landais, Henry gained Francis's support for an expedition and this was publicly demonstrated at a formal oath-swearing ceremony in Vannes Cathedral in the presence of the Duchess of Brittany, whose chaplain, Master Arthur Jacques, presided at the service. Duke Francis provided Henry with fifteen ships, according to Vergil, including three bigger vessels, and these were made ready to carry 5,000 Breton soldiers to England. The accounts of Francis's receiver general record the precise cost of at least half of the fleet. Seven ships are named, two other ships came from St Malo, two others from Brest and Auray, one was supplied by Alain de la Motte, Vice-Admiral of Brittany, and another one came from the Admiral of Brittany and commander of the fleet, Jean Dufou. The commissary-general of Duke Francis of Brittany, Yves Millon, provided Jasper and Henry with 13,000 livres tournois during October and November for wages and provisions for their expedition, in addition to a loan of 10,000 ecus d'or.[47]

Several accounts affirm that the fleet was ready to disembark on 1 September,[48] but this date is far too early. In fact, when Henry and Jasper received Duke Francis's loan on 30 October, they were still at the fishing port of Paimpol on the north coast of Brittany. There is a possibility that the journey had earlier been postponed because of the weather, but it is more likely that the fleet sailed soon after this, early in November, from Paimpol. As soon as they did the strong northern wind scattered the ships in different directions – some to Normandy, most others back to the Breton coast, except for Henry's ship and one other. These two remaining ships were battered all night in the severe storm but the next morning both came in sight of the Dorset coast near Poole. Just before they had set foot ashore, they noticed that the coastline was full of armed men drawn up waiting for them.

Henry therefore sent a boat to scout what was actually going on. The men in the boat were encouraged to land by the armed forces – 'They were informed that they were sent from the Duke of Buckingham to be ready to accompany Henry safe unto the camp' because, it was said, Richard III was defeated.[49] Henry, however,

47 Vergil, p. 197. AD Loire-Atlantique E 212 no. 18 fos. 17v–19.
    British Library MS 19,398 fo. 33.
48 Dominici Mancini, *The Usurpation of Richard the Third*, pp. 236–7
    ed. C.A.J. Armstrong (2nd ed., Oxford, 1969)
49 Vergil, pp. 201–3. Croyland Chronicle, p. 495.

seems to have remained suspicious and, after waiting in vain for the other ships to arrive, he and Jasper set off back across the English Channel, having been forced to leave behind some of the Bretons, presumably the scouts. These Bretons were taken prisoner and just before Christmas four of them were released to go home and arrange ransom for themselves and for their fellows who had stayed behind in England. The two ships had to encounter further storms at sea, but finally they reached the northern coast of France, some accounts say at St Vaast-la-Hogue, others at Dieppe. Jasper, Henry and their entourage must have been exhausted. After three days of rest, the group resumed their journey overland through Normandy back to Brittany. Henry sent some envoys to the court of the new thirteen-year-old French King, Charles VIII, who had succeeded to the throne following the death of his father on 30 August. The young King, whose elder sister Anne acted as regent, kindly gave his permission for the party to cross his lands and even provided some money to meet expenses. It is significant that Charles did not grasp this opportunity to seize Henry when it would have been so very easy. Certainly, his father would not have hesitated to do so. Perhaps Louis' death in August and the political uncertainty that followed paralysed the new king's ministers. Instead Charles VIII, Jasper's second cousin, took pity on his two kinsmen and accepted a substantial sum of money sent by Margaret Beaufort to purchase their safe conduct. An escort was provided by Henry Carbonnelle, one of King Charles's own esquires. Henry was the son of Jean Carbonnelle, who was Lord of Sourdeval and the king's chamberlain, and his grandfather Pierre de Brezé, a friend of Margaret Beaufort, had fought for the Lancastrians in the 1460s. Jasper, Henry and their followers returned to Brittany on foot accompanied by Henry Carbonnelle all the way to the Abbey of Saint-Sauveur at Redon (which still stands today), thirty-five miles east of Vannes. Jasper and Henry probably rested for a while at the abbey before they resumed their journey to the court of Duke Francis.[50] Back at the Breton court Jasper and Henry learned the details of the Duke of Buckingham's failure. Frustrated by a lack of support and hampered by unusually bad weather, Buckingham had fled, only to be betrayed by one of his servants when hiding at his home. The duke was taken to King Richard III, now at Salisbury, but Richard denied

---

50   B.N. Clairambault 473, f. 213. Fonds Français 23266 f. 35.

Buckingham's request for an audience.[51] Henry Stafford, 2nd Duke of Buckingham, was executed in the town's market-place on Sunday 2 November 1483.

If Henry Tudor's prospects a month or so previously had never seemed so bright, after his return to Brittany they can hardly have looked dimmer now. As an impoverished exile whose biggest ally, the Duke of Buckingham, had suffered total defeat, Henry himself now feared that Duke Francis might become reconciled with Richard III and hand him over to the English king. The only remaining hope and comfort lay in the support of fugitives trickling in from England, who came looking for Henry as soon as they arrived in Brittany. Elizabeth Woodville's son, Thomas Grey, Marquess of Dorset, and around 400 Englishmen came to Vannes in search of him and to offer their support.[52] This must have cheered him up and made him confident enough to recognise that he must swiftly reassemble his limited forces, before Duke Francis decided to abandon him and his cause for good.

---

51 Vergil, pp. 201–2. Grande Chroniques, pp. 459–60.
52 Vergil, p. 200.

Figure 32   Chateau de Suscinio, the place where Jasper and Henry
                 where imprisoned from 1472 until 1474.
                 (© 2015 Debra Bayani)

Figure 33   Plaque in 'Henry's room' commemorating
                 Henry's imprisonment.
                 (© 2015 Debra Bayani)

Figure 34   Prison Keep at the Chateau de Josselin. Jasper was
                imprisoned here from 1474 until 1476.
                (© 2015 Debra Bayani)

Figure 35   The 14th Century façade of the Chateau de Josselin, which
                still remains as it was when Jasper was imprisoned there.
                (© 2015 Debra Bayani)

Figure 36   Tour d'Elven.
                (© 2015 Debra Bayani)

Figure 37   Original medieval door which leads to Henry's room in
            Tour d'Elven.
            (© 2015 Debra Bayani)

Figure 38   Henry's tiny room in Tour d'Elven. The room is
            approximately 10ft by 6ft.
            (© 2015 Debra Bayani)

Figure 39   Medieval town and town walls of Vannes in Brittany.
                   (© 2015 Debra Bayani)

Figure 40   Portrait of Charles VIII of France.
               (© 2015 Debra Bayani)

12
EXILE IN FRANCE
November 1483 – August 1485

HENRY GATHERED together his exiled supporters and made every effort he could to inspire them with a sense of mission. Jasper's whereabouts during the following months are not recorded, but we can be confident that he still took part in the events unfolding and remained close to his nephew. At this time, Jasper was around fifty-one and it is almost certain that he played a key role as his nephew's closest adviser, confidante and mentor. However, the most comprehensive account of the exiles in Brittany is that of Polydore Vergil, written after Jasper's death and possibly with an eye to flattering Henry VII, which is primarily the story of one man, Henry Tudor, who is portrayed as a courageous young leader. But, as would be later demonstrated by the rewards granted to Jasper, to say nothing of the trust placed in him and the powers granted to him after 1485, greater than those enjoyed by anyone else, it is clear that Henry owed an enormous part of his success to his uncle.

Henry used the winter in Brittany to make plans for a new invasion. About a third of the supporters who joined him in exile in Vannes can be identified by name, mainly because they were rewarded the year after Bosworth. Without doubt, the majority of the others did not live to tell the tale, dying either on the journey or in the battle ahead, and perhaps a few remained in Brittany for unknown reasons. As far as is known, most of the exiles were among the miscellany of noble attendants recruited to the conspiracies of the late summer of 1483.

Margaret Beaufort's role is reflected in the presence in Brittany of the many attendants of her and her husband, Lord Stanley. These of course included Bishop John Morton, Reginald Bray and the priest Christopher Urswick (of whom the latter two served in Margaret's household), but also John Cheyne (former standard-bearer, esquire of the body, master of the horse and master of the bodyguard to Edward IV), John Browne and Richard Pigot. Other exiles that had a connection with Lord Stanley are notably John Edward, John Risely and Seth Worsely.[1]

Queen Elizabeth Woodville's party was represented by her son Dorset and her brothers Lionel, Richard and Edward, together with the many loyal servants of her husband, Edward IV, who were without any doubt outraged and shocked by the deposition and disappearance of Edward V and his younger brother. These last included William Brandon, Sir Giles Daubeney, Edward Poynings, William Knight and John Welles, half-brother to Margaret Beaufort. William, Lord Hastings, Edward IV's dearest friend, was represented by John Harcourt. Also, most of these men had additional connections to each other in one way or another. All this evidence of loyalty and service confirms the many reports about plots and rumours during the summer of 1483. It suggests that a secretive network linking Buckingham, Beaufort, Stanley, the Woodvilles and Edward IV's loyal servants did in fact exist. Henry Tudor could now present himself as the unifier of the rival houses of Lancaster and York.

Henry called a meeting at Rennes with Dorset and the other exiles. The discussions took several days and on 25 December 1483, in Rennes Cathedral, Henry solemnly promised to marry Elizabeth of York, and so unite the houses of Lancaster and York, as soon as he became King of England with Richard's crown on his head. With the help of his mother, Henry unified the Woodville conspiracy with his own. In return, all those who were present swore their loyalty and duty to Henry as if he were already their sovereign, placing their lives and possessions at his disposal on his mission to become king.[2]

On 2 February 1484, Henry and his followers, including Dorset, Peter Courtenay and the Bishop of Exeter, had returned to Vannes

---

1   Vergil, pp. 195–196, 212.
2   Vergil, pp. 203–4. The Grande Chroniques reports the Christmas Day ceremony as taking place at Vannes Cathedral.

and celebrated the feast of the Purification of the Blessed Virgin at Vannes Cathedral.[3]

As so many Englishmen were fleeing abroad, Richard III took what measures he could to reduce the effect of Henry Tudor and the dynastic threat he stood for. He began by ordering the execution of Sir Thomas St Leger, and many other loyal servants of his brother Edward. After the many executions of the previous months, Richard publicly attainted all rebels, especially those that had fled, at the parliament that met on 23 January 1484. Jasper and Henry were particularly singled out as the king's greatest enemies. At the same time Margaret Beaufort was stripped of the right to hold her estates and, as her husband Lord Stanley had proved himself a supporter of Richard, they were confiscated and given into his custody,[4] making Margaret a prisoner in her own house. It is difficult to believe that Richard did not suspect Lord Stanley of involvement in any of his wife's plots, for there was no doubt in Richard's mind that Margaret was doing everything in her power to destroy his dynasty. It may have been that Richard did not want to take a chance by challenging Stanley's considerable power in north-west England and Wales. Richard did, however, take a big risk by offering reconciliation. He even granted a general pardon to two of Margaret's close servants and conspirators, Richard Edgecombe and Reginald Bray.

In March, Richard III tried to win Queen Elizabeth Woodville's trust by formally assuring her that neither she nor her five daughters would come to any harm, if only they came out of sanctuary. He promised they would be treated as honourably as his own family and that they would not be sent to the Tower.[5] This was an astounding change of heart given that Richard had declared the marriage between Elizabeth and his brother to be invalid and their children illegitimate, and a vital promise so soon after the disappearance of the Princes in Tower.

Around the same time that he made these promises Richard received information that another invasion attempt was being planned. He became increasingly anxious that Henry and the other exiles should remain on the far side of the Channel and offered Duke

---

3   Allanic, p. 38.
4   RP, VI, pp. 250–51. Vergil, p. 204.
5   Harleian MSS 433, BL vol. 3, p. 190.

Francis II all revenues from the English estates of Henry and the other refugees in Brittany if Francis would keep them under guard.[6]

Jasper and Henry's next task was to persuade Duke Francis to support yet another voyage to England. Money was the main priority because the recent failure had exhausted their resources. Henry again promised to repay Duke Francis whatever was provided and the duke agreed to help with gathering another fleet. According to Duke Francis's receiver-general, the new fleet comprised six ships provided by Henry and Jasper's former custodian, the Admiral of Brittany and Lord Auray, and carried 890 men who were from St Pol de Jean, Brest and Morlaix. Payments were made and provisions collected by March, suggesting the ships were ready to set sail soon. Strangely, nothing happened and the English exiles continued to while away their time in Vannes.[7]

Henry Tudor and his supporters formed an uncomfortable collection of exiles. They had all been robbed of the positions and wealth they had previously enjoyed in England, they were separated from their loved ones, had prices on their heads and were largely cut-off from reports from England. To these exiles Henry Tudor appeared as a fresh wind, maybe even a blazing meteor in the heavens – or, quite simply, their only way home. Henry, for his part, felt a great sense of obligation and publicly acknowledged his appreciation of the danger and suffering his fellow exiles had experienced for his sake. In the accounts of the procurator of the chapter of Vannes Cathedral, Jean Avallenc, brief observations of the exiles can be found. Led by Henry Tudor, Dorset and the bishops of Salisbury and Exeter, Lionel Woodville and Peter Courtenay, they attended mass in Vannes Cathedral, and made small offerings on the high altar on 8 February, 15 August and 8 September 1484.[8] Such snapshots suggest that Henry, Jasper and their exiled friends were not restrained from liberty and lived comfortably at the Breton court, even if in a state of frustrating expectations. According to Philippe de Commynes, the exiles were a financial weight to Duke Francis, and in particular after Buckingham's rebellion in late 1483 the number of fugitives was considerably swollen. In June 1484, for example, Francis paid 3,100 livres to the English exiles in Vannes and an additional 2,500 livres

---

6   Vergil, p. 205.
7   R.A. Griffiths and R.S. Thomas, *The Making of the Tudor Dynasty*,
     Sutton Publishing (Stroud 2005), p. 116.
8   Allanic, p. 38.

was given to his 'impoverished English guests' when the burgesses of Vannes saw the shabby state they were in. Duke Francis also made personal financial gifts: to Dorset 400 livres a month; to John Halewell 200 livres; to Edward Woodville 100 livres. On one occasion the duke even had to pay 200 livres to a Vantaise widow because one of the exiles had killed her husband, a man called Georget le Cuff.[9]

In the intervening months Richard tried everything he could to obtain the surrender of Henry Tudor. In March 1484 he sent several diplomats to France, Brittany and the papal courts, supposedly to inform the leaders of his accession. On 1 May, Richard warned all the counties in his kingdom about a possible rising so that, when necessary, every officer would be ready to launch an attack.

Finally, on 8 June, Francis negotiated a truce that was to Richard's advantage. In fact, this truce was approved by the doing of Henry's former guardian Pierre Landais, who at this time had need of allies to reinforce his own unpopular position at the Breton court.[10] As Duke Francis was then too ill to deal personally with this matter, Landais, his treasurer, could use this opportunity all too well to strengthen his own position against some of the Breton nobility who resented his influence over Francis. Richard assured Landais his protection from the Breton nobility, if he would urge Duke Francis to accept Richard's proposals and his offer to grant him Henry's earldom of Richmond.

John Morton, who at the time was spending his exile in Flanders, got wind of the rumours, and send his protégé Christopher Urswick, who was also in Flanders, to warn Henry and to advise him to flee into France. Henry was fortunate to receive this warning just in time. From Vannes, Urswick was rapidly sent to the new King of France, to discover whether Henry would be given asylum there. Charles VIII agreed so, as soon as Urswick returned from the French court, Henry and Jasper started to make plans for their flight and to work out the fastest, safest and best way to France.[11]

It was in the first half of September 1484 that they made their move. Jasper, with a few of the exiled English noblemen, travelled ahead, to give the impression they intended to visit Duke Francis at Rennes, which lay not too far from the French border. As soon as they approached the French border, Jasper and his attendants made

9   AD Loire-Atlantique E 212 no. 17 fo. 17v. E 209 no. 23 fo. 7v. E 212 no. 18 fo. 16.
      E 212 no. 93 fo. 15r. 17v.
10   Foedera, XII, pp. 221–2, 226.
11   Vergil, pp. 206–8.

a final run for it and successfully arrived in the province of Anjou.[12] Between then and 22 August 1485, Jasper's presence is only recorded a few times but he must surely have been there every step of Henry's way to Wales and England. Having watched over and cared for his nephew for the previous fourteen years, there was no way he would now sit back at a distance and leave the course of unfolding events, and Henry's fate, to be decided by others.

In the meantime, Henry, accompanied on horseback by a small entourage of just five servants, left Vannes two days after his uncle. According to Polydore Vergil, Henry pretended to be visiting a friend who owned a nearby manor house. Most of the English exiles were still in Vannes, so no suspicion was aroused by his departure. After five miles, Henry, with help from his servant Mathew Baker,[13] withdrew into the forest and disguised his appearance by changing into servant's clothing. They then travelled on to Angers in Anjou, only stopping to let the horses drink. Henry's precautions and the urgency to escape were not in the least unfounded. Pierre Landais got wind of Henry's departure not long after he had left and immediately sent men in all directions to find him and bring him back. In fact, Landais' men are said to have been only an hour behind.[14] Henry was lucky once again and by probably the end of September or the beginning of October he was able to join his uncle Jasper and the other English noblemen at the French court at the Chateau of Angers.

Henry's escape placed the remainder of the English exiles in Vannes, who still numbered around 400, in great danger. However, as soon as Duke Francis learned how Landais had dealt with them with regard to the truce with Richard III, he sympathised with them and, in a remarkable act of generosity, allowed all the exiles to rejoin their leader. Edward Woodville, Edward Poynings and John Cheyne were summoned to Francis's presence and the duke promised that he would help them to travel to France. He also granted each of these leaders 100 livres to cover the expenses of the journey and paid one livre to each of the other 408 exiles for their maintenance in Vannes and their lodgings.[15] Henry was deeply grateful for this sincere gesture of regret for Landais' ill-treatment of him and his followers and sent a

---

12 Vergil, pp. 206–8.
13 *The Channel Islands, 1370–1640*, Tim Thornton, p. 60.,
    The Boydell Press (Woodbridge 2012)
14 Vergil, p. 206–7.
15 Vergil, p. 208. Archives de Loire-Atlantique, E 212, 93, ff 15t, 17v.

message of thanks to the duke who, once again, had shown himself to be an honourable man, a man of his word who, sadly, was no longer capable of ruling his own duchy.

At the time of Jasper and Henry's arrival in Anjou, King Charles VIII was actually at the ancient town of Montargis, seventy miles south of Paris, a considerable distance. Christopher Urswick was again sent by Henry to Charles VIII and informed the king on 11 October of the English arrivals. Gilbert de Chabannes, Lord of Curton and governor of the province of Limousin, was immediately ordered by the French government to meet and welcome the exiles. Chabannes was to receive them and to arrange accommodation for them in the towns through which they had to pass on their journey of around ten days to the illustrious cathedral city of Chartres where the Tudors and Charles VIII would meet. Arriving there, Henry explained why he was throwing himself on his mercy. Charles was supportive of the idea of Henry's endeavour and encouraged him, arranging for the financial support and the lodging of Henry's 400 followers from Brittany. On 4 November the arrangements were complete and Henry's exiled faction were accommodated in the town of Sens, thirty-five miles north-east of Montargis. A fortnight later Charles VIII granted Henry 3,000 francs towards clothing for his men. Furthermore, Henry received permission to recruit men to raise an armed force for his mission to invade England.[16] The remainder of the autumn and the beginning of winter was spent at the French court at or near Montargis.[17]

Naturally, relations between England and France worsened even further during that autumn and winter and Richard responded to the news of French support for Henry's cause with the same anger as he had done the previous year. On 7 December 1484, he issued a major proclamation against Henry, Jasper and some other leaders of the exiles in France, Bishop Peter Courtney of Exeter, Edward Woodville, Thomas Grey, Marquess of Dorset and the 13th Earl of Oxford, John de Vere. They were condemned for desiring 'one Henry Tydder son of Edmond Tydder son of Owen Tydder', who had the audacity to style himself Earl of Richmond, to be their commander. In addition both Owen Tudor and Margaret Beaufort were declared illegitimate, while Charles VIII, 'calling himself King of France', was

16 Gairdner, *Richard III*, pp. 169–70.
17 Vergil, p. 208.

described as England's ancient enemy.[18] These condemnations were accompanied by detailed orders for special commissions to muster men in every county at short notice. In order to retain as much loyalty and support as possible, Richard was also quick to offer general pardons to some leading rebels, most notably to John Morton and Elizabeth Woodville's younger brother Richard.[19]

The staunch Lancastrian supporter John de Vere, Earl of Oxford, had just escaped from Hammes Castle near Calais, after being imprisoned there for the last decade. Oxford's custodian at Hammes was Sir James Blount, a former Yorkist who, according to the Burgundian chronicler Jean Molinet, was informed by Lord Thomas Stanley that Richard III had sent a man named William Bolton to transfer Oxford back to England.[20] The strict instructions given to Bolton betray not only Richard's anxiety to remove Oxford into more secure custody but perhaps also some doubt about Blount's loyalty. Richard was justified in his suspicion because Blount preferred to declare for Henry instead of complying with Richard's orders. At the same time, in England, there were signs of revolt led by several men connected to Oxford. On 2 November 1484, there were minor uprisings involving some men who had connections to Oxford, and treasonous words were uttered by Sir Thomas Brandon, his sons William and Thomas Brandon, and several others, who, it was alleged in a later indictment, were conspiring with Henry and the Earl of Oxford.[21] Some of these men had connections to Oxford and others to Lord Stanley. It therefore seems fairly clear that there had been some sort of correspondence between Oxford and the activists in England prior to his escape from Hammes. It should be noted that Lord Stanley's loyalty towards Henry's cause was already apparent before his decisive intervention at Bosworth. John Morton can also be connected to many of the conspirators.[22] Moreover, all these men mentioned above, and Oxford and Blount, arrived at Henry's small court in France soon after their escape, nearly at the same time.[23]

It is no surprise that Henry was ecstatic at the good fortune of Oxford's arrival and his willingness to join his cause. John de Vere

---

18   *The Paston Letters*, vol. 3, p. 316.
19   Harleian MSS. 443. BL F. 273v–274. Chrimes, Henry VII, p. 106.
20   Fabyan, p. 672.
21   KB27/908, rex. Rot. 8. *Norfolk Archaeology*, vol. 38 (1981–3), p. 143.
22   Accession of Henry VII; EHR, cii (1987), pp. 7–8.
23   Vergil, p. 208–9. Molinet, vol. 2, p. 406.

was an important addition to the swiftly growing group of supporters and Polydore Vergil describes Henry's reaction to his arrival:

> Whan Henry saw therle he was ravished with joy incredible that a man of so great nobilytie and knowledge in the warre, and of most perfyte and sownd fydelytie, most earnestly bent to his side, was at the last by Gods assistance delivered owt of ward, and in so fyt tyme coommyd to help him, in whome he might repose his hope, and settle himself more safely than in any other; for he was not ignorant that others who had holden on to King Edward side yealdid unto him by reason of the evell state of tyme, but this man who had so oft fought for King Henry was he thowght delyveryd from that ward by the hevenly help, that he might have one of his owne faction to whom he might safely commit all things; and therfor rejoysing above all measure for therle of Oxfoorthis coming, he began to hope better of his affaires.[24]

Other Englishmen that settled for Henry were John Fortescue, the porter of Calais, and John Risely. Also English students at the University of Paris offered their services, the most prominent among them being Richard Fox, who would later become one of the leading figures in Henry's government. William Bret, a London draper, personally delivered several suits of armour costing £37.

On 27 January 1485, Richard III once again offered a general pardon, his usual strategy in a crisis – combining resolution with reconciliation to prevent catastrophe. This time the offer was to William Blount, his wife Elizabeth, Thomas Brandon and the entire garrison at Hammes.[25]

Meanwhile Henry, Jasper and their growing party of supporters travelled further north, reaching the French capital by the beginning of February 1485.

To Richard III the desertions at Hammes Castle were more than alarming and he sent part of the Calais garrison to take over control of it. The rebels inside then appealed to Henry Tudor and Oxford

24 Vergil, pp. 208–9.
25 CPR, Edw.IV/Rich.III 1476–1485, p. 528.

returned to help the besieged by way of returning a favour, especially by rescuing his friends and also Blount's wife (who had been left behind in the rush to escape). According to Polydore Vergil, Oxford was able to get inside and unite with the besieging force, while Thomas Brandon moved quietly into the castle with thirty men to strengthen the garrison, which now numbered seventy-two. The Calais garrison was forced to agree terms by which the men of the Hammes garrison were allowed to leave, and the Earl of Oxford brought them all to Paris, to join Henry Tudor.[26]

On a political front, Richard continued negotiations with Francis II and by March 1485 the Anglo-Breton truce had been extended for a further seven years. One of its terms provided that neither side would support the enemies of the other. Richard was fully aware that an invasion was coming and he became ever more desperate in his endeavours to unsettle and undermine Henry's position. On 16 March, Richard's queen, Anne Neville, died, but even before her death, while she was ill, gossip about the king's marriage was spreading. Rumours were publicly denied but soon it was widely circulating that Richard III intended to marry himself to his niece (and Henry's betrothed) Elizabeth of York, and thus circumvent Henry's plans. Richard was troubled by the rumours and the reactions to them and so he found a solution. Having already found a marriage candidate for Elizabeth's younger sister Cecily, Sir Ralph Scrope, a man far below her rank, he now began to negotiate a marriage for Elizabeth to a cousin of the Portuguese king, Manuel, Duke of Beja. For himself, he offered his hand in marriage to the Portuguese king's elder sister, Joana. Richard knew that by arranging these marriages he might not only be able to destroy the rumours about a marriage between himself and his niece but that, more importantly, he would destroy Henry's position as the foremost claimant on behalf of the house of Lancaster, for there were living descendants of Henry IV's sister Philippa, who had married John I of Portugal, in the Portuguese royal family.

By the spring of 1485, Henry was in close touch with the French court and at some stage he had at least one lengthy conversation with Philippe de Commynes, which may have taken place when Jasper and Henry accompanied Charles VIII to Normandy in March. They entered Rouen on 14 April, just before the opening of parliament.[27]

---

26 Vergil, pp. 212–13.
27 Entrée de Charles VIII à Rouen en 1485 (Rouen 1902) pp. 9, 22–4.

According to Polydore Vergil, Henry, Jasper and the rest of their supporters had already moved to Rouen while a fleet was still being equipped at Harfleur when rumours of the plans for the marriage of Elizabeth of York reached Henry. Henry feared that rebellious Yorkists would now abandon him and his cause and understood that, if Richard did marry Elizabeth himself or marry her off, his own plans for a union between the houses of Lancaster and York would be jeopardised. The presence of Elizabeth Woodville's son Dorset and also her brothers Edward and Richard in France with Henry Tudor was a great embarrassment to her. Elizabeth managed to persuade her son to desert Henry and return to England. One night Dorset secretly left Paris and hastened towards Flanders.[28] This, of course, threatened disaster since, over the past couple of months, all of the exiles' plans had been under discussion and, if Dorset did reach Richard's court, he would naturally reveal them all. Having requested and been granted King Charles VIII's consent, Henry promptly sent in pursuit two of his own supporters, Matthew Baker and Humphrey Cheyne. At Lihorns-sur-Santerre, seventy-five miles north of Paris, between Amiens and Saint-Quentin, they overtook Dorset and persuaded, or perhaps compelled, him to return to Paris.

Confiding in the Earl of Oxford, Henry discussed with him a possible solution to the marriage problem. Both agreed that Henry's second-choice candidate would be Katherine Herbert,[29] the daughter of his former custodian William Herbert. Henry had known Katherine and her brothers and sisters in the days when he was growing up in her father's household at Raglan. Among these had been Maud, to whom Henry would have been married had William Herbert been still alive, and her brother William, who in 1479 had been forced to surrender his earldom of Pembroke and been given the earldom of Huntingdon instead. Maud Herbert had been married to her father's other ward, Henry Percy, Earl of Northumberland, who had also been Henry's companion while growing up. Henry may have hoped that the prospect of his marriage to a Herbert might move the Earl of Northumberland to come to his aid.

On 4 May, Charles VIII, having requested financial aid from the estates in order to assist Henry 'to recover the realm to which he had better right than anyone else living', granted him 40,000 livres. By 3

---

28 Vergil, p. 210.
29 Vergil, p. 215. *Herberts of Raglan*, pp. 218–19, 287–8.

June, King Charles returned to Paris, seemingly leaving Jasper and Henry in Rouen. There, some initial preparations may already have been underway for the collecting of a convoy at the River Seine. In the early summer, naval and military preparations at Harfleur neared completion

On 22 June, Richard ordered the commissioners who had been nominated in every county the previous winter to muster their men and to make sure they were properly paid and ready for service. Richard also issued a new proclamation that betrayed the urgency of the moment. He heaped fresh personal insults on Jasper and Henry, and in particular on Henry, saying: 'for he is descended of bastard blood both of father's side and of mother's side'.[30]

By 26 June, Richard was preparing to send 1,000 archers from Southampton to Brittany, under the command of John Grey, Lord Powys.[31] These men were to help secure Duke Francis's power against both the rebellious Breton nobility (who detested Landais as a presumptuous commoner) and the French. In return for Richard's support, Landais was to arrange the capture and extradition of Henry and Jasper. Within a week Richard learned that Pierre Landais had fallen out of favour and that Duke Francis had been forced to hand him over to the Breton rebels who had the backing of Anne de Beaujeu, King Charles VIII's elder sister and the regent of France. Landais was arrested and accused of extortion and many other alleged crimes and on 19 July he was hanged on the gallows of Biesse in Nantes. Richard III's troops never arrived. However, his interference in Franco-Breton relationships greatly offended the French government.

Charles VIII had granted Henry 40,000 livres on their joint arrival in Rouen but, according to the receiver-general's account of 1484–85, it seems that so far Henry had only received a quarter of this amount, and there is no sign he ever received the rest.[32] Henry realised he would need to look elsewhere to finance his invasion and turned to one of Charles's councillors, Phillippe Lullier, pleading his overwhelming need for money. On 13 July 1485, at the office of the notary Pierre Pichon on Rue Saint-Antoine in Paris, a private contract was signed between Henry and Lullier, by which the latter agreed to lend Henry 30,000 livres. As security for the loan, Henry was to hand over all his personal belongings and, in addition, two hostages

---

30 The *Paston Letters*, Gairdner, vol. 6, pp. 81–4.

31 Nottingham Medieval Studies 37 (1993) pp, 110–26.

32 B.N., fonds française 23.266, f. 38. Kendall, pp. 339–40.

- Thomas Grey, Marquess of Dorset (who was, in any case, no longer a trustworthy supporter) and John Bourchier, Lord FitzWarin - and to promise to refund the cost of their custody in the Bastille Saint-Antoine.

Soon after this Jasper and Henry and their party left for Harfleur. As they journeyed they were intercepted by John Morgan, who was sent by Henry's mother Margaret and came with good news. Morgan could confirm that both John Savage, Lord Stanley's nephew, and Rhys ap Thomas were preparing to lend their aid and would be 'strong supporters' of the Tudor cause, and that Reginald Bray had managed to collect a sum of money that would be handed over to Henry on his arrival in Wales so he could pay his men. He also brought the message that Henry should make for Wales as soon as possible.[33]

Henry was delighted by the news and realised that any further delay could only increase his supporters' uncertainties. It was now time to finalise the strategy for the invasion. To some extent, because of the assurances of assistance and partly because of Henry's Welsh origin, but without question mostly because of Jasper's roots and past authority there, it was decided to land in Wales.

Many of Jasper's supporters in Wales were aware of the likelihood of their hero's long-awaited arrival in the land of his fathers. In several poems Jasper is called upon to put an end to the Yorkist claim to the throne.[34] Even the Welsh bard Robin Ddu ap Siencyn Bledrydd of Anglesey, who had been an adherent of Owen Tudor, called for Henry 'our little bull' to conquer Richard III (see Appendix L).

At Harfleur, there was now assembled an increased group of 500 Englishmen,[35] together with around 1,000 Scots, accompanied by the noble knight Sir Alexander Bruce of Ershall and Bernard Steward, an emigrant Scot who had joined the French royal household, as well as another large group of Scottish footmen and, finally, the French troops under the command of the nobleman Philibert de Chandée (described by Henry as 'our dear kinsman, both of spirit and blood'), which made up the majority of Henry's supporters. The exact number of French troops supplied by Charles VIII can be argued, but they probably constituted around half of the armed flotilla that was to leave from Harfleur.[36]

33 Vergil, pp. 215–16.
34 Gwaith Lewis Glyn Cothi, pp. 477–9, The Cymmrodorionn (Oxford 1837)
35 Spont, 'La marine française sous le règene de Charles VIII', p. 393.
36 Commynes, pp. 355, 397. Molinet, p. 406.

Richard was already keeping a close eye on the most dangerous elements in the kingdom, notably the Stanley-Beaufort household. From the moment Lord Stanley wished to excuse himself from court sometime in July, King Richard's distrust of him increased. Richard accepted the request but only if Lord Stanley's son, George Lord Strange, remained at court, in effect as a hostage.[37]

After fourteen long years of waiting, Jasper and Henry's exile was finally over. By 1 August 1485, Lord Strange was in Richard's company at Nottingham Castle, while his father, Lord Stanley, was in the North West, and Henry and Jasper with around 4,000 allies – made up, according to Commynes, of the dregs from Norman gaols – were ready to embark. With their flotilla of around thirty ships containing English exiles and French and Scottish troops, under the command of the notorious naval commander Guillaume de Casenove aboard his flagship the *Poulain of Dieppe*, they left Harfleur on a soft southern wind and sailed out towards the Channel. They had one aim – to claim the English crown.[38]

---

37   Vergil, p. 216. Croyland Chronicle, p. 501. Analles, p. 467.
38   Vergil, p. 216.

13

THE ROAD TO
BOSWORTH
1 August – 22 August 1485

'In what seas are thy anchors, and where art thou thyself?

When wilt thou, Black Bull, come to land;
    how long shall we wait?'[1]

'This is a world that loves to behold thee
    and to call thee a second Jasper'.[2]

THIS TIME the weather was on their side and, without encountering any obstacle at sea, on 7 August, after a journey of six days the fleet landed safely at Mill Bay, six miles west from Milford Haven along the rocky coastline of Pembrokeshire.[3]

Preparations had been going on for their arrival. As soon as word of Jasper and Henry's landing began to spread the Welsh bards started to exercise their talents in circulating prophecies which foretold the victor of the forthcoming engagement but also reflected the impatient

---

1 Lewis Glyn Cothi, Dos, VIII, 5. (Cited in *Welsh Nationalism and Henry Tudor*, p. 18) The bard addresses Jasper, expressing the anxious expectation of his countrymen concerning the arrival of the fleet.

2 Hywel Eurddrein ai Kant, *Welsh Nationalism and Henry Tudor*, pp. 30–32.

3 S.B. Chrimes, 'The landing place of Henry of Richmond, 1485', *Welsh History Review*, 2 (1964), pp. 173–80.

expectations there were in Wales. Amongst the most influential bards was Dafydd Llwyd ap Llewellyn ap Gruffydd of Mathafarn, whose poetic exhortations anticipated Henry's triumph:

> [...]when the Bull comes from the far land to battle with his great ashen spear, to be an earl again in the land of Llewelyn, let the far-splitting spear shed the blood of the Saxons on the stubble. Then the Boar, in Harry's day, will snarl when it comes to fighting with us [...] When the long yellow summer comes and victory comes to us and the spreading of the sails of Brittany and when the heat comes and when the fever is kindled, there are portents that victory will be given to us. When we sing together on the heights of Caergylchwr then there will be fire in Manaw and a proud progress through Anglesey [...] and Denbigh awaits us and flames in Rhuddlan and Rhos. Entangled will be the fight and wonderful will be its end [...] And the world will become happy at last to blessed Gwynedd.'4

In another poem the bard Dafydd Llwyd writes:

> The Bards have befooled the world; God knows it, but he will save. Everyone speaks of a reckoning between our race and the foreigners, were we but to wait for one who will strike, a high-born Briton of the stock of Maegwn, the peacock of Tudor, greatest of sires who will gild all with solid gold [...] The Knell of the Saxon, when we win, will give a chief judge of our race [...] Cadwaladr shall come home, with his eightfold gifts, from his deeds [...] Woe to the black host beside the wave! When ill fortune comes – strangers! – Jasper will breed for us a Dragon-of the fortunate blood of Brutus is he

---

4   Hist. MSS. Com. Rept., vol 1, pt. II, pp. 408–9. Contrary to what is stated by
     W.G. Jones in his *Welsh Nationalism and Henry Tudor*, where this poem by Daffydd
     Llwyd is cited (p. 34), 'The Bull' who is to come 'to be an earl again' symbolizes Jasper,
     and the reference in the poem to Denbigh and 'the flames in Rhuddlan and Rhos'
     alludes to the siege and the destruction of the area back in 1459–60 and 1468
     (see Chapter 10)

> [...] A Bull of Anglesey to achieve; he is the hope
> of our race. A great gift is the birth of Jasper of
> the line of Cadwaladr of the beautiful spear.
> Horsa and Hengist were strangers to the Brut of
> Greece and the Round Table; Vortigern brought
> shame on us by giving them a share of our land.
> Jasper was ordained for us, he will draw us out of
> the net and set us free [...] After travail will come
> the Lily Crown to Beli of Anglesey.[5]

Amongst those waiting on the shore was likely Jasper's half-brother and Henry's uncle, the twenty-six-year-old David Owen, illegitimate son of Owen Tudor, who had spent the first years of his life with Henry at Pembroke Castle.[6]

Henry's mingled sense of relief and anxiety was obvious. According to the chronicler Robert Fabyan, 'when he [Henry] was come unto the land he incontently kneeled down upon the earth, and with meek countenance and pure devotion began this psalm: Judica me deus, et discerne causam meam' (Psalm 43: 'Judge me, O God, and distinguish my cause'). He then 'kissed the ground meekly, and reverently made the sign of the cross upon him'.[7] Soon after landing Henry also decided to knight eight of his foremost followers – his uncles David Owen and John, Lord Welles; Philibert de Chandée; James Blount; Edward Courtenay; John Cheyne; Edward Poynings and John Fort.[8]

Soon after all the soldiers had disembarked, the French commander of the fleet, Guillaumme de Casenove, put out to sea again bound for his next adventure (less than three weeks later he was to be found in southern Portugal). With Casenove's fleet fading out into the Atlantic Ocean, there could be no turning back for Henry and Jasper.

Their first task was to climb the steep cliff from the rocky shore. This was soon followed by the decision to go as far as the village of Dale and its castle. Dale did not prove to be difficult to suppress[9] and Henry ordered his men to set up camp in the village, possibly near

---

5   Brut, Bleddyn MS. 3, fos. 48–49, Jones, *Dafydd Llwyd, Welsh Nationalism and Henry Tudor*, pp. 32–3.
6   W.H. Blaauw, '*On the effigy of Sir David Owen*', pp. 25, 38, 39, vol. 7, History and Antiquities of that county, The Sussex Archaeological Society, vol. 7 (London 1854)
7   Fabyan, p. 672.
8   Harleian 78 fo. 31v.
9   Vergil, p. 216.

the castle. According to Bernard André, Henry, perhaps especially mindful of his French troops, now admonished his men, warning them not to do anything to others, 'either by word or by deed, that you not wish to have done to yourselves'. Rules of war were crucial if authority was to be maintained and order kept.

Both Jasper and the Earl of Oxford inspected the French troops in order to determine what gear and weaponry they were short of. Except for a few sporadic accounts, Jasper's own activities are not documented, but he may have been occupied with restoring and rekindling old friendships and associations in an attempt to generate further support.

It was probably the constable of Pembroke, Richard Williams, who hastened 200 miles over four days to King Richard at Nottingham and gave him news of their landing. But Arnold West brought them good news, that the people of Pembroke 'were ready to serve Jaspar ther erle'.[10]

Although King Richard had kept a close watch on the area during the winter period, he was informed that Henry landed at Angle, which is about a mile across the bay from Mill Bay, as perhaps a detachment did. The following morning, 8 August, at the break of dawn, Henry began his march to Haverfordwest, twelve miles away, crossing a branch of the Western Cleddau River at what now is Old Bridge. Arriving rapidly at Haverfordwest Henry and his army were received 'with great goodwill of all men'.[11]

On the same day, John Morton came with disappointing news. Contrary to what Jasper and Henry had been told in Normandy, Rhys ap Thomas and John Savage were keeping their distance for now. This was quite likely because they feared the possible consequences of King Richard's wrath. John Savage had already been arrested in May at Pembroke, probably for intriguing for Henry's cause, and although he had been released he needed to be extremely careful.[12] Also, Reginald Bray, who had promised a large sum of money for Henry to pay his troops, had yet to arrive. There was also good news. Arnold Butler, who had been Henry's servant when he fled to Brittany in 1471 but had been removed from his company by Duke Francis and forced to return home, 'came to tell him that the entire nobility of the County of Pembroke was prepared to serve him, provided that

---

10 Vergil, p. 216.
11 Vergil, p. 216.
12 Harleian MSS 433, BL vol. 3, pp. 172–3.

he would grant pardon for and wipe out the memory of anything they had done against him and against Jasper during the time when they were both in Brittany. In accordance with his nature and for the benefit of his enterprise', Henry 'with Jasper easily forgave them. At which they came voluntarily to him and bound themselves by the military oath'.[13] The support of Arnold Butler was important, not only because Pembrokeshire would follow his lead, but also because Butler himself was a long-time associate and close friend of Rhys ap Thomas, which had made Henry more certain of Rhys' support. King Richard's supporters, Richard Williams and Sir James Tyrell, had long controlled the region with a firm hand. For now, Rhys ap Thomas remained aloof in the Tywi Valley and may have wished or thought it wise to practise a cautious strategy by following Henry's progress from a distance and shadowing him as he moved northwards.

That same afternoon Henry and his troops departed from Haverfordwest, heading for Cardigan, twenty-seven miles away. At some point, having made good progress, Henry is said to have decided to set up camp 'at the fifth milestone' so that his soldiers could have a rest. Then a sudden rumour sprang up and spread throughout the camp that Sir Walter Herbert, son of Henry's childhood custodian William Herbert, and Rhys ap Thomas were encamped near Carmarthen and preparing to challenge them with a large force . Uproar immediately ensued and since 'a stirre rose straightway, every man mayde ready his armor'.[14] As Rhys ap Thomas and Walter Herbert had been ordered to suppress any uprising, this fear amongst the soldiers was not without logic. Henry decided to send out some scouts on horseback to find out what was going on. Soon they returned with the information that no danger was to be expected from Carmarthen and that the news was probably false, and the mood of anxiety dissolved. Shortly afterwards, another of Rhys ap Thomas's associates, Gruffydd Rede, joined Henry's camp, perhaps to discuss Rhys's conditions for defection. In addition, John Morgan of Gwent and Richard Griffith, both possible associates of Rhys ap Thomas, came to join Henry and Jasper.[15] Rhys ap Thomas may have been cautious and seemingly reluctant to announce his allegiance to Henry in public. It was even reported by

---

13 Vergil, Vatican Urbs. Lat. 498, fo. 230r (cited in C. Skidmore,
    Bosworth, the Birth of the Tudors (London: Weidenfeld & Nicolson, 2013)
14 Vergil, pp. 216–17.
15 Vergil, p. 217. Hall's Chronicle, p. 410.

several accounts that Rhys and Herbert intended to confront Henry's army and obstruct their passing or even to attack them.[16] It is quite likely that this was part of a strategy to deliberately confuse King Richard and his advisers, and Rhys may have communicated precisely this to Henry after he landed. It is hard to believe that many of Rhys's associates defected one-by-one to Henry's side, while Rhys himself was still hesitating to do so. *The Life of Sir Rhys ap Thomas*, first published in 1796 and authored by Rhys ap Thomas's direct descendant Henry Rice (c. 1590–c. 1651), even states that Rhys had already met with Henry soon after the landing at Mill Bay and was committed to his cause.[17]

By now it was probably late in the day and so the army remained encamped at the fifth milestone. The following morning, 9 August, Henry felt confident enough to begin the next difficult part of the journey, leading his army up over the rough Preseli Hills to reach the farmstead of Fagwr Llwyd, probably in the evening – a twelve-mile trek.

Continuing his journey the next day Henry and his men crossed the River Teifi at the fortified town of Cardigan after a march of ten miles. Tradition has it that Henry stopped at the Three Mariners Inn and decided to pause there to gather further support. Letters were written to be sent out across the region. Messengers were dispatched to the Stanleys and Talbots, and Henry also wrote to his friends and supporters in North Wales. A copy of one of these letters has been preserved. It is written to Jasper's second cousin, John ap Maredudd ap Ieuan ap Maredudd, who lived in the area of south Caernarvonshire. In the letter Henry urges him in a tone of authority to come faithfully to his aid and not to fail in this if 'ye will avoid our grievous displeasure and answer unto at your peril'.[18] However, as John ap Maredudd was not rewarded after Henry's succession it is possible that he did not respond to the request.

Henry and his force left Cardigan and moved northwards, proceeding along the coastline. After stopping for water at Ffynnon Dewi north-east of Cardigan, they arrived at a country mansion at Llwyn Dafydd, fifteen miles further north-east. Henry rested that

---

16 Hall's Chronicle, p. 411. Holinshed, vol. 3, p. 435. Grafton, p. 542.
17 Sir Rhys ap Thomas, Griffiths, Cromwell Press (Wiltshire (reprint of 1981)2014) p. 210.
18 An Unpublished letter by Henry, Earl of Richmond, in *Miscellanea Genealogica at Heraldica*, 4th series, vol. 5, G. Grazebrook and J. Ballinger eds. (1914), pp. 30–39. Gwydir Family, pp. 55–6.

night at a house called 'Neuadd', the home of Dafydd ap Ieuan, a descendant of the ancient Welsh nobility, where Henry was lavishly entertained. Henry would later reward Dafydd ap Ieuan for his trouble with a precious 'Hirlas Horn', a drinking horn that rested on a silver stand decorated with the Welsh dragon and a greyhound, and had images of a the Beaufort portcullis and Tudor roses engraved on a silver band around its rim.[19]

There were good reasons why Henry chose this particular route. Richard III's loyal adherent Richard Williams had wide-ranging authority in the south-west as well as Sir James Tyrell. A route towards Brecon was also quickly eliminated because Henry's army would have had to cross the River Severn and, as this area had fallen into the hands of Sir Thomas Vaughan, son of that Sir Roger Vaughan of Tretower who had been executed by Jasper in 1471, this would have been too risky. Moreover, Henry had great hopes of North Wales and Cheshire, where the Stanleys ruled. There just was no other option than the route he was now following.

The following day, 11 August, Henry continued his march northwards and, according to tradition, stopped at the home of Einion ap Dafydd Llwyd at Wern Newydd in the parish of Llanarth, only four miles from Llwyn Dafydd, probably to enjoy some hospitality.[20] After this they marched on to spend the night at St Hilary's Church in Llanilar, where Henry is supposed to have slept at the old mansion of Llidiardau, overlooking the Ystwyth Valley.[21]

The next day, Henry and his supporters reached Aberystwyth with the ancient Monastery of Llanbadarn close by.[22] Aberystwyth Castle was held for his opponents by Walter Devereux, Lord Ferrers, but the garrison was not large and the castle was taken with very little trouble.

The news that Aberystwyth had fallen must have been a significant blow to Richard III, for he had at first considered Henry and his forces as being of little consequence. For Henry it must have seemed as if his onward march was unstoppable. Even so, to maintain such an advance across rough and possibly hostile country, and then to accomplish his goal of grasping the throne, was not something

---

19 Thomas and Griffiths, *The Making of the Tudor Dynasty* (Stroud 2003), p. 162.
20 Thomas and Griffiths, *The Making of the Tudor Dynasty* (Stroud 2003), p. 162.
21 Vergil's *Anglia Historia*, Vatican Urbs. Lat. 498, fos. 230r–231r. The house was completely rebuilt in the 18th century.
22 Vergil's *Anglia Historia*, Vatican Urbs. Lat. 498, fos. 230r–231r.

that could be taken for granted. After Aberystwyth was taken, Henry possibly stayed the night in the town and paused to send scouts to locate the armies of Rhys ap Thomas and Sir Walter Herbert. After consultation with some of his advisers, possibly Jasper and the Earl of Oxford, Henry recognised that he had pushed as far north as he could and it was now time to turn inland towards the English frontier.

The following morning, 13 August, Henry's army continued their march, heading up the Dyfi Estuary and making for Machynlleth, twenty-three miles away. Henry arrived at the town in the evening and spent the night there, where, the following day, 14 August, he wrote several more letters. One of these, addressed to Sir Roger Kynaston, a Shropshire knight and a nephew by marriage to John, Lord Grey of Powys, still survives.[23] A local powerful magnate and supposed to be one of Richard III's allies, Lord Grey was absent from Wales at the time and Kynaston had been left in charge in his place. In the remarkable letter to Kynaston, Henry writes that Lord Powys had every intention of supporting him, saying 'forsomuch as we be credibly informed and ascertained that our trusty and well beloved cousin the Lord Powys hath in the time passed be of that mind and disposition that at this our coming in to these parts he had fully concluded and determined to have do us service'. Had Grey somehow secretly promised Henry his allegiance? Henry certainly claimed so in the letter.

Rhys ap Thomas's allegiance would come at a price. According to Vergil, Henry was willing to pay and promised either by messengers or letters 'the perpetual governorship of Wales if he came over to his side'.[24] The same day other letters were written, one to William Stanley at Holt Castle, one to Gilbert Talbot, 'and some others'. In addition, Henry's chaplain Christopher Urswick was sent to Thomas Stanley and his mother at Lathom.[25]

According to tradition, Henry, and probably Jasper, spent the night at the home of the elderly Welsh bard Dafydd Llwyd, five miles east of Machynlleth, at Mathafarn. There the story of Henry's request for a prophecy was born when, it is said, he asked whether he would be successful in his campaign. Afraid to answer this straight away, Dafydd promised the outcome in the morning and retired to his bed

---

23 Thomas and Griffiths, *The Making of the Tudor Dynasty*, p. 163. The letter is in private ownership.
24 Vergil, p. 217.
25 Vergil, p. 217.

somewhat disconsolate. The bard's wife asked him the reason for his melancholy and after hearing his explanation she recommended that her husband should tell Henry what he mostly wanted to hear.

If Henry was not successful, he would not return to accuse Dafydd of being a false forecaster; but if he was successful, Dafydd could only be rewarded.[26]

Resuming his journey the next day, 15 August, encouraged by the bard's prediction, Henry knew that this part of the journey would be a tough one. Marching through the mountains of Snowdonia, amidst some of the most rocky mountains in Wales, must have been physically challenging. After an exhausting thirty-mile march they reached Henry's intended destination, Dolarddun, just a few miles west of Welshpool and close to Castle Caereinon. Local tradition says that Henry spent the night at Dolarddun, and was presented with a fine white horse that carried him all the way to Bosworth.[27]

The following morning, Henry's men marched the six miles to Welshpool and, without stopping in the town, carried on up to the top of the Mynydd Digoll, known in English as Long Mountain. There the first meeting between Henry and Rhys ap Thomas took place. Rhys was finally willing to pledge his loyalty openly to Henry and 'submitted to his authority'. He brought with him from mid-Wales, under his Black Raven standard, a force estimated at between 1,800 and 2,000 men, which swelled Henry's troops significantly.[28]

The messages sent by Henry over the past few days were now at last bearing substantial fruit. That same night a number of other Welshmen joined him before he reached Shrewsbury. One of them was Rhys Fawr ap Maredudd (also known as Rhys the Mighty) from Golgynwal in the Conwy Valley, who brought not only a contingent of men but also many fat cattle. Henry also received support from, among others, William Gruffydd of Penrhyn, Adam ap Evan ap Jankyn and several members of the Howell family who had been loyal supporters to Jasper in the past – for example, Richard Howell of Mostyn and

---

26 Thomas and Griffiths, *The Making of the Tudor Dynasty*, pp. 158–9.
27 Details of Henry's march to Shrewsbury are taken from Vergil's *Anglia Historia*, Vatican Urbs. Lat. 498, fos. 230r–231r and *also Vergil*, pp. 217–19. Other accounts that cover the march are *Bosworth Feilde* and the *Ballad of Lady Bessie*. All are cited in *The Making of the Tudor Dynasty*, pp. 147–66.
28 Sir Rhys ap Thomas and his Family, p. 42, Griffiths. Vergil, p. 217. Hall's Chronicle, p. 411.

Philip Howell and his wife, who had been Henry's nurse in childhood when he was at Pembroke Castle. [29]

Sir Walter Herbert joined Henry and Jasper at about the same time and brought with him a number of officials from south-east Wales and Monmouthshire, including Hugh ap Howell, John ap Howell, Evan Lloyd Vaughan, constable of Neath and Aberavon, the constable of Caerphilly Mathew Cradock, and William Herbert, receiver of Monmouth, Whitecastle and Skenfrith.

Henry's stepfather Lord Stanley still kept his distance for, if he and his brother had made it clear that they stood behind Henry, it would have put his own son's life in great danger. The brothers kept in touch by messengers but their awaiting armies remained separate. This final part of the journey was very rough, through the mountains of Snowdonia.[30]

The next day, 17 August, Henry and his party rose very early and pressed on from Long Mountain to cover the eleven miles to Shrewsbury with its gate to England. It was essential they should enter the town to be able to cross the River Severn across its Welsh Bridge. Henry could not afford a repeat of what had happened at Gloucester in 1471, when the town refused to permit the Lancastrian troops to enter, thus frustrating their crossing the Severn and forcing them to undertake a strenuous march to face disaster at Tewkesbury.

History did, however, repeat itself in part. On arrival at Shrewsbury they found the portcullises down and the town's bailiffs, Thomas Mitton and Roger Knight, refused them permission to enter the town and march through. Thomas Mitton had been Richard's loyal servant and upon the command to open the gate 'to their right King', Mitton insisted he 'knew no king but King Richard to whom he was sworn, whose life tenants he and his fellows were, and before he should enter there he should go over his belly'. Upon this, Henry and his force retreated five miles north-west to cross the river at Montford Bridge and that night the army camped in the nearby village of Forton, where Henry and probably Jasper stayed in the house of Hugh of Forton.[31]

---

29 Vergil, p. 218.
30 Details of Henry's march to Shrewsbury are taken from Vergil's *Anglia Historia*, Vatican Urbs. Lat. 498, fos. 230r.–231r. and also *Vergil'*, pp. 217–19. Other accounts that cover the march are *Bosworth Feilde* and the *Ballad of Lady Bessie*. All are cited in *The Making of the Tudor Dynasty*, pp. 147–66.
31 Owen and Blakeway, *A History of Shrewbury*, vol. 1, pp. 246–8. *The Early Chronicle of Shrewsbury*, ed. W.A. Leighton (1888), pp. 249–50.

The next morning, 18 August, Henry decided to send his messengers to Shrewsbury to negotiate with Mitton, assuring him that, if permission was given, he and his men would march through the town quietly and without causing any damage or injury to any and would respect the oaths of loyalty sworn to Richard III. This probably did remove some of the anxiety of the townsmen but the decisive factor in changing the bailiff's mind was the arrival of one of Sir William Stanley's men, Rowland Warburton, in response to Henry's message. Along his way, Sir William Stanley had been alerted to Shrewsbury's resistance and therefore sent Warburton to encourage the bailiffs to open the gates. The full story of how Warburton delivered this message tells that he wrapped it around a stone and this was launched over the town walls by means of a sling. That day Shrewsbury did surrender to Henry and added a number of men to his supporters. A local chronicler captures the scene with Mitton maintaining his oath sworn to Richard III. As Henry's men entered through the gate to pass through the town, Mitton 'lay along the ground with his belly upwards and so the said Earl, Henry, stepped over him' and marched forwards. Sir William Stanley's assistance at this stage again proves that the Stanleys' alliance with Henry existed before the decisive battle that would shortly take place and not just from a crucial moment during the battle, as has been maintained by many historians. Henry and his troops likely did not stay the night at Shrewsbury but a strong tradition has it that Henry stayed in a fifteenth-century house called Wyle Cop that is still to be seen today. Perhaps Henry and his supporters just paused for refreshment at Wyle Cope before resuming their journey.[32]

The incident at Shrewsbury had been rather embarrassing for Henry. The townsmen did not display any recognition of his right to the crown and for him it was also a reminder of the difficulties ahead of him and the importance of winning new supporters.

From Shrewsbury Henry took the road through Shropshire and marched fifteen miles north-east into Staffordshire, where they spent the night of 18 August in a tent on a hill close to the town of Newport.[33] The following day, 19 August, Sir Gilbert Talbot, uncle of the Earl of Shrewsbury, joined them with about 500 armed Shropshire

32 Owen and Blakeway, *A History of Shrewsbury*, vol. 1, pp. 246–8. *The Early Chronicle of Shrewsbury*, ed. Leighhton,, pp. 249–50.
33 Vergil, p. 218.

men.[34] This brought the total from Shropshire close to 800. That they were commanded by Sir William Stanley's stepson Sir Richard Corbet was another assurance for Henry of the Stanleys' loyalty prior to the battle. From there the entire force moved a bare twelve miles east to Stafford, being joined by more and more important supporters along the way. From Hertfordshire came Thomas Croft, a staunch supporter of King Edward IV. From Worcestershire there was John Hanley, probably one of the Duke of Clarence's old servants and his men. And from Gloucestershire, Robert Pointz. Yet more came to join Henry from other neighbouring Welsh marcher lordships. This was the kind of support Henry needed to challenge Richard III. The last few miles of the road to Stafford were completed rapidly and there in the town a most encouraging meeting with Sir William Stanley took place.[35] Henry met Stanley and a small entourage and was told that Richard III was based at Nottingham and was also given some crucial strategic advice. From Stafford his army moved fifteen miles south-east to Lichfield, where they spent the night just outside the cathedral city.

The following morning, 20 August, Henry entered the city of Lichfield and was, according to Vergil, 'honorably receavyd'.[36] This was a significant moment for Henry. Even more significant is the fact that it was his stepfather, Thomas Stanley, who made this honourable entry into Lichfield possible. Three days earlier, Thomas Stanley had entered the town with an entourage of around 5,000 armed men.[37] By constantly shadowing Henry's movements supposedly to keep watch on him on King Richard's behalf, Stanley was able to remain near his stepson without giving Richard cause to execute Stanley's son, Lord Strange.

It is apparent that Stanley's sympathies, as reflected in his promises, lay with Henry. But for the present the risk of openly defecting to Henry's cause was too dangerous.

It was only now that Richard learned how close his rival was and immediately left for Leicester to hinder Henry's direct route into London. And at this point two noblemen on whom Richard had hoped to depend were missing – Thomas Stanley and the Earl of Northumberland.

---

34 Vergil, p. 218. Vergil's *Anglia Historia*, Vatican Urbs. Lat. 498, fos. 230r–231r.
35 Vergil, p. 218.
36 Vergil, p. 218
37 Vergil, p. 219. *Bosworth Field*, pp. 249–51.

Henry gave the impression of 'noble courage' as his forces increased in number 'wherever he went', but in private he continued to be nervous. Having been informed by his scouts of the size of Richard's army and been told that nothing was stronger and more ready, Henry was in doubt as to whether he was able to defeat Richard. Needing to rethink his strategy, he allowed his troops to continue their march while he remained behind with twenty armed men, presumably intending to catch up with the main force later on horseback. Henry somehow lost track of his army and, according to Polydore Vergil:

> [...] after long wondering he could not finde his company, he came on to a certain towne more than thre miles from his campe, full of feare; who least he might be betrayed, durst not aske questions of any men, but taryed there all night, no more afraye; for he was afeard that the same might be a signe of soom maner plaque to ansew. Nether was the army less heavy for the suddane absence of ther captane, whan as Henry the next day after, in the gray of the morning, returned to the host, excusing himself that he was not deceavyd in the way, but had withdrawen from the camp of set purpose to receave soome goode newys of certane his frindes.[38]

Meanwhile, late in the evening of 20 August, after Henry's troops had marched on for seven miles and had reached Tamworth, it was decided to pitch camp by the river, in the shadow of Tamworth Castle. At Tamworth Henry's numbers were further increased by men led by Thomas Bourchier and Walter Hungerford.[39] Richard III had ordered Sir Robert Brackenbury to travel up from London and to bring Hungerford and Bourchier with him, but along the way to Leicester Brackenbury was deserted by both men and many others. According to the *Great Chronicle*, Brackenbury did little to prevent their departure.[40]

Whatever had been the real reason for Henry's vanishing that night, early the following morning, 21 August, he marched across

---

38 Vergil, p. 221.
39 Vergil, p. 220.
40 Great Chronicle, p. 237.

the River Anker to Atherstone for a secret meeting with the two
Stanley brothers at the Cistercian Abbey at Merevale, where he finally
met Thomas Stanley.[41] According to Vergil, Henry and Stanley took
each other 'by the hand, and yielding mutual salutation', both were
'moved to great joy', after which 'they entered in counsel in what sort
to arraigne battle with King Richard, if the matter should come to
strokes, whome they had heard to be not far off'. After plans were
made for the positions of both Henry's and Stanley's armies, there
was further good news for Henry, for Stanley ordered four knights,
Sir John Savage, Sir Robert Tunstall, Sir Hugh Persall and Sir
Humphrey Stanley, to strengthen Henry's front line. Henry and his
troops parted from Stanley, but before the day came to an end more
defectors arrived at his camp, including Simon Digby, the younger
John Savage and Brian Sandford, who appeared with a band of armed
men.[42] A gentleman called John de Hardwicke, who was the lord of
the nearby manor of Lindley, had also joined Henry that day with
men and horses. Night fell and a camp site was found between the
neighbouring villages of Witherley, Fenny Drayton and Atterton, just
outside Atherstone.[43]

By now Richard had been well informed about Henry's approach
and location and the King now prepared himself to face his enemy. It
is said that King Richard struggled to find peace in sleep that night.
The following morning he spoke of how he had had 'a terrible dream'
where 'he was surrounded by evil demons, who did not let him rest'.
Did Richard know what was about to come?[44]

Early on the morning of 22 August, Henry sent a messenger to
Thomas Stanley. Stanley had moved his force, along with that of his
brother, between the armies of Richard and Henry. Henry requested
that Stanley permit his men to join Henry's troops, which would
allow Henry to place his men into formation. He also asked Stanley
to lead the vanguard. Stanley's reply was not what Henry hoped for,
being that 'the earle showld set his owne folks in order, whyle that he
should come to him with his army well apoyntyd'. For the sake of his
son, Stanley would keep his distance. For now.[45]

41 Campbell, *Materials*, vol. 1, pp. 188, 201, 233.
42 Vergil, p. 221.
43 Campbell, *Materials*, vol. 1, pp. 188, 201, 233.
44 Vergil, p. 221. BL Additional MS 12060 fos. 19-20v.
45 Vergil, p. 222.

Henry recognised that his troops were too few to defeat Richard's army. According to Vergil, Henry's estimated force of around 8,000 soldiers was around half the size of Richard's impressive army. However, sources for the actual number of armed forces at the Battle of Bosworth vary. Many accounts have been written about the action of 22 August, but the majority of them are based on non-contemporary reports. Polydore Vergil's is one of the very few writers who had direct eyewitnesses of the march and battle, including Christopher Urswick.

All would now depend on whether the Stanley brothers with their combined forces of an estimated 6,000 men, would come to Henry's aid. It is said that Henry became 'anxious and began to lose heart' and that he was advised by the Earl of Oxford to draw up a single battle-line, given how few men he had compared to Richard. Oxford had been placed in charge of the military leadership of Henry's army and commanded the vanguard. Henry had Gilbert Talbot on his right and Sir John Savage on his left. Behind this line, Henry was positioned, surrounded by just one squadron of cavalry and a few infantry, including his loyal friend William Brandon, his standard-bearer. It is said that Henry remained on foot.[46] Jasper's presence during the battle is recorded by the sixteenth-century historian and antiquarian John Stow, who writes that Henry 'assigned Sir John Savage, and hee with the ayde of the Lord Stanley accompanied with the Earle of Pembrooke having a good company of horsemen and a small number of foot-men'[47]

Both Richard and Henry's forces included companies of cavalry and infantry and were supplied with handguns and cannons as well as the more traditional bows and blades.

Richard positioned the elderly but experienced John, Duke of Norfolk, and Sir Robert Brackenbury in his vanguard, leading the archers. His rearguard was to be commanded by the Earl of Northumberland, with the king himself at the rear of the extended battle line.

When the two vanguards saw one another, final preparations were made, helmets were put on and finally, a shout for battle sounded. It was Oxford against Norfolk. The two leaders were old rivals, jostling for the leadership of their East Anglian region, and they had fought against one another fourteen years before at Barnet, where Norfolk

---

46 Vergil, p. 223.
47 Stow, Annales p. 469, ed. E. Howes.

had been victorious thanks to Oxford's own military failure that day. It was now Oxford's chance for revenge.

When the battle was well commenced, Richard caught sight of Stanley's motionless forces in the distance. Furiously, he ordered Lord Strange to be brought to him at once to pay the ultimate price for the behaviour of his father and uncle. Sir William Harrington urged Richard that now was not the time for executions and urged the king to delay until both Lord Stanley and Sir William Stanley were captured.[48] Another possible reason for delaying Lord Strange's execution could be that the Earl of Oxford, supported by Talbot, renewed his attack on Norfolk's vanguard.

Within a short period of time, Oxford was able to separate Richard's forces from Northumberland's.[49] The fighting had now swung around its axis, with the ensuing advantage that Henry's enemy now had the sun shining directly into their eyes. It was not long before Norfolk's troops had been completely routed and many of his men killed in the flight. According to many sources, men started to defect to Henry's side, or to flee the field, even before it was clear who held the winning hand. Northumberland's troops on Richard's left flank remained immobile; and according to Molinet, Northumberland had made a secret agreement with Henry before the battle. Several accounts suggest that Northumberland now actively turned on Richard's men, passing in front of the king with his back to Henry and, according to the Spanish account, with 10,000 men began to fiercely fight against the king's front line. Mainly because of treachery, the battle now turned against the king and it was at this point that some of Richard's army believed the best course of action was to encourage the king to flee.[50] According to Vergil, whose account of the battle seems confirmed by other accounts, 'the battle had manifestly turned against him', and now there was great need to 'procure a fast horse'. King Richard was exhorted to escape and to take revenge another day. But, according to the Spanish account written shortly after the battle, and also many others, Richard replied to Juan de Salazar: 'Salazar, God forbid I yield one step. This day I will die as a King or win.'[51] By now Richard must have realised that

48 Vergil, pp. 223–4. *'Lady Bessie'*, pp. 360–61. Hutton, p. 129.
49 Vergil, Vatican Urbs. Lat. 498, fos. 234r–235r.
50 Molinet, p. 408.
51 BL Harleian MS 433 fos. 210v, 213, 214, 219.

his day of judgement had arrived. He placed his royal crown upon his head before making his final charge.

Henry was still unmounted because he 'wanted to be on foot in the midst of us'.[52] Richard was informed about the location of Henry's standard and that it was surrounded by only a few armed men. Oxford's tightly grouped infantry now pushed forward and a gap opened up between the two battles – to the advantage of Richard, who was now ready to charge. With just a few men around him and Oxford too far away to come quickly to his aid, Henry must have feared the worst as Richard bore down on him. When the onrush made contact with Henry's first ranks, Richard fought courageously for his crown. Having managed to reach Henry's standard-bearer William Brandon and instantly kill him, it is said that Richard was then confronted by John Cheyne, six foot eight inches tall, who tried to retrieve the standard. Richard managed to unhorse him by striking him around the head so that, without his helmet, Cheyne fell unconscious to the ground.[53] The fighting was now ferocious and intense. Coming under attack in the thickest press of the enemy, Richard's own standard-bearer, Sir Percival Thribald, is recorded as continuing to hold on to the king's standard 'till both his legs were cut from him'. Richard continued to cut his way through Henry's ranks and it became clear that Henry was at great risk. Vergil claimed that Henry himself 'withstood the attack longer than even his soldiers thought possible' for a comparatively young man with no real military experience. Having so far remained at the top of the hill watching as events unfolded, it was now that Lord Stanley ordered his brother William to charge into the battle, allegedly together with Rhys ap Thomas. Their attack caught Richard by surprise and it was not long before the king was killed.[54]

Later there would be many who claimed the credit for the death of King Richard III, including Rhys Fawr and one Thomas Woodshawe.[55] However, according to many Welsh bards, including Tudur Penllyn, Lewis Glyn Cothi and Guto'r Glyn, it was a Welshman – in fact Rhys ap Thomas himself – who was personally responsible for delivering the fatal blow with a halberd:

---

52 C. Skidmore, *Bosworth, The Birth of the Tudors*, p. 305.
53 Vergil, p. 224.
54 Vergil, pp. 224–5.
55 *The Richardian* IX, no. 121, pp. 417–25.

The ravens of Urien prepared it.
King Henry won the day
through the strength of our master:
he killed Englishmen, capable hand,
he killed the boar, he chopped off his head,
and Sir Rhys like the stars of a shield
with the spear in their midst on a great steed
The Ravens of Urien prepared it.

King Henry won the day.
Through the strength of our master.
He killed Englishmen, capable hand.
He killed the boar, he chopped off his head.
And Sir Rhys like the stars of a shield.
With the spear in their midst on a great steed.[56]

There is no doubt that Richard had fought bravely to the very end, whether out of determination or desperation. All chroniclers and accounts agree on this, even John Rous, who was no admirer of Richard, wrote that 'though small in body and feeble in limb, he bore himself like a gallant knight and acted with distinction as his own champion until his last breath'.[57]

Henry now ordered his men to take care of the wounded and bury the dead.[58] Many of the fallen were buried at the nearby church of St James in Dadlington. Among the casualties from Henry's side, Brandon was the only one from the nobility to die.[59] There were, however, many wounded, including Gilbert Talbot, Sir Rhys ap Thomas, Sir Humphrey Stanley, Sir Robert Poyntz, Ralph Bigod and Roger Acton.

Estimates of the number of men killed in the battle vary greatly. The casualties from Richard's side were, of course, the heaviest. Walter Devereux, Lord Ferrers; John Howard, Duke of Norfolk; Sir Robert Brackenbury; Sir Richard Ratcliffe; Sir Robert Percy and

---

56 Gutor Glyn,, 'Moliant i Syr Rhys ap Tomas o Abermarlais', lines 34–40
    (ed.by Dafydd Johnston, at: www. gutorglyn.net)
57 John Rous, cited in Skidmore, *Bosworth, The Birth of the Tudors*, p. 310.
58 Vergil, p. 226.
59 Vergil, p. 225.

John Kendal, together with at least thirty others of the nobility and gentry who can be identified, were killed.[60]

As for Richard himself, an examination of his remains, which were found in the Grey Friars dig of 2012, has shown that he suffered a number of head wounds, two of which would have been fatal. Other wounds, which included a wound to the pelvis believed to have been caused by a dagger driven through the right buttock, are likely to have been 'humiliation' injuries inflicted after death. The report of the Grey Friars team confirmed many of the contemporary accounts of the death of Richard III.[61] Following his death on the battlefield, Richard's naked body was thrown across the back of a horse, 'with the armes and legges hanginge downe on both sydes', and taken to Leicester where it was displayed for two days.[62]

How shocking and barbaric the results of the Grey Friars dig prove to be for modern day readers, but we have to consider them in a historical context. Certainly the death of Richard III was a brutal event and the treatment of his remains appears distasteful, but we need to understand that such treatment was common practice in the Middle Ages when a king or significant figure was killed. Henry VI's body was displayed at St Paul's following his murder at the Tower of London, as was the Earl of Warwick's following his death at the Battle of Barnet. Such display aimed to suppress rumours of their survival.

The almost unbelievable victory at Bosworth had taken around two hours to accomplish. Not since the Norman conquest of 1066 had an invasion resulted in a king's death on the battlefield and Bosworth would be the last battle on British soil that would cost the life of a king.

Henry was 'replenyshydd with joy incredible' when he realised that Richard was defeated and all was over and so immediately gave 'thanks to Almighty God' with many prayers for receiving the victory he had won. He also 'gave unto the nobylytie and gentlemen immortal thankes, promising that he wold be myndfull of ther benyfyttes'. Henry's soldiers began to praise him and, raising a great shout, they cried 'God save King Henry, God save King Henry!'[63]

---

60 Great Chronicle, p. 193. Vergil's *Anglia Historia* is used for the entire battle: Vat. Urbs. Zlat. 498, fos. 234r–235r. Vergil, pp. 224–5.
61 University of Leicester Press Pack, 4 February 2013.
62 Vergil, p. 226.
63 Vergil, p. 226.

Figure 41   Mill Bay near Dale. Landing place of Jasper and
                Henry Tudor.
                (© 2015 Debra Bayani)

Figure 42   Mill Bay.
                (© 2015 Debra Bayani)

Figure 43   Plaque at Mill Bay
               (© 2015 Debra Bayani)

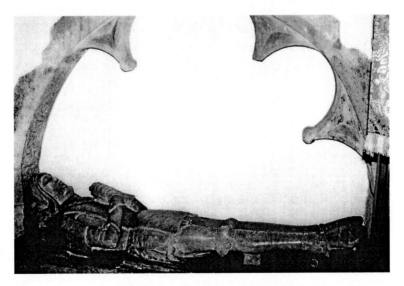

Figure 44   Tomb of Jasper's half-brother, Sir David Owen (d. 1542)
               in St. Mary's Church in Easebourne, Sussex.
               (Courtesy of Jean McCreanor)

Figure 45   Old Bridge in Haverfordwest was constructed in the 18th century at the site of the ford that Henry and Jasper Tudor crossed with their army in 1485.
(© 2015 Debra Bayani)

Figure 46   Tomb effigies of Sir Rhys ap Thomas (1449-1525) and his wife at St. Peter's Church in Carmarthen.
(© 2015 Debra Bayani)

14

'THE HIGH AND MIGHTY PRINCE JASPER' [1]

August 1485 – March 1486

Blood like that which flowed of old
through the veins of Griffith Maelawr
is the life-soul of Henry VII, Jasper
and Sir Rhys ap Thomas.
It flows alike in each of them,
and enjoins upon them duties of the highest responsibility,
The British Isle has now been entrusted to
    men of kindred blood,
to Henry, Jasper and Rhys.
The former two are descended
from Ednyvyd Vychan,
and sir Rhys is related to them by intermarriage,
wherefore the Goronwy's and the Gruffydd's side with
the descendants of Ednyved Vychan.
In consequence of which
the offspring of Rhodri the Great
will have no longer any cause of alarm.

---

1   *The Complete Peerage*, vol. 2, pp. 72–3.

And may the lineal descendants of the mighty three
become the most powerful of any under heaven.
Henry will maintain his right,
his uncle Jasper Tudor will defend us from harm,
and sir Rhys is our pledge
for the prosperity of the Rose.
May Christendom, in spite of infidel lands,
become under the sway of the descendants of Tudor.
The stars as well as the prophetic songs,
have long ago assigned this kingdom to Northwallians.
For from Gwynnedd it has been foretold,
from the towers of Idwal has Heinyn,
the bard, foretold the overthrow of the Saxon monarchy.[2]

THESE LINES by Lewis Glyn Cothi are just one of the highly flattering poems composed by many bards in celebration of Henry, Jasper and also Rhys ap Thomas. In the original Welsh, 'Siars' recurs many times, as this word is an altered form for Jasper, whose name in Welsh is Siaspar, also written as Siasber or Siasbar.

After thirty years of turmoil, Londoners had become accustomed to preparing a welcome for the victor of the latest battle. Henry's mother had sent appropriate fabrics, velvets and silks for her son's official entry into London and when, at the beginning of September, Henry and his troops arrived at Shoreditch on the outskirts of London, he was splendidly dressed from head to toe. Hundreds of official representatives from London were waiting for Henry's arrival in the capital. As soon as he arrived Henry went to London's St Paul's where he offered at the altar his three standards – the Red Dragon, the Cross of St George and the Dun Cow – and also gave thanks to God and the Virgin for his triumph. Afterwards Henry stayed at the house of Thomas Kempe, Bishop of London, and there he was happily reunited with his mother, whom he had not seen for fourteen years.

The general feeling of insecurity and danger that followed Bosworth and the killing of Richard III was still prevalent when a sudden outbreak of sweating sickness struck just two weeks after Henry's arrival in the city. The illness, said to have been brought from France along with Henry's army, took the life of London's mayor

---

2   'Molliant Syr Rhys ab Thomas, un o gynghoriaid unchav brenin Harri VII; Siaspar, Dug Bedford', part 1, in Gwaith Lewis Glyn Cothi (Oxford: The Cymmrodorion, 1837), pp. 163–6.

two weeks later and that of his successor the week after. It was now too dangerous to remain in the crowded capital and Henry left the city to stay for some weeks with his mother at her manor at Woking. Slight traces of the manor can still be seen today at the village of Old Woking.

By the summer of 1485, Jasper had been a political refugee for nearly a quarter of a century. He had been in constant exile ever since Edward IV usurped Henry VI's crown in 1461, with only a brief return to Wales and England at the time of Henry VI's return to the throne in October 1470 until spring 1471.

Now Jasper finally returned as a free man, once more able to serve a king according to his conscience and to enjoy his position as one of the most important men in the kingdom, not only as the king's uncle, but also as one of his closest and most trusted advisers. Furthermore, Jasper could at last look forward to the rewards that he so abundantly deserved, though one senses that his key role in bringing down the Yorkist dynasty and seeing the nephew he surely regarded as a son succeed to the throne was his greatest reward of all. In a poem the bard Lewis Glyn Cothi congratulates Henry and initiates Jasper's name with flattering compliments (see Appendix M).

The period from the end of August 1485 until the early winter was largely used to establish the new dynasty and Jasper was closely involved in those activities. On 15 September, the king summoned his first parliament, which would meet on 7 November, and Jasper naturally was one of those called on to attend.[3] The other councillors included Oxford, Lord Stanley, Reginald Bray, John Morton and Richard Fox. Henry had yet to be crowned and on 19 October Jasper, Peter Courtenay, the Bishop of Exeter, the Earl of Nottingham, the Lords Stanley and Fitzwalter, and Richard Croft were commissioned 'to do all that pertains to the office of steward of England at Henry's coronation', which would take place in eleven days' time.[4] Satisfying to Jasper as it must have been to have his old title of Earl of Pembroke restored to him, the title and its endowment were at this point of little value to him because of the 1461 act of attainder by which all of his lands, wealth and offices had been bestowed on others. Henry took immediate steps to undo this and similar acts. The king, 'understanding that his deerest beloved Uncle Jasper Duke of Bedford,

---

3   CCR, 1485–1494, p. 15.
4   CPR, 1485–1494, p. 49.

by the name of Jasper Erle of Pembrock attainted of high Treason, and the said Duke disabled of hys Name of Erle, Preeminence and Dignitee', made sure that the act passed by Edward IV was annulled with effect from 23 August, and those originally drawn up 'by the most blessed Prince King Herrie the VI' were reinstated 'of as good strength, force and effecte [...] as they should or might have been, if noon Act of Resumpeon, ne other Act of Parlement, had been made to the hurte or adnullation of the same lettres Patents.'[5]

The supporters of the Houses of Lancaster and Tudor were restored but those of the house of York were in their turn attainted. Henry dated the beginning of his reign from 21 August, instead of from Bosworth on 22 August, making all that had fought against him guilty of treason and answerable to attainder and forfeiture. Henry thought about the rewards he was to bestow upon his many friends and supporters, and he certainly had good reason to show gratitude to all those who had served him, but his uncle Jasper was at the top of the list. Henry decided that even before his own coronation took place, another ceremony should have precedence. On Thursday 27 October 1485, the king rode from Lambeth to the Tower of London. After mass on the next day, the feast of St Simon and St Jude, his uncle Jasper, arrayed in the robes of a duke, was presented before him in his presence chamber in the Tower. With traditional pomp Jasper was led:

> [...] by the Duke of Suffolk [John de la Pole], and therle of Lincoln [his son John], therle of Nottingham [William Berkeley] bearing next before him his cape of estate, and therle of Shrewsburie [John Talbot] bearing his sweard the pommel upwards, having officers of Armes before him. And in the entering of the chamber dore he [Jasper] did his first obeisaunce, and in the middest of the chamber the seconde, and in the Kinges presence the thirde. Garter [John Writhe] delivered to therle of Oxforde [John de Vere] as great chamberlayn of England his patent which he delivered to the King. And the King delivered it to his Secretarie [Richard Fox] commanding him to reede it openly. And when

he came to Cincturama gladii, the King put his
girdell about his neck, and hanged the sweard
before him. And likewise the cape on his head,
and all things according to his Patent. And
when his patent was red, the King received it,
and delivered the said patent of the creation of
the annuitie of the duchie of Bedforde to his said
uncle the duke of Bedforde.[6]

From that day on until Jasper's death, whenever heralds cried out
his name, in the opening of his own letters or even on the legends of
his seals, he was exaltedly styled 'The high and mighty prince, Jasper,
brother and uncle of kings, Duke of Bedford and Earl of Pembroke'.
The choice of titles could hardly have been more prominent. There
had only been two earlier dukes of Bedford and, while the second
owner of the entitlement, George Neville, son of John Neville, the
Earl of Northumberland, was rather obscure, it was the first duke of
Bedford, Henry V's younger brother John, a pillar of the royal house
who had enjoyed great popularity, whom Henry must have had in
mind when seeking an appropriate title for his beloved uncle. It also
signalled the link between the Houses of Lancaster and Tudor. But,
most of all, it shows Henry's gratitude towards the uncle who had
devoted his life to his nephew, and without whom Henry's kingship,
possibly even his very survival, would have been out of the question.

That same day, Lord Stanley was granted the earldom of
Derby and Edward Courtenay was created Earl of Devon. After the
ceremonies were complete, Jasper and the newly created earls of Derby
and Devon took their seats at the dining table in the king's great
chamber in celebration. The festivities were splendid, the king being
'nobly accompanied with the Duke of Bedforde, therle of Oxenforde,
therle of Darbie, therle of Devonshire with many other noble Lordes,
knightes and esquieres'.[7] The next morning, 29 October, the dubbing
of six new Knights of the Bath took place at the Tower when:

> [...] the King in a riche gowne enterid into
> the hall, and stoode under the clothe of estate,
> to whom the duke of Buckingham was presented
> by two estates. And the henchman that bare the
> sweard, the spurres presented them to therle of

6   B.M., Egerton MS. 985, ff. 41v–42. CChR. 1427–1516, p. 267.
7   B.M., Egerton MS. 985, ff. 42v–46v.

Oxenforde, and he toke the right spurre and
presented it to the King, and the King toke it to
the duke of Bedforde, commanding him to put
it upon the duke of Buckingham's heel of his
right legg. And in likewise therle of Darbie the
lift spurre. And the King girde the sweard about
him, and dubbed him knight.[8]

This was repeated five more times until all six men were knighted,
including Reginald Bray.[9]

After attending mass together, they all returned to the hall where
the king and his nobles dined at a single table. That afternoon, in
preparation for the coronation the next day, the customary impressive
procession from the Tower of London to Westminster Hall took
place. As tradition prescribed, Henry rode bare-headed, on a horse
caparisoned with cloth of gold trimmed with ermine. He himself wore
a long gown of purple velvet trimmed with ermine, and four knights
held a royal canopy above his head. At the head of the procession rode
Thomas Stanley, the newly created Earl of Derby, and the earls of
Oxford, Lincoln and Nottingham, and behind them – 'next after him
[the King] on the right hande somwhat before, his courser trapped in
the same sute, as the king's trapper was' – came Jasper and 'on the left
hande' the Duke of Suffolk, 'his courser also richely trapped'. Then
came six henchmen and Sir John Cheyne, who led a riderless horse
caparisoned with cloth of gold embroidered with the king's arms, and
behind them rode what must have been a splendid procession made
up of the nobility, knights and esquires, together with the heralds and
kings of arms.

When they awoke the following morning both Henry and Jasper
must have been acutely aware on this most momentous day that it was
also a day that three months earlier had looked to be nearly impossible
to achieve. Now finally, on 30 October, the stage was set for the
king's coronation at Westminster Abbey. The king sat in state at
Westminster Hall and from there went in procession to Westminster
Abbey. Massive crowds witnessed the public ceremony from platforms
especially erected for the occasion. Oxford bore the king's train and
behind him came Stanley holding the sword of state, while Jasper was
given the greatest honour of all, that of carrying the crown before the

8   B.M., Egerton MS. 985, ff, 42v–46v
9   B.M., Egerton MS. 985; fos.41v–42r

king himself. In the midst of this setting of magnificent pomp it was Jasper, the king's uncle who played the leading role in the coronation of his nephew.

When Henry was officially proclaimed 'Henricus Sept Rex Angliae et Franciae et Dominus Hiberniae' ('Henry VII, King of England and France and Lord of Ireland'), the crown was placed upon his head by Archbishop Thomas Bourchier of Canterbury, and the king's mother, Margaret Beaufort, wept marvellously. It is said her tears were not just of joy, but above all for fear of the danger that this crown could bring to her son.[10]

After the ceremony, King Henry VII and his train returned to the Tower of London in preparation for the coronation banquet at Westminster Palace. Once more, Jasper had the most important role, this time as steward of the feast, riding 'before the Sewer' on a horse caparisoned with cloth of gold embellished with ermine.[11]

The final part of the ceremony – the traditional coronation jousts, which were initially planned for the following Sunday, 6 November – was postponed to the following Sunday,[12] probably because of another important occasion that was scheduled during this time: Jasper's marriage ceremony. Although the marriage is traditionally dated to 7 November, there is actually no contemporary source that confirms this as fact. It is simply the date of the first day of parliament where Jasper and his wife are for the first time officially stated to be married.

Henry's desire to benefit his uncle even further was demonstrated by his choice of a bride for him – Jasper was to marry Katherine Woodville, the dowager Duchess of Buckingham, widow of Henry Stafford, 2nd Duke of Buckingham. Katherine was also the youngest sister of dowager Queen Elizabeth Woodville. At twenty-seven, she was half Jasper's age and, moreover, a very wealthy woman, in large part because Richard III had never permitted her the dower she was entitled to after her husband's execution in November 1483 and which was now forthcoming.

This choice was also fortunate for Katherine. Since Buckingham's execution two years earlier, the dowager duchess had found herself in the difficult position of being attainted by Richard III and having

10   J. Fisher, *The Funeral Sermon of Margaret Countess of Richmond and Derby, Mother to King Henry VII, and Foundress of Christ's and St. John's College in Cambridge, Preached by Bishop Fisher in 1509*, ed. J. Hymes (Cambridge 1840), p. 127.
11   B.L., Egerton MS; 985 fo. 45v.
12   B.L., Egerton MS, 985 fos. 48r.

four young children to raise with an uncertain future ahead of them. Just before Henry's coronation, Katherine's oldest son, seven-year old Edward, had been created a Knight of the Bath. The wardships of both Katherine's sons, Edward and Henry Stafford, being now a very attractive proposition, were given to the king's mother and the boys would grow up in her household. In parliament, which opened on 7 November, the duchess was granted both the jointure of 1,000 marks per year bequeathed to her in her late husband's will, as well as the extensive lands in both England and Wales that had belonged to Katherine and her first husband.

These properties comprised six major groups: in the county of Kent – the lordship, castle and borough of Tunbridge and the manors of Hadlow, Brasted, Yalding, Edenbridge, Penshurst and Bayhall, with the office of bailiff of the liberty of the honour of Gloucester in Kent and Surrey; in Surrey itself – the manor, borough and lordship of Bletchingley and the manors of Titsey and Oxted; in London – a dwelling or public housing and its rent in Thames Street, also the manors of Writtle, Boyton, Hatfield Broad Oak, Broomshawburry, Fobing, Ongar and Harlow with 'a marsh called Palmers Things in the Hundreds of Ongar and Harlow'; in Norfolk – the manors of Wells, Warham, Wiverton Sherringham, Stafford and Barningham; in Huntingdonshire and Bedfordshire – the castle, manor, soke and lordship of Kimbolton and the manors of Tilbroke, Swineshead and Hardwick and also the office feodary of the honour of Gloucester in those counties; in Gloucestershire – the manors of Thornbury, Haresfield, Eastington, Alkerton and Rendcomb, as well as the office of the bailiff of the liberty of the honour of Gloucestershire in that county. This more than impressive list was completed with the lordship of Callilon in Cornwall, the castle and lordship of Newport in the Marches and the office of the honour of the liberty of Hereford in Herefordshire.[13]

Jasper would be unable to acquire the manor of Tilbroke in his wife's name. Tilbroke had been bought by the late Duke of Buckingham and Sir William Catesby between 1477 and 1478, and in the normal way of things the manor would have passed to Duchess Katherine, which is what officially happened. However, by mistake Henry VII had granted the manor on 9 March 1486 to his kinsman Sir Charles Somerset, the only surviving, albeit illegitimate, son of the

13 CPR, 1485–1494, pp. 100, 405.

late 4th Duke of Somerset, Edmund Beaufort, and his mistress Joan
Hill. Naturally, Jasper felt that he had a better claim to the property
in right of his wife, and a dispute developed with Somerset. It would
take until the end of 1489 – and the intervention of the king – to settle
this dispute. Henry said that 'right and title of the same manor had
long hanged in travers and demaunde' between Jasper and Sir Charles
Somerset, and for the 'fynall discussing thereof [we] have late doon
to be assembled certain of oure and oure said Uncles counsaill which
upon thaire examination of the same matier have founde that our said
knight is rightfully entitled unto the same manor'. It seems that, after
Henry and Jasper had discussed the matter in person, Jasper agreed
that Charles should retain possession.[14]

In theory the acts of parliament allowed Jasper to recover all
the estates and lands he had held between 1453 and 1461. In spite
of this, in practice it was impossible for him to be restored to all of
his lands, because of how they had been granted to others over the
previous twenty-five years. In 1469 the honorial lands of the earldom
of Pembroke had been inherited by the Yorkist Earl of Pembroke's
son, William Herbert, but in 1479 he was forced to exchange the
title and lands with Edward IV's son for the less valuable earldom
of Huntingdon. The lordships of Pembroke, Cilgerran, Llansteffan,
St Clears, Ystlwyf and Trane Clinton were still in royal hands in 1485
and could therefore be restored to Jasper without any problem. The
manor of Westley in Suffolk was last owned by John Howard, Duke
of Norfolk, but following his death at Bosworth the estate reverted to
the crown and was restored to Jasper.[15] The lordship of Caldicot and
the manor of Magor in Monmouthshire, the latter jointly granted to
Jasper and Edmund in 1453, had still been in the hands of the dowager
Countess of Pembroke, Anne Devereux, and probably continued so
until her death around 1486. On 9 March 1486, the lordship and
manor of Caldicot were granted, along with others and the earlier
mentioned manor of Tilbroke, to Charles Somerset, but since the
grant was made in tail male, it may have even been the case that
Somerset made an arrangement with Jasper to exchange the manor
of Tilbroke with the lordship and manor of Caldicot, as they were
certainly in Jasper's hands on 1 March 1490 when he concluded an
agreement as Lord of Caldicot with Henry for better government of

14 CPR, Henry VII 1485–1494, pp. 100, 405. V.C.H. Bucks., vol. 3, pp. 172–3. N.L.W.,
    Bad, Deeds and Docs. 1194.
15 Thomas, p. 256.

the Welsh Marches to ensure peace and stability in that region.[16] Most
of Jasper's other previously owned lands and properties were restored
to him before the first half of 1486. A few others, however, were not.
Those were the Manors of Cloigyn and Pibwr in Carmarthenshire
plus the lordship of Caernarvonshire, all held by the well-known
Welshman John Dwnn.[17] Dwnn had originally been a loyal Yorkist
but after Bosworth had embraced Henry VII's cause. The service of
such a man was too valuable to lose and to enforce the return of these
remaining lands and estates would be asking for a new war. The young
Tudor government simply could not afford to alienate such nobles.

Concerning the lordship of Aber in Caernarvonshire, there is
no evidence for its restoration to Jasper.[18] The manor of Bonby in
Lincolnshire which, in 1453, was jointly granted to Edmund and
Jasper, was held by Edmund Skern and could not be restored to
Jasper.[19]

The lordship of Moor End in Northamptonshire had also been
jointly granted to Edmund and Jasper, but had been surrendered by
them in 1453, in exchange for more extensive lands in Derbyshire and
Northamptonshire. Although there is no record of it being granted to
Jasper, it was in his possession in 1495.[20] Another grant to Jasper was
the manor of Yorkhill in Herefordshire. Again, there is no record of
a formal grant, but it is clear he held it from 1485 until his death.[21]

In addition to the reinstatement of most of his former possessions,
Jasper obtained very valuable new lands, by royal grant for his
dukedom of Bedford. But since there were no estates attached to the
title, Jasper was given instead an annuity of £40 for the county of
Bedford, just as he had received when he was granted the earldom of
Pembroke in 1452.

Furthermore, during the first parliament that November,
provisions were also made for the king's income by a grant for life for
'tonnage and poundage', with Jasper and Elizabeth Woodville being
the only persons granted the favour of exclusion should this assignment
have any negative consequences.[22] On 19 November, Henry ordered
an oath to be sworn by the lords in parliament, including Jasper, that

---

16 Thomas, p. 256.
17 Thomas, p. 257.
18 Thomas, pp. 257–58.
19 Thomas, p. 259.
20 CPR, Henry VII 1494–1509, p. 39, cited in Thomas, p. 260.
21 Thomas p. 314.
22 RP, vol. 6, pp. 303–4.

they would keep his peace and endeavour to avoid lawlessness and disorder against King Henry VII.[23]

More bounty came Jasper's way when, on 2 December, he was granted for life the office of steward of the duchy of Lancaster lands in Gloucestershire and Herefordshire, Monmouth, Grosmont, Whitecastle and Skenfrith, together with the constableships of the castles of Monmouth, Grosmont, Skenfrith and Whitecastle, as well as the posts of porter and janitor of Monmouth Castle, and keeper of the woods of Whitecastle, Skenfrith and Grosmont.[24] On 13 December, Jasper received the office of justiciar of South Wales for life,[25] while Sir Rhys ap Thomas became chamberlain of South Wales. Under Richard III's government the office of justiciar of South Wales had belonged to only one man, the Duke of Buckingham. This had proved to be a disaster as Buckingham had failed to keep order, so now the duties of the office were divided into two, to prevent the same thing happening again. There was much work to do in South Wales for both Jasper and Sir Rhys.

One final matter had to be dealt with during this parliament, that of the king's own marriage. During his exile in Brittany, Henry had promised, on Christmas Day 1483 in the cathedral of Rennes, that when he became king he would marry Edward IV's eldest daughter, Princess Elizabeth. Now, during the final sitting of this parliament, on 10 December the lords petitioned the king to marry the princess.[26] Henry agreed and parliament was prorogued until 23 January 1486.[27] For the time-being, Wales seemed to be at peace and so Jasper and his wife remained at court in the king's company to celebrate Christmas and New Year and the king made a Christmas gift to Katherine of a golden goblet.[28] On 18 January 1486, the day came for the Houses of Lancaster and York to be officially reunited by the marriage of King Henry VII and Princess Elizabeth of York. There is no record of Jasper's attendance at this event, but there is no reason to think that he and his wife Katherine, the bride's aunt, did not take part. Jasper and Katherine were still in the capital until at least 6 March, when the king was at the Hospital of St John of Jerusalem in West Smithfield

23 RP, vol. 6 , pp. 278–88.
24 Duchy of Lancaster Chancery Roll 62, m.ld. Materials, vol. 1, pp. 594–5, 603.
25 CPR, 1485–1494, p. 47.
26 Croyland Chronicle, p. 195.
27 R.L. Storey, *The reign of Henry VII* (London, 1468), pp. 60–62.
28 Exchequer, Warrants for Issue, 79/312–13.

for the appointment of his chancellor, in the presence of Jasper, Peter Courtney, Bishop of Exeter, and Christopher Urswick, the new royal almoner, and delivered the great seal to the new chancellor, John Morton.[29] A priest, Thomas Betanson, wrote to Sir Robert Plumpton in mid-February of rumours that 'the Duke of Bedford goes into Wales to see that country'.[30]

Soon after Bosworth, either at Henry VII's command or at least with his approval, Jasper seized a number of estates from the attained Francis Viscount Lovell and Sir William Berkeley, and on 2 March 1486 Jasper was rewarded with a substantial part of those properties. Lovell's estates included the manors of Minster Lovell (which would become one of Jasper's favourite residences), Brize Norton, Cogges, Hardwick, Rotherfield Grey, Somerton and Banbury, Widford and Little Rissington (Oxfordshire); Acton Burnel, Holgate, Langdon, Woolstaston, Smethcott, Abdon, Millichop and Uppington (Shropshire); and some meadow land at Wanborough in Wiltshire.[31] Berkeley's forfeited lands included the castle and lordships of Weoley and Northfield (Worcestershire); the manors and lordships of Stoke, Kingsweston, Aylburton, Rockhampton, Sheperdine and Uley and the manor of Bradley (Gloucestershire); and the manors of Brigmerston (Wiltshire) and Kingsmoor (Somerset). Other grants Jasper received included the very wealthy lordships of Glamorgan, Morgannok and Abergavenny in the Marches of Wales and the lordship of Sudeley in Gloucestershire.[32]

Included with the last-named was Sudeley Castle, which became one of the Duke and Duchess of Bedford's private residences. The castle had been rebuilt by Ralph Butler, Lord Sudeley, but due to his support of the Lancastrians, the property became forfeit. Butler died in 1473 and after his wife Alice died the year after with no surviving heir, the castle remained in royal possession. In June 1486, Jasper let the farm of Sudeley to Sir John Hudleston, to hold during Jasper's lifetime, and Hudleston was also appointed constable of Sudeley Castle.[33]

---

29 CCR, Henry VII 1485–1500, p. 18.
30 *Plumpton Correspondence*, ed. T Stapleton, Campden Soc. old series, vol. 4 (1839), p. 50. Cited in Thomas, p. 330.
31 CPR, Henry VII 1485–1494, pp. 64–5. Materials, Vol. 1, pp. 334–5.
32 CPR, 14811485–1494, pp. 64–5.
33 Thomas, p. 315.

A few weeks earlier Jasper, together with Thomas Savage (chancellor of the Earl of March), Sir Edmund Montfort, Hugh Hunteley and some others, had been ordered to investigate thoroughly all administrative affairs relating to the tenants of lands of the earldom of March.[34] On 11 March, Jasper was granted, during the king's pleasure, the power to appoint justices to enquire into treason and all other offences and also to hear and determine such cases in the counties of Worcester, Hereford and Gloucester, the Marches of Wales and all of South Wales.[35] Jasper was also authorised to select men-at-arms and archers in Wales, for his own safety as well as for the oppression of lawbreakers and, if necessary, to bring the arrayed men to the king. Jasper was also ordered to deal with similar offences outside his jurisdiction. On that same day, he was appointed to the lieutenantship of Ireland. This was initially for two years, but eventually Jasper held the office for eight years. In fact, it was the Earl of Kildare, as deputy-lieutenant, who was the real governor of Ireland. As Jasper had no experience in Ireland, the office was actually just a titular assignment and there is no evidence that he ever crossed the Irish Sea to carry out any duty in person.[36]

Somewhere near the end of March, Jasper finally left London and arrived in South Wales. Katherine's whereabouts are rarely recorded, or more likely those records, like so many of Jasper's, have not survived the test of time. However, it is clear that, on this occasion, while Jasper visited South Wales, Katherine remained near the capital, for Jasper sent £50 to his wife who was staying at the Abbey of Stratford near London.[37] Jasper's arrival in Wales seems to have coincided with the first major rebellion that threatened the fledgling Tudor dynasty.

The Wars of the Roses were not yet over.

34 CPR, Henry VII, 1485–1494, pp. 85–6.
35 CPR, Henry VII, 1485–1494, p 84.
36 CPR, Henry VII 1485–1494, pp. 84, 252, 376.
37 Staffs. R.O. D641/1/2/192 m.8d. Cited in Thomas, p. 278.

Figure 47   (ABOVE) Stained glass image of Sir Reginald Bray in
St. Mary Magdalene Church in Taunton, Somerset.
(Courtesy of Rex Harris)

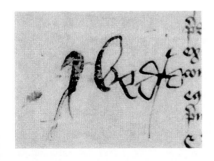

Figure 48   (LEFT and
OPPOSITE)
Jasper's signature.
Original document
LEST/NA 49.
*(Courtesy of Norfolk
Record Office)*

Figure 49   Tomb effigy of Sir John Cheyne in Salisbury Cathedral.
(Courtesy of Walwyn, professor-moriaty.com)

Figure 50   Victorian stained glass image of Jasper Tudor and
Katherine Woodville in Cardiff castle.
(© 2015 Debra Bayani)

Figure 51   Victorian Stained glass image of
Henry VII and Elizabeth of York in Cardiff Castle.
(© 2015 Debra Bayani)

15
'THE GOOD DUKE'[1]
March 1486 – December 1495

B Y NOW, six months after Bosworth, Jasper had become the
undeniable ruler of South Wales and pre-eminent among the
ranks of British magnates. Henry VII relied heavily on his uncle to
bear the weight of Welsh affairs. With the receipt of the lordship of
Sudeley, Jasper had gained a foothold in the Severn Valley and, in
addition, some of the far-flung Lovell and Berkeley properties gave
him considerable territorial power along the Welsh Marches, across
the Cotswolds and into Oxfordshire as well.

One might perhaps have expected Jasper to return to live in
Wales again, the place where he had faithfully laboured so long
during the reign of his half-brother Henry VI, but now with all
the additional properties, the strategic centre of his widespread
domain had become the Severn Valley at the English-Welsh border.
From there he was able to travel much faster to the capital for court
sessions, and also elsewhere for matters concerning administration of
his estates, and it was there that he would now spend most of his
time. Jasper's presence at the court councils is, however, infrequently
recorded, presumably because he had many other obligations away
from court. But according to R. S. Thomas, who wrote a thesis about
Jasper's political career, it was also because the king seems to have

---

1   Merrick, p. 143. In describing Jasper in this manner, Rice Merrick appears to following
    a 16th-century Glamorgan tradition.

preferred the services of other men.[2] Unfortunately, only fragments of information about Jasper's council and household survive. From what does exist it is clear that Jasper's household was dominated by his wife's former servants from her first marriage to the Duke of Buckingham. The most senior member of Jasper's household was probably his chamberlain, Sir Edmund Montfort of Coleshill, who had first seen service in the household of Henry VI. Montfort had fought for the Lancastrians at Towton in 1461, afterwards joining the king and queen in their exile in Scotland and probably also in France, where he had then been in Jasper's company. It appears that Montfort made his peace with Edward IV by 1475, when he became steward of the household of the Duke of Buckingham; and since he received a pardon by Richard III on 8 November 1484, he was possibly involved in Buckingham's rebellion the previous year.[3] Sir Edmund Montfort was also Jasper's steward in the lordship of Thornbury, MP and JP for Gloucestershire, and in 1491 and 1492 is described as one of Jasper's councillors.[4] Until his death in 1494 Montfort remained a loyal and devoted servant to Jasper, as he had formerly been to Lancaster.[5]

Others known to have been members of Jasper's staff are Richard Pole; Thomas Garth, who was Treasurer of the Duke and Duchess; John Tomlyn, controller of the household who was, for example, in charge of all the provisions of food, drink and other day-to-day necessities coming into the house, making sure the merchants received payment, etc; John Raulynson alias Foteman, keeper of Thornbury manor; John Mace, Jasper's avener (responsible for providing grain and fodder for his horses); the Welshman Owain ap Jankyn, one of the grooms of the horses; Robert Cocke and Philip Ricard, clerks of the kitchen; John Russell of Strensham, one of Jasper's clerks; and Thomas Lucas, Jasper's personal secretary.[6] Young Thomas Lucas would become a very close and devoted servant to Jasper and would later be promoted to councillor and solicitor general to Henry VII. Other members of Jasper's council were Morgan Kidwelly, William Fisher and Ralph Bampton. Morgan Kidwelly was a lawyer who began his career as attorney-general to Richard of Gloucester and rose to prominence as Edward V's attorney-general in 1483, and also for

2   Thomas, p. 326.
3   Pugh, p. 295, cited in Thomas, p. 269.
4   Thomas, p. 269.
5   Wedgewood, pp. 602–3.
6   Thomas, pp. 270–75, 286.

Richard III when he usurped the throne. Morgan quickly adapted himself to Henry VII's regime and was granted a pardon by the end of 1485. He was one of the best legal brains around and therefore an obvious choice for his council. Undoubtedly there were many more officials in Jasper's household, but unfortunately the identities of these individuals are now lost. How large his household may have been can perhaps be deduced, if only tentatively, from a fragmentary glimpse that is shown in a document of 1491 where an entry dated 24 September tells us that for two months that year the groom of the horses, along with six others, looked after Jasper's horses at Thornbury manor.[7] This does gives some sort of slight insight as to the numbers of staff that were necessary to keep Jasper's household running.

An impression of Jasper's lifestyle is provided by his payments for food, wine, furs and rich fabrics such as silks, taffeta, damask, velvet and cloth of gold. It appears that the duke and duchess's daily meals included bread, beer and wine, mutton, pork and salt fish.[8] Evidently on other, more special, occasions Jasper spoiled himself and others with more exotic and luxurious foods. Early in 1494, for example, he entertained the king at his manor of Minster Lovell, with 'ginger, oranges, conserva lymonis and mermelade', and Henry rewarded Jasper's tumbler with 13s. 4d for his performance at the same occasion.[9]

Much more information about Jasper's local officers can be found in Thomas's thesis. However, we include here only the names of these individuals and the offices they held: Ralph Hakeluyt, steward of the lordships Clifford, Winforton and Glasbury in the Marches; John Walshe, receiver between 1485 and 1495; John Arnold, keeper of Eastwood park; Walter Mildmay, parker of Marlewood; Thomas Sligh, parker of Haresfield; Henry Wogan, steward of the lordship of Pembroke and treasurer of Pembroke, and his successor Richard Newton; Sir Henry Heydon, steward of Jasper's Norfolk estates from 1493, and his son John; Thomas Jenyns, keeper of Writtle from 1493; John Beverley, bailiff of Fobbing from 1494; William Walron, janitor of Kimbolton Castle, keeper of parks and woods in Huntingdonshire;

7   Staffs. R.O., D641/1/2/193 m. 10, /194 m.lid, /195 m.ll, /196 m.ll.
     Cited in Thomas, p. 273.
8   Exchequer, K.R., Memoranda Roll 264, adhuc commissioned, hi., m.9. Staffs. R.O.,
     D641/1/2/193 m.9d., /195 m.10. Cited in Thomas, p. 277.
9   Staffs. RO, D641/1/2/197 m.14d. Sydney Anglo, 'The Court Festivals of Henry VII: A
     study based upon the account Books of John Heron, Treasurer of the Chamber',
     B.J.R.L., XLIII (1960), 28. Cited in Thomas, pp. 278, 351.

Thomas Hill, parker of Kimbolton from 1486; Robert Partsiol, steward of Kimbolton from 1486; John Smyth, bailiff of the lordship of Solilhull; Thomas Slade of Maxstoke Hall, receiver in Shropshire, Nottinghamshire and Derbyshire; Jankyn ap John, receiver of the lordship of Newport;, Thomas Morston; Sir Walter Herbert, son to the late Sir William Herbert, steward of the lordship of Abergavenny between 1488 and 1492; Thomas Percival, receiver and escheator of the lordship of Pembroke; Henry Willoughby, steward of Nottinghamshire, Derbyshire and Warwickshire and sheriff and JP of Staffordshire between 1486 and 1487; Sir Thomas Leighton, steward of Shropshire; William Harcourt of Witham, receiver of Jasper's manor of Minster Lovell; Simon Milborne, steward of the manor of Little Rissington (who, it should be noted, refused the order of knighthood in 1494 thus risking a fine of £500); Sir William Norris, receiver of the manor of Rotherfield Grey; Hugh Hunteley, attorney-general in Glamorgan; Ralph Bampton, coroner of Glamorgan; Richard Meuric, receiver of the lordship of Glamorgan between 1491 and 1492 and steward of the manor of Newton Nottage; Sir Mathew Cradock, constable of Aberafan, Caerphilly, Kenfig and Neath; Nicholas Baryngton, forester and woodward of Hatfield; Richard Lusher and John Gunter, auditors; and Sir John Hudleston, constable and parker of Sudeley Castle, and bailiff and steward of Glamorgan,

There are, however, a few persons whose circumstances merit more particular mention here because they give us an insight about Jasper himself. Those include the appointment of Sir Richard Croft of Croft Castle as sheriff, steward chamberlain, master forester and constable of Cardiff Castle in replacement of Sir James Tyrell. Tyrell had been appointed to the office by Henry VII in 1486, but Jasper clearly did not agree with the assignment and replaced him with Croft as soon as he was granted the lordship of Glamorgan.[10] John de Vere, the Earl of Oxford, was steward of Jasper's estates in Essex between 1495 and 1496.[11]

King Henry had probably left London for the North at about the same time as Jasper headed for Wales. Henry travelled via Waltham, Cambridge, Huntingdon, Stamford and Lincoln, where on 26 March 1486 he spent Easter. It was here that the king was informed that Lord Lovell, Thomas and Humphrey Stafford had broken out from

---

10   H.M.C., Var. Colls., 317. Cited in Thomas, p. 290.
11   Thomas, p. 285.

sanctuary at Colchester, where they had been hiding ever since Bosworth. Henry continued his progress northwards, perhaps not taking this possible uprising too seriously. Lovell had the intention of capturing the city of York, while the Staffords aimed to take Worcester. Rebellion broke out around the old Yorkist stronghold of Middleham. The Staffords even claimed to have been pardoned by Henry in their attempts to recruit supporters. Another rumour was spread that the king had been captured by Lovell in Yorkshire and that Edward, Earl of Warwick, who had been imprisoned by Henry to safeguard his throne, had been released and was at liberty. As the only remaining son of the late George, Duke of Clarence, the young Earl of Warwick had a strong claim to the throne and was from the start the biggest threat to Henry's rule. It was therefore Lovell's intention to kill Henry and place the young Warwick on the throne. On 23 April, Henry was nearly captured at York but ultimately this was a poorly planned rebellion that failed to achieve its aims.

Jasper at this time was still in Wales, probably in the border shires from where he may have directed his attention to the Staffords in Worcester. Rebellion had spread as far as South Wales and in mid-April Sir Thomas Vaughan of Tretower, along with his kinsmen the Herberts, raised rebellion against the king at Brecon, Hay and Tretower. 'Arrayed in manner of war' they managed to seize Brecon Castle, burning the rolls and muniments that were kept there, and even stole an old missal that had belonged to the late Duke of Buckingham.[12] According to Hall, the king 'comaunded the duke of Bedforde with III Thousand men not strongely armed to do a great enterpryce (for their brest plates for the moost part were made of tanned lether) to encounter & set upon them [the rebels] with all hast and diligence. And made him prevy what he him selfe had entended to doo'.[13] It is not recorded exactly where this rebellion was based but it can be assumed to have originated with the Vaughans and Herberts, also the Duke and Duchess of Bedford held many estates in this vicinity. Jasper 'settyng forwarde after the fassion, eger & fierce captaine came nigh to the tentes and campe of his enemyes where he consulted and communicated his mynde with certayne capitaynes & suge souldioures of his compaigny, by what waye he might treyne & allure them to peace, without battaill or bloodsheddyng'.

12 B.M., Egerton Roll 2192, m.5.
13 Hall's Chronicle, p. 427. Vergil's Anglica Historia, pp. 10–11.

Accordingly while negotiating, it was Jasper who proposed, after careful consideration, that a pardon would be provided to all who would lay down their weapons, and this seems to have worked, for 'by this pollitique wisdom & ingenious meanes of the good duke, this great rage and fierce route of sturdy and valyaunt traytours which was prepared against the kyng, and were lyke to have to have been the slaughter of many a man, were pacefyed & repressed and brought to good conformytie and obedient subieccion'.[14] Jasper was highly respected and praised for the way he dealt with this problem.

Soon other branches of rebellion were also suppressed. On 1 May, Humphrey and Thomas Stafford, having seen support for their rising crumble, fled into the abbey of Culham, near Abingdon, for sanctuary. The next day, however, Sir John Savage forced them out of hiding and they were conducted to the Tower of London. During the trial that spring, the elder Stafford, Humphrey, was sentenced to a traitor's death by hanging drawing and quartering, which was performed on 5 July. The younger brother, Thomas, was spared. [15]

On 3 May, Jasper, along with twenty-one others, was commissioned to investigate all cases of treasons, felonies and conspiracies in the counties of Worcester and Warwick.[16] A week later another group was similarly commissioned for Herefordshire. Sir George Neville, son and heir of Lord Edward of Abergavenny, was one of several to be deceived by Vaughan's revolt. Neville wrote a petition in which he stated that he held the lordships of Ewyas Harold and Ewyas Lacy. According to Neville, false allegations were made against him by the rebellion's leaders concerning the withholding of payments, whereas it was actually Vaughan who was to blame. In his petition Neville writes that they:

> [...] made other untrue suggestions to my
> lord of Bedford and wold have had hym to sease
> these lordships into the hands of yor good grace
> and for nothing else but to restrain the arrerages
> in their hands. And all the maere and causes
> shewes unto my said Lord Bedford he of his grace
> and goodness hath sent thider his lettres that
> they shuld not restrain any deuties for any entres

---

14   Hall's Chronicle, p. 358.
15   King's Bench, Ancient Indictments, 957/8. Plea Roll 900, Rex, m. 8–8Ad.
16   CPR, Henry VII 1485–1494, pp. 106–7.

mader or any othr else. Yet notwithstanding they
disobeid his lettres and wool noth pay noon of
their dewties.[17]

It is unknown what the conclusion of the enquiry was, but
the petition clearly proves that Jasper was putting into practice the
authority granted to him the previous 11 March to establish and
maintain order in South Wales and the border shires.[18] King Henry
travelled southwards from York and reached Worcester on 13 May.
There Jasper joined the king on either the same day or the next. It
was Whitsunday, and the king, Jasper and some other peers heard a
sermon at Worcester Cathedral concerning the papal bull confirming
Henry's marriage to Elizabeth of York. After this Henry resumed
his journey southwards towards London, passing through Hereford,
Gloucester and Bristol, very likely with Jasper in attendance.

For now the kingdom remained reasonably quiet and the birth
in September of Henry's first child, a boy named Arthur, brought
considerable strength to the newly founded dynasty. But when
autumn changed to winter, there were fresh rumours of a plot to put
the Earl of Warwick on the throne. The instigators were Margaret
of Burgundy, Francis, Viscount Lovell, and John de la Pole, Earl
of Lincoln, who was the son of Elizabeth Plantagenet, sister to
Edward IV and Richard III and also to Margaret of Burgundy. It
appears that Richard III had named Lincoln his heir after the death
of his son Edward of Middleham in 1484, but Margaret felt that the
House of York could only be restored through the male line and,
although Lincoln had a strong claim, he and Margaret knew that
someone else still had a better claim: the twelve-year-old Edward, Earl
of Warwick. The allegedly simple-minded adolescent earl was safely
locked up by Henry in the Tower and so the conspirators were unable
to gain possession of him. They therefore used a foolish impostor,
called Lambert Simnel, to impersonate him.[19] Early in March 1487,
Lincoln, Lovell, Simnel and some 2,000 German soldiers landed in
Ireland, which was still significantly supportive towards the Yorkists,
and were well-received there. When Henry learned about Lincoln's
escape from England, he realised this increased the likelihood
of imminent invasion and ordered a close watch to be kept on the

---

17 Leland, *Collectanea*, vol. 4, p. 192.
18 Leland, *Collectanea*, vol. 4, p. 192.
19 Bennet, *Lambert Simnel and the Battle of Stoke*, pp. 7, 33–40.

east coast. He himself travelled to Norwich and to the shrine of Walsingham. Jasper took similar precautions for the coast of South Wales and was in Carmarthen on 4 April. Although Henry had made an attempt to defuse matters by parading the real Earl of Warwick through the streets of London, the pretender was crowned king in Dublin on 24 May.[20] On 4 June, the Yorkists invaded England and landed in Lancashire. Jasper joined the king and his troops in the Midlands, where he and the Earl of Oxford were given joint command of the royal army, which also included the Earl of Shrewsbury, Sir Rhys ap Thomas and the king's stepfather Lord Stanley, Earl of Derby. They encountered the rebels in the Nottinghamshire village of East Stoke on 16 June.[21] The Yorkists were considerably outnumbered and Lincoln's troops were butchered, including Lincoln himself, to Henry's frustration. Henry had felt that by seizing Lincoln alive he would have been able to get to 'the bottom of his danger', that is, to the origin of the conspiracy.[22] Francis, Viscount Lovell escaped, or at least disappeared without a trace and was never seen again, and Simnel was captured. Surprisingly, Henry thought it appropriate to provide the boy with a job, as a turnspit in the royal kitchens, which, of course, did not do him any harm. The Battle of Stoke marked the end of an era. It was, as we would later say, the end of the Wars of the Roses. But old loyalties still simmered.

Henry VII remained in the North for the rest of the summer and autumn of 1487, restoring royal authority in the area. On 1 September, the king summoned Jasper and the other peers to attend a session of parliament on 9 November, which lasted only nine days. Henry had returned to London a few days before the opening of parliament and had decided that the time had now come to crown his queen. On the first or second day after the opening of parliament, Henry issued a commission to Jasper, the earls of Oxford, Nottingham and Derby and three others, charging them with the duties of stewards for the coronation.[23]

Only one other item of parliamentary business was of any concern to Jasper. The Act of Resumption to be passed in parliament was not to adversely affect him in any way. There was general agreement that

20 Busch, pp. 32–6.
21 Vergil's Anglica Historia 1485–1537, p. 22. Hall's Chronicle, p. 433. Staffs. CRO, D641/1/2/193 m. 9d.
22 Vergil's Anglica Historia, pp. 26–7.
23 CPR, Henry VII 1485–1494, p. 196. BM, Egerton MS. 985, f. 11v.

such a worthy person was entitled to this immunity. And so Jasper, unlike the other peers, emerged unscathed from these proceedings.[24]

On 23 November Henry's queen travelled by barge up the Thames from Greenwich to the Tower. The boats of Elizabeth of York's little fleet were richly decorated, but it seems that one boat in particular stood out, 'passing al other, wherein was ordeynede a great red Dragon spowting Flamys of Fyer into Temmys'. Arriving at the Tower, the queen was welcomed by Henry and on the following day, 24 November, she went in procession to Westminster Palace. 'And there rode next before the lytter, the Right High and Myghty Prince the Duc of Bedeforde, Great Stuarde of Englande for the Tyme being of this fest.' The next day, the 25th a final procession took Elizabeth from the palace to Westminster Abbey. Jasper and Katherine again performed central roles in the events. In the parade, after the chamberlain, the Earl of Oxford, came:

> [...] the high and myghty Prince Duc of Bedeforde, in a Gown of Clothe of Golde richely furrded, mounted on a goodley Courser richely trapped with a Trapper embroderde with red roses, a Border of Golde Smythes Werk encompashede with rede Dragons, a longe white Rodde in his Hande, a riche Cheyne about his Nek [...][25]

And when they reached the abbey Jasper yet again played a leading part:

> [...]the Duc of Bedeforde bar hedede in his Roobees of Astate [bore] a riche Corowne of Golde. Then followed the Quene [...] And next her my lade Cecill, which ar her Trayne. Next her folowd the Duchess of Bedeforde, and another Duchess and Comtesse apparelled in Mantells of Sircoots of Scarelet, furred and powdered, the Duchesses having on ther Heds Coronatts of Golde richely garnysshed with Perle and precious Stones.[26]

---

24 CCR, Henry VII 1485–1500, p. 69. RP, vol. 4, p. 407.
25 BM, Egerton MS. 985, ff. 12–22. Leland, *Collectanea*, vol. 4, pp. 216–33.
26 BM, Egerton MS. 985, ff. 12–22. Leland, *Collectanea*, vol. 4, pp. 216–33.

The press of those eager to catch sight of all this splendour led to the deaths of several among the crowd of spectators. Nonetheless, the coronation itself carried on smoothly and the party returned to the palace. The rest of the day was given over to feasting and dancing.

For Christmas 1487, Jasper had a gown made of cloth-of-gold, at a cost of £33 6s 8d and, presumably for Katherine, a silk dress at a cost of £38 16s 8d[27] Christmas and the New Year were spent with the king and queen at Greenwich Palace. On New Year's Day the king gave the officers of arms a sum of £6 as 'largesse', and the heralds proclaimed his title. Similarly, Jasper made a gift of £2, proclaimed as 'de hault et puissaunt Prince, frère et uncle de Roys. Duc de Bedeforde, et Counte de Pembroke, Largesse'. And likewise for Katherine.

On the feast of Epiphany the king and queen sat in state and 'the Duc of bedeforde bare the cappe of estate next before the king'. These ceremonies were followed by a feast where Jasper again played a prominent part.[28]

In general, Jasper resided mostly at Thornbury manor but he also spent a considerable amount of time at Sudeley and Minster Lovell.[29]

By the end of January 1488, Jasper was in residence at Baynards Castle. He was still in London on 6 March when he witnessed a charter in favour of Queen Elizabeth.[30]

On 21 March 1488, Jasper was granted the castle, town and lordship of Haverfordwest in Pembrokeshire.[31] In December 1489, there was a fresh attempt to overthrow the king, a plot by supporters of the former and late Earl of Lincoln. Although few facts are known about this episode, it would appear the problems affected Jasper's territory in the Welsh Marches and, despite the lack of surviving information, it is clear that Jasper was able to suppress the rebels.[32]

During the spring of 1490, tensions increased between England and France, caused by French ambitions towards the duchy of Brittany. Nevertheless, that July a truce with France was signed for six months. Charles VIII of France named Admiral Louis Malet de Graville as the conservators of the truce on the French side, while Henry named his trusted and experienced uncle Jasper as his guarantor and placed

27 Staffs. R. O., D641/1/2/193 m.9d. Cited in Thomas, p. 277.
28 BM, Egerton, 985, ff. 27–29. Leland, *Collectanea*, vol. 4, p. 234.
     Cited in Thomas, pp. 346–7.
29 Thomas, p. 319.
30 Staffs. CRO, D641/1/1/193, m.10. Materials, vol. 2, p. 270.
31 CPR, 1485–1494, p. 220. Materials, vol. 2, p. 281.
32 Busch, p. 84. PSO, Warrants, 2nd serie, 3. Cited in Thomas, p. 349.

him temporarily in charge of the lieutenancy of Calais.[33] Even so, affairs between both countries deteriorated and on 5 and 8 May Jasper and the Earl of Oxford were commissioned to gather an army at Warwickshire and Hampshire.[34] On 15 May Henry granted his uncle the castle and lordship of Builth, in the Marches. This grant would be Jasper's final official reward from his nephew.[35]

On 4 July 1491, Jasper, Sir Rhys ap Thomas, Gruffydd Rede of Carmarthen and Jasper's own servants Morgan Kidwelly, Richard Newton and Thomas Garth were ordered to raise money in the earldom of Pembroke and in the counties of Cardigan and Carmarthen for the fight that was at hand. Jasper attended the great session on 2 and 8 August at Carmarthen and Cardigan in his capacity as justiciar, for which he received an annual salary.[36] The conflict was delayed for a while by negotiations between the two countries, but at the beginning of 1492 war seemed inevitable. The once supportive French king, Charles VIII, who had been essential to Henry's cause and who could have been considered to be his friend, now became his enemy. King Henry drew up a will on 20 February 1492 in which his uncle Jasper is named as one of the executors who is to carry out his wishes.[37] On 17 September that year, Jasper was again at Carmarthen to attend a council session and a week later he did the same at Cardigan. There is no known surviving document that records another visit by Jasper to Wales after this date.

On 2 October 1492, the king at last set sail for Calais, having given joint command of his huge force of 15,000 men and 700 ships to Jasper and the Earl of Oxford. [38] This is the only proof that Jasper took part in the invasion. No other source mentions him or his actions. The campaign itself was no more than a military parade through Normandy and eventually Henry allowed himself to be bought off by the Treaty of Etaples on 3 November. Shortly afterwards Henry and his army returned to England with no glory but with a massive sum of money – 745,000 gold crowns.[39]

The first five years of Henry's reign had been hectic and action-packed for everyone involved, not least for the king's trusted uncle,

33 Materials, vol. 2, p. 334. Busch, pp. 40–43.
34 CPR, 1485–1494, pp. 353–5.
35 CPR, 1485–1494, p. 345.
36 SCMA, Henry VII/1615 m. 9.
37 RP, vol. 4, p. 444, 521.
38 Vergil's Anglica Historia, p. 52. Hall's Chronicle, p. 456.
39 Busch, pp. 61–66.

but from around 1492 Jasper slowly moves to the background. After the expedition to Calais, Jasper carried out only occasional public duties to serve his sovereign, but no regular employment or long-term periods of service. Now in his sixties, Jasper's advancing years had probably begun to take their toll. After so many years of danger, exile and trauma and now, in contrast, the establishment of a new dynasty with comparative peace and security, the time had come to settle down in retirement, to take a step back and leave the hard work to a younger generation.

There is no evidence that Jasper enlarged his income through trade but he did, however, receive fee-farm annuities from Bedford, Hereford and London, and also an annual salary as justiciar of South Wales.[40] In his declining years Jasper's link with Wales and the Marches remained strong. His routine work in Wales mainly comprised maintaining law and order there and, for example, if a Welshman felt he had a grievance he had to apply to the council or in their absence, to Jasper himself.[41] But since Jasper's presence in Wales is not recorded after 1492, it may be that he carried on his work there by ordering others to attend meetings, and so on, in his place. Or perhaps it is simply that the records of his visits have not survived. He continued to be nominated to various administrative commissions but it is clear from the records of these bodies that most of the duties entailed were not performed by Jasper in person. However, on 20 March 1493, he was commissioned to deliver the gaols of Gloucester, Hereford, Shrewsbury and Worcester, and was also granted a commission of oyer and terminer for these shires and for Wales as a whole.[42] It is very likely that he did fulfil some of these duties because he certainly visited Gloucester between 1493 and 1494 when he was 'wined and dined by the mayor with capons, woodcock, Malmsey and Gascon wine'.[43]

The first ten years of Henry VII's reign had been full of plots to overthrow the new Tudor dynasty. After the conspiracies of Lovell, Lincoln and Lambert Simnel in 1487 and the vague plot in 1489,[44] the next few years were full of smaller plots and even a new pretender.

40 Spec. Coll., Min. Acc., HenVII/1613 m. 1. /1614 m.3. / 1615 m. 9. /1616 m.8.
    Cited in Thomas, p. 320.
41 T.B. Pugh, *The Marcher Lordships of South Wales*, pp. 20–30.
42 CPR, Henry VII 1485–1494, pp. 434, 441.
43 H.M.C., Beaufort and Donoughmore MSS., Twelfth Report, appendix, pt IV,
    pp. 423–4. Cited in Thomas, p. 350.
44 W. Busch, *England under the Tudors*, Vol, I, *King Henry VII* (London, 1895), p. 84.

Relations between England and the Low Countries deteriorated as the Holy Roman Emperor Frederick III seems to have felt humiliated at being left out from negotiations for the Anglo-French Treaty of Etaples in 1492. Margaret of Burgundy was a close friend of the emperor's son and heir Maximilian, and despised Henry VII, and this just was the opportunity she needed to destroy the House of Tudor.

By early 1493, a new pretender emerged, claiming to be Richard, Duke of York, the younger prince in the Tower. This pretender, Perkin Warbeck, was in and out of England until 1495, instigated by the support of Duchess Margaret of Burgundy and supported by Emperor Maximilian, John de la Pole, Duke of Suffolk and others.

By the autumn of 1494 the Warbeck conspiracy had penetrated to the heart of Henry's royal household. Two of Henry's most powerful and trusted household officials – his lord steward Lord Fitzwalter and, even worse, Henry's chamberlain Sir William Stanley, brother of Henry's stepfather, the man who had helped him to victory at Bosworth – were involved. This conspiracy was at its peak between late 1495 and 1497 and if Jasper was aware of the seriousness of this situation he may have been frustrated at no longer being able to serve his king.

Eventually these political problems were overcome and Jasper must have been pleased to see how firmly his nephew ruled the kingdom compared to the king Jasper had formerly served. Henry VII indeed differed in many ways from Jasper's half-brother, the weak but kind-hearted Henry VI he had once served with all his devotion. Notably different from Henry VI's single child was Henry VII's growing family tree. Jasper could be reassured and contented by the thought of how Henry and his queen were expanding their family and creating a stronger dynasty.

Jasper appears to have spent most of 1494 at his castle at Sudeley, his services for royal duties being no longer called upon. It seems probable that he was not able to carry out such tasks as previously and it is likely that by this time he was already suffering from poor health. From a fragmentary household account drawn up in December 1495, it is clear that Jasper was living at his manor house at Thornbury and the huge sums of money being spent suggest that he was seriously ill.[45]

---

45 Nearly £130, representing the running cost during this period for one week, a staggering amount of money if one considers that Jasper's yearly income as earl of Pembroke in the early 1450s was around £1,000.

Figure 52   Bust of Henry VII made in c. 1509-1511 by Pietro
                Torrigiano in the Victoria and Albert Museum in London.
                (© 2015 Debra Bayani)

Figure 53   Thornbury Castle.
                (© 2015 Debra Bayani)

Figure 54   Remains of the oldest parts of Sudeley Castle, home of
                Jasper Tudor and his wife Katherine Woodville.
                (© 2015 Debra Bayani)

16
JASPER'S LEGACY
December 1495 and after

A S THE year 1495 approached its end, so too did Jasper's life. On 15 December, at his manor at Thornbury, he drew up his last will. At first glance it resembles most contemporary wills, but a more careful look at its content does provide some insights into Jasper's character.[1]

Jasper starts his last testament by committing his soul to Almighty God, the Blessed Virgin Mary and all the saints. He then asks for his body to be buried 'in a place convenient' at the Abbey of Keynsham, located eighteen miles south of Thornbury, and requests that his tomb be honourably made, to suit 'the estate it hath pleased god to call me to', at a cost of 100 marks (a considerable sum of money). Jasper then goes on to make provisions at a cost of £40 for the endowment of chantry priests to sing 'perpetually' for his soul, as well as for the souls of his father and 'of the noble memorie Kateryne some tyme Quene of England my moder', for Edmund his brother and for all his ancestors, but if this is not possible he then wishes that two benefices at a cost of £50 or £40 per year shall be assigned to the

---

1   To the medieval mind, debts were a burden that held the soul in limbo for a long time, something that was best avoided, and so it was of utmost importance that any dues one might have were amortized. The same went for requesting that prayers should be said for one's soul and making bequests to or for certain places, particularly those places important to an individual during his or her lifetime, whether because of warm memories or some family tie, or for more practical reasons. For a full transcription of Jasper's will, see Appendix A.

Abbot of Keynsham Abbey (at that time John Gybryn), for five or six priests to sing daily for the same purpose. If neither of these two requests could be accepted Jasper then desired for the same intention that the abbot would be given 'in redy money' a sum of £100 in order to endow two permanent chantry priests, with the surety that the offer would be arranged and supervised by his appointed learned council. Jasper took this matter very seriously. His appointed executors were John Morton, now Archbishop of Canterbury; Richard Hill, Bishop of London; Giles, Lord Daubeney; Dr Owen Poole; John Browne; and Jasper's two servants Morgan Kidwelly and Richard Newton. (It was to Morgan Kidwelly that the administration of the will was committed on 2 July 1496 when the testament was proved.) Jasper then goes on to make several donations to churches and religious houses in Wales and in the West Country, both areas he had considered his home. To Keynsham Abbey he bequeaths his best gown of cloth of gold for vestments to be made to honour God and his Blessed Mother. Furthermore, Jasper directs that on the day of his interment, all poor men and women who would accept it were each to be given alms of 2d and this was to be repeated a month later. He then makes a donation to Winchcombe Abbey of £20 for building work as well as his long gown of crimson velvet for a cope to be made to honour God and the venerated Anglo-Saxon saint Kenelm. To St Mary's Church in Thornbury Jasper bequeaths £10 for repairs and a gown of black velvet for a cope and vestments, and for the vicar of the same church another 40s for unpaid tithes and other duties. Bequests to religious foundations continue: to the four orders of the Friars in Bristol £8; to the Black Friars at Hereford 40s; to the Grey Friars at Hereford 'where my father is interred' £20 as well as his second best gown of cloth of gold to be made into a cope or vestments; to the three orders of Friars at Gloucester £6; to the two orders of Friars at Cardiff £4; to the Friars of Newport 20s; to the Friars of Haverfordwest 40s, to the vicary or church of Winchcombe 40s; to the Blessed Trinity of Christchurch in Bristol his jacket of cloth of gold to make two jackets for vestments; to the church of Pembroke his black velvet gown for a cope or vestments to be made there. It is not clear to which church in Pembroke Jasper is making the bequest, but St Mary's Church in Pembroke dates back to the thirteenth century and is alleged to be the church where Jasper's nephew was baptised in 1457, although there is no concrete evidence of this event.[2]

Jasper follows these bequests by saying that every parish church that his body is carried into on the journey from Thornbury to his final resting place at Keynsham is to receive 20s and two torches. Further, Thomas Okeley, parson of Sudeley is to receive payment from Jasper's executors for unpaid tithes and duties, and the Crotch Friars of Gaunt's St Mark's Hospital in Bristol are left 40s. Jasper authorises his executors, for twenty years from the date of his death, to use the income from the lands he holds in fee simple to settle his debts, including carrying out the provisions in his will. At the end of that period the lands are to 'remayne to my saide soverayn Lord the King and to hie heires Kings of England for ever'. Then follows a generous bequest – Jasper instructs that his household servants shall be paid a whole year's wages and his household is to be maintained until that Easter, In effect, none of his servants would be cast out without money and before they had an opportunity to find a new employer. Nearly at the end of the will Jasper, although briefly, mentions Katherine – 'my Lady my wife and all others persons [who] have such dueth as shalbe thought to theym appereyning by right lawe and conscience'. As Katherine was a very wealthy woman in her own right, it is likely that her financial affairs were already securely tied up.

It is impossible to know whether Jasper and Katherine's marriage was a happy one. However, we do know from brief references in the records as to Katherine's whereabouts that they spent at least some of their time together at the manor of Thornbury and Sudeley Castle. Their union of Tudor bridegroom to Yorkist bride, made when Jasper was around fifty-four and Katherine in her late twenties, was clearly, like Henry's own marriage, one forged for political purposes rather than based on romantic attachment. Nor did it produce any living children. We can only speculate as to their actual relationship. What is a fact is that, less than two months after Jasper's death, his widow married, without royal licence (which gave Henry VII a reason to

---

2   Besides these bequests to churches, it is thought that Jasper earlier had a hand in embellishments made to St Mary's Church in Tenby; however, other attributed projects such as the founding of a university in Neath in Glamorgan or one in Oxford, or that he was responsible for the building of the tower of St Woolos Cathedral in Newport (which features a headless statue said to depict Jasper), are probably the works of others. See W.G. Thomas, 'The Architectural History of St Mary's Church, Tenby', Archaeologia Cambrensis, CXV (1966), pp. 159–61. Cited in Thomas, p. 356.

fine the couple £2,000),[3] Sir Richard Wingfield, at that time only
a mere knight far below her rank, a younger son and around twelve
years her junior,[4] which suggests that Katherine's third marriage was
likely to have been a love match. Perhaps the couple had known one
another for a long time. Two of Wingfield's brothers, and possibly
he himself, had served in Katherine's household and there was also
a blood tie between Wingfield's mother, Elizabeth FitzLewis, and
Mary FitzLewis, Anthony Woodville's wife.[5] The marriage, however,
did not last long for Katherine died on 18 May 1497. The cause of her
death, which took place when she was around the age of thirty-nine,
is unknown. It is tempting to speculate that she may have died
because of a later life pregnancy. However, there is no evidence of her
becoming pregnant by Wingfield. Years later Wingfield remarried, to
the daughter and heiress of Sir John Wiltshire, Bridget Wiltshire, and
went on to have a large family. He also advanced to have a successful
career as a diplomat at the court of Henry VIII. On a delegation to
Emperor Charles V, he fell ill and died on 22 July 1525 in Toledo,
aged around seventy. In his testament he asked for masses to be said
for the soul of his 'singular good lady Dame Katherine'.

Jasper concludes his own will with the modest request:

> 'I ordeyne and desire my sovereyne Lord
> the King to be Supervisour of this my testament
> beseching humbly his highnes for myne olde
> since devotion to his grace to see the same duely
> executed'.

Six days after making his will, Jasper died at Thornbury, on
21 December 1495, at the age of about sixty-four. His body was
apparently embalmed and his entrails buried in the parish church
at Thornbury. The medieval, mainly fifteenth-century, church of
St Mary the Virgin which can still be seen today, some fifty yards
from where the manor house stood, must have been a frequent place
of worship for Jasper while in residence there. In May 1497 King
Henry issued a licence to Robert Slimbridge to found a perpetual
chantry in the chapel newly built in the church– 'for two chaplains

---

3   S. Higginbotham, *The Woodvilles, The Wars of the Roses and England's Most Infamous Family,* The History Press (Stroud 2013), p. 176.
4   Sir Richard Wingfield b. 1469, ODNB (October 2008).
5   Higginbotham, *The Woodvilles*, p. 176. C.S.L.,
     Davies, 'Stafford, Henry, Second Duke of Buckingham (1455–1483)'.

to pray for the good estate of the King, Queen Elizabeth and Robert Slymbrigge and for their souls after death, and for the souls of the king's uncle, Jasper Duke of Bedford whose entrails are buried in the said chapel'. [6]

On the way from Thornbury to the market town of Keynsham close to Bristol, Jasper's funeral procession halted at Kingswood, where they were met by 'the Maire and his brethren [...] with iiml men on horsebake, all in blake gownes, and so brought his body to Keynsham, for the which the said Maire and his brethren had grete thankes of the King'.[7] The king and queen, with an escort of spiritual and temporal nobles, also travelled to Keynsham for the interment in the abbey. Only part of the foundations of the twelfth-century Augustine abbey now survive. The abbey and Jasper's tomb were not spared by Henry VIII and did not survive the dissolution of the monasteries in 1539. A plaque commemorating the abbey can be seen with the remaining foundations in the, somewhat neglected, Abbey Park in the town.

A few near-contemporary reports about Jasper survive, including that of an anonymous sixteenth-century observer who described him as 'a very benevolent prynce an a lovynge frynde'.[8] Rice Merrick, also writing in the sixteenth century, refers to Jasper as 'the good duke'[9] and, according to Edward Hall, Jasper was 'a wise and gifted soldier'.[10] Minuscule as the surviving fragments are, they do reveal that Jasper made an impression in the hearts of the people who were close to him.

It appears that the association between Jasper and his servant Thomas Lucas grew into a fairly strong friendship. Between 1490 and 1491, Jasper granted Lucas 'the manor of Pembroke, or Dunham Hall, in Westley [Suffolk]'.[11] Some years after Jasper's death, in 1513, Thomas Lucas ordered a manor house to be built in Suffolk. Called Little Saxham Hall, it was said to have been built on the land that Jasper bestowed in 1490 on his beloved and faithful servant. Unfortunately, not much is known about the building, as no drawing or painting of it is known to exist and for unknown reasons it was pulled down in 1773. What we do know is that Lucas was very

6   CPR, Henry VII 1494–1509, p. 114.
7   Ricart's Kalendar, p. 48.
8   BM. Additional MS 6298, f. 290.
9   Marrick, p. 143.
10   Hall's Chronicle, p. 338. Cited in *The Political Career*, p. 358.
11   J. Gage, *The History and Antiquities of Suffolk: Thingoe Hundred*, pp. 131–2.

grateful to his master and, although Jasper had already been dead for eighteen years by the time Little Saxham Hall was built, he was held in loving remembrance by the Lucas family, and for this reason the building was lavishly decorated with Jasper's coat of arms and 'all the windows of the mansion being powdered throughout with the broom code in compliment of Jasper, Duke of Bedford'.[12] And to honour his master even more, Thomas Lucas named his eldest son Jasper. In his will, Thomas gives £30 to the Crossed Friars in London for 'reparations and building of that virtuous house and to pray specially for Jasper, Duke of Bedford'. He also gives donations to several churches, amongst them the churches of Sudeley and Thornbury, the places where he had served Jasper. Furthermore, Thomas Lucas bequeaths to a little chapel of Our Lady and St John Evangelist in the parish of Little Saxham six pounds a year for two years, to sing for Jasper, as well as for himself, his wife, family and daughter Margery.

Nor was Jasper forgotten by his half-brother David Owen and his family. Sir David Owen married as his first wife the Bohun heiress Mary de Bohun in around 1489 and together they had one son named Henry after Henry VII, who may have been the baby's godfather. Henry Owen in turn had several children, one of whom, born to his second wife Dorothy West, was named Jasper. From his second wife, Anne or Alice Blount, daughter of William, Lord Mountjoy, Sir David had two surviving children, a daughter called Anne and a son named Jasper. And from his third marriage, to Anne Devereux, Sir David had several more children of whom the eldest was another Henry. Sir David's will was already drawn up in 1529 and was proved in 1542. In it he writes that 'he wold that his Executours shulde make a tomb to the value of tenne [pounds?] at the Grey Freers in hereford where his Father ys buryed to be a perpetuall memory of hym'.[13] Sir David Owen also requests for 'prestes quarterly and yerly for evermore to keep an obite with placebo and dirirge by note with the said twelve prestes and masse on the morrow for the sowles of King Henry VII, Edmund sometime Erle of Richmonde, Jasper, Duke of Bedford, my fader and moder soules, my wiffes and all christen soules'.[14]

During Jasper's lifetime the king and queen were blessed with more children following the birth of Arthur in 1486: Margaret in

---

12   Gage, *The History and Antiquities of Suffolk: Thingoe Hundred*, pp. 139, 152.
13   W.H. Blaauw, 'On the Effigy of Sir David Owen', *Archaeologia Cambrensis*, vol. 18 (1854), p. 42.
14   Blaauw, 'On the Effigy of Sir David Owen', p. 31.

1489, who was named after her Beaufort grandmother; Henry in 1491, who was given the name of the Lancastrian kings, including his own father; and Elizabeth in 1492, named after her Woodville grandmother. One might wonder why none of Henry's children was named after his beloved uncle Jasper. Although we will never know for sure, it is very likely that after Arthur, Henry and Edmund (b. 1499), there would have been a Jasper if another son had been born. Henry named his youngest son after his own father, the father he never knew. Neither did he forget his father's remains in Carmarthen and, sometime after the fortieth anniversary of Edmund's death, Henry assigned £43 10s 0d to Sir Rhys ap Thomas for 'the making of a newe tombe for our most dere fadre'.[15] The top of the Purbeck marble tomb was ornamented with an engraved brass image of Edmund. The nineteenth-century brass that can now be seen is presumably a replacement of the one that was put there in 1496. During the dissolution of the monasteries, Edmund's grandson, the illustrious Henry VIII transferred the tomb from the Grey Friars Church in Carmarthen to the cathedral of St David's in Wales, where it can still be seen today.[16] Unfortunately, he did not do the same for the remains of his great-uncle Jasper. It is surprising and somewhat saddening to realize that Jasper has never attracted the attention he so richly deserves - how soon he was forgotten and his career, and the fundamental part he played in the foundation of the Tudor dynasty became overlooked by his contemporaries as well as by more modern historians. A substantial part of this neglect can probably be assigned to the fact that so little of Jasper's archives has survived.[17] From what does remain we can see a man whose steadfast loyalty and courage cost him the best years of his life but eventually brought him peace and reward. If any man was responsible for the triumphant rise of the Tudor dynasty, that man was surely Jasper Tudor, Duke of Bedford and Earl of Pembroke.

At the time of his death, Jasper could have surely closed his eyes for the last time, satisfied and without regrets, knowing that he had done everything within his power, and more, to follow his conscience and to do what was right. His mission was accomplished.

---

15   PRO, E404/84. Cited in Griffiths, *Sir Rhys ap Thomas and his Family*, p. 49.
16   E. Allen, 'The Tomb of the Earl of Richmond in St. David's Cathedral', *Archaeologia Cambrensis*, vol. 13 (1896), pp. 315–20.
17   Thomas, p. 358.

Wherfor we crye,
Suffer not Jasper to dye,
But to lyve;
For eternally that he shall lyve
Is oure byleve.[18]

---

18 'The Epitaffe of the Moste Noble and Valyaunt Jaspar Late Duke of Beddeford', in *The
    Poetical Works of John Skelton*, ed. Alexander Dyce (London, 1843), vol. 2, pp. 388–98.
    This eulogistic elegy was once attributed to John Skeleton (c. 1463–1529) but is likely
    written by a member of Jasper's household, his falconer whose name is said to be Smert
    or Smart.

Figure 55   St. Mary's Parish Church in Thornbury.
                Jasper's entrails were buried here.
                (© 2015 Debra Bayani)

Figure 56   The remains of Keynsham Abbey.
                (© 2015 Debra Bayani)

APPENDIX A
The Will of Jasper Tudor,
Duke of Bedford and Earl of Pembroke

(Source: PROB 11/10/401. Transcribed by S. T. Moore)

'In the name of God Amen.

I Jasper Duke of Bedford and Earl of Pembroke make my testament and last will in this forme following

First I bequeath my soul to almighty god to our blessed lady his mother the virgin Mary and to all saints

My body to be buried in the monastery of our Lady of Keynesham in a place convenient where I will that my tomb be honourably made after the estate that [line 5] it hath pleased God to call me to and thereupon to be employed a hundred marks

Item I will that certain my Lordships manors lands and tenements with their appurtenances which I have in fee simple as well in the counties of Nottingham Derby and Warwick as in the March of Wales and elsewhere the some of £40 yearly of the same with licence and agreement of my sovereign Lord the King be amortised for the finding of 4 priests to sin perpetually in the said church and monastery as well for my soul and for my father's soul as for the souls of the noble memory Katherine some time Queen of England my mother, and of Edmund late Earl of Richmond my brother and of all other my predecessors

Item I will then that in default hereof one or 2 benefices of the value of £40 or £50 yearly above all charges of the patronage of my said sovereign lord of mine as of my other where the same may be best obtained by special labour and means of me or my executors be impropried to the abbot and convent of the said monastery perpetually for the time being to the intent 5 or 6 priests shall be found daily to sing in the said monastery as well for my soul as the souls aforesaid

Item I will that in default of both the premises £100 to be delivered to the said abbot and convent by my executors in ready money to the intent that 2 priests shall be perpetually found in the said monastery to sing daily for me and the souls above rehearsed according to an office made by the said abbot and convent in that behalf and that the surety hereof to be devised by my counsel learned

Item I bequeath to the said monastery my best gown of cloth of gold for vestments to be made to the honour of God and his blessed mother

Item I will that the day of my internment at Keynesham there be distributed among every poor man and woman there will take it 2d a piece and likewise at my months mind

Item I bequeath to the monastery of blessed Saint Kenelme of Winchcombe toward the building of the same £20 and my long gown of crimson velvet to make a cope there to the honour of God and the saints

Item I bequeath to the church of Thornbury toward the reparation of the same £10

Item I bequeath to the said church a gown of black velvet for a cope to be made there and vestments

Item I bequeath to the vicar of the said church of Thornbury for tithes unpaid and other duties 40s

Item I bequeath to the 4 Orders of Friars of Bristol £8 equally to be divided

Item to the Black Friars of Haverford 40s

Item to the Gray Friars of Haverford where my father is interred £20

Item to the 3 Orders of Friars at Gloucester £6

Item to the 2 Orders of Friars at Cardiff £4

Item to the Friars of Newport 20s

Item to the Friars of Haverford West 40s

Item I bequeath to the house of Grey Friars of Harford East my second gown of cloth of gold where my father is interred for a cope or vestments there to be made

Item to the vicary of the parish church of Winchecombe or the church there 40s

Item I bequeath my jacket of cloth of gold to make 2 jackets to the blessed Trinity of Crichurch

Item I bequeath my other black velvet gown to the church of Pembroke for a cope or vestments to be made there

I bequeath to every parish church that my body shall be carried into between this and Keynesham 20s and 2 torches

Item I will that my executors content Thomas Okeley parson of Sudley for his duty of the herbage of the park there impound since the time that he was parson all that shall be found yearly due unto him for the same with all other such duties and tithes of hay as to him of right belong

Item I bequeath to the Croch friars of the Gaunts of Bristol 40s

Item I will that my executors have and pertain all issues profits and revenues of my said fee simple land in case the same be not amortised from the day of my death unto the end and term of 20 years next immediately following for the contentation of my debts and performance of this my last will and after the same 20 years complete I will that the same fee simple land remain to my said sovereign Lord the King and to his heirs kings of England for ever

I bequeath to my household servants a whole year's wages and my house to be kept from the day of my death unto East now next coming

Item I ordain my said executors the most reverend father in God John through God's sufferance Cardinal and Archbishop of Canterbury the right reverend father in God Richard Bishop of London Giles Lord Dawbeney Doctor Owen Poole Richard Newton John Browne and Morgan Kydwelley unto whom I bequeath and give the residue of all my goods to the intent that they shall ordain and dispose every thing as the shall think best and most necessary and expedient for the well of my soul and discharge of my conscience as they will answer in that behalf by whose oversight I will that my Lady my wife and all other persons have such dues as shall be thought to them appertaining by right law and conscience

Item I ordain and desire my sovereign Lord the King to be supervisor of this my testament beseeching humbly his highness for my old since devotion to his Grace to see the same duly executed

Given at my manor of Thornbury the 15th December the year of our Lord God 1495 and the eleventh year of the reign of our sovereign Lord King Henry VII

Item I will that the lands of the Abbey be recompense for such duties and tithes of hay as to them of right belong'

Probate granted at Lambeth 2 July 1496 sworn by Morgan Kidwelly executor

Appointing Lord Giles Daubeney Lord Daubeney and the said Morgan executors.

APPENDIX B
In praise of Owen Tudor in gaol

We know to keep silent and suffer,
we pray to the worthy God in heaven,
the great One God will save us,
Welshmen all, and woe to us!
The one man from [good] parents
– a flower that was our protection –
is in gaol in London,
sorrowful grief, misguided wrath,
with the terrible turreted towers in the land yonder
closed about him.
Woe to me that Owen Tudor
is under a roof's eaves in their chains!
What news if a leader descended from
Tudur the father is in Newgate?
who's descended from the royal blood of Edeirnion
two cold and very unpleasant shackles.
If it's true that a shackle
was hastily placed on the heel,
I myself with my praise, brilliant tongue,
will enmesh it about his leg,
and I'll break it with my tongue,
the second miracle [= after Taliesin's], if he pleads for praise.
He was no thief, he wasn't billeted,
nor was he a traitor, Tudur Llwyd's lineage;

he wasn't ashamed
to be caught in the town yonder,
not because he stole a horse with an eloquent bridle
in an act of surreptitious misrule,
not because of the law, idle talk
(trouble of a man second to innocent Abel),
not because of debt, if I'm to be believed,
is there a tall, slender man under arrest,
[but] because he once, on a feast day,
showed his affection, fearful business,
to the king of the wine-country's daughter,
who was a beautiful, worthy, gentle and tall maiden;
if my brilliant, golden man touched the maiden's skin,
it was by her consent.
It's slander, his escape is fearful,
against the daughter of the king of France's rich wine;
a hundred thousand swear, gift's medium,
that a fearful proposition preceded her act.
Of high status in his absolute ability,
it was a second marriage of Melwas.
He has lively children from her,
so they tell me,
who are brothers of baronial blood to a king [= Henry VI],
shield-men of battle,
and also grandsons to another king [= Charles VI],
wise council.
May God have a part in protecting the lives
of Tudur's grandsons against the turmoil of pain!

The lad will be released from captivity
before long, we have hope;
the generous, handsome duke from the banks of Gloucester
will save us always [= Humphrey of Lancaster];
he's a Welshman's equal
and his relation, a brilliant, fine black stag.
May God give long life
to my proud, white-tower hawk to that end!
May the wrath of his axe's sharpness
liberate Owen entirely,
and easily by all accounts,
and freely to Penmynydd on Anglesey! [1]

---

1   Gethin, *'In praise of Owen Tudor in gaol'*; trans. Eurig Salisbury.

APPENDIX C

*In praise of Edmund Tudor and
Jasper Tudor, sons of Owen Tudor*

The two lordly men
good is the root from Troy and Greece
from the region (they'd come thither)
of Rhodri Mawr, Anglesey's emperor:
Edmund, earl of Richmond,
from Cadwaladr's nation and his region,
fresh offshoot of the king of Paris
with golden leaves and fleur-de-lis;
Jasper is the one who's prepared for the dance,
Charles's nephew from the city of Orleans,
he's the brave earl of Pembroke from the lineage
of Llŷr r Llediaith, the greatest of the nation.

Kingship resides
in the two men's grasp wherever it goes.
A finely-wrought crown with gold and precious stones
was placed on their mother,
and both her father and great-grandfather
bore the gold of two crowns,
and so too the king of the immaculate Island
of Great Britain, their brother from the same mother.
They'd peruse their father's portion,
they'd come with steel, Tudur's grandsons;
thirty kings of his lineage
came lineally.
After Camber there were three diadems
of the nation as far as Rhyd Helyg,
and twice shall lord Owain come
from each one of these.

Helmets are the arms they'll provide
from the land of Gwynedd, three white ones,
and a black chevron before hosts,
and a field of roses, it was time,
Madog ap Maredudd's escutcheon
in the green colour, a lion in hiding,
and a tame lion on the shield,
and a black gown and a fiery claw.
There was a painted shield against a man's thrust
above the head of Tewdwr,
and his hand bore steel nails
and his fingers azure armour.
May a grandson of Maredudd bear
a golden lion and the red hand,
Cynan, prince of Gwynedd,
and all his arms on his grave,
and a depiction of the three white lions
treading on the sanguine.

May these receive the lions
on a banner, earls of Owain;
if the father appoints a day
to place the banner on a mountain top,
it will enable the support of sixty thousand men
as far as Maelor, great prophecy.
For us, for a hundred summers in succession,
for a hundred springs before they were born,
there was talk by men of yore,
so it is again because of what they'd do:
before long a yellow dragon
and a white dragon will strike each other,
and the yellow dragon's clutches
will cause the white dragon to fall.
When the fire was extinguished completely
in Llywelyn's hall (every night it retreats),
a spark was found from Anglesey,
from France and from fair Aberffraw;
Owain and his children in one family
are the firebrands of the Britons.
May Jesus (after permitting it)
keep Cadwaladr's hall powerful![1]

1   'In praise of Edmund Tudor and Jasper Tudor, sons of Owen Tudor', in T. Roberts and
     I. Williams (eds), *The Poetical Works of Dafydd Nanmor* (Cardiff and London, 1923),
     poem XIII. Exclusively translated for this book by Eurig Salisbury.

APPENDIX D

Elegy for Edmund Tudor, earl of Richmond
- Dafydd Nanmor

Jasper is with Henry,
he's a sorrowful man for one of the three,
Jasper the fair – every day, indeed,
he's in need of a brother;
his nephew, more's the pity
(he died), is in need of an uncle.
They die as far away as the sea of Mwnt,
eighteen thousand men, because Edmund was taken.
Even though both he and the old hay
departed off the land from the place of reaping,
his lineage will survive in the bud
(with no less growth),
a bud of note, blessed are we,
the crown's nephew who sustains us,
one lad who exhilarates a thousand men,
and from one lad to a hundred thousand.

It was well that a bronze man
was fashioned from stone for the city of Rome;
I'd place a load of gold on the grave
to fashion a likeness of the earl of Gwynedd
above Milford Haven, no less than complete,
conspicuous for them,
his brave likeness beside the wave,
an obstruction there against foreigners.
That's how a likeness of pious Gwrthefyr
was fashioned near Dover.

For us it's sad to see how happy his enemies are,
they obliterate us.
There was no sadness for even a moment
without joy and a leader.
As another Jasper of yore
came with the myrrh for wise Mary's son,
so too Jasper (no less of a man)
for our sake brings healing for a kinsman.
The South, Gwynedd and the kingdom of Gwennwys
will place their force on one side,
then they, the Britons and the healthy man,
will take the Croes Naid.
Look, Hywel's governance,
Wales will have a brilliant Welshman.
We'll make ready a speckled spear and his brother's pennon
(proper nation), and the white and coloured banner,
and vigorous men will drive it into a skull.
An immortal man in supremacy,
by the grace of God he'll come in full one day.
Call before him his daring, brave men
and his brother's men,
with his spear he'll be able to
win the world from one end to the other
in order to end the race of Frenchmen in France
and smite the royal bough into an old stump;
if we'll be wise we'll have
a conqueror from the other bough.

Even though the eldest brother of the Britons
was taken from the land of his grandfather,
the God of the Trinity will bless
the younger Owain (I'll follow him).[1]

---

1   Here 'the younger Owain' is an allusion to Edmund's son Henry Tudor. 'Elegy for
Edmund Tudor, earl of Richmond' in *The Poetical Works of Dafydd Nanmor*, ed. T
Roberts and I Williams (Cardiff and London, 1923), poem XV. Exclusively translated
for this book by Eurig Salisbury.

APPENDIX E

Elegy for Edmund Tudor,
earl of Richmond - Lewis Glyn Cothi

The Welsh were enslaved,
once they were free;
every Welshman of lineage as far as Gwent
was taken away after [the death] of Edmund.
Edmund, earl of Richmond, God gave him to mankind,

God takes away his life;
oh God, why don't you give two lifetimes
to a monarch, or even a third of a lifetime?
No one enjoys life as they consider their desire

for the lord of Pembroke's brother;
Owain Tudor, he pines
for his son.
It is he, without hindrance, who'll lead us from the front

deservedly, Britain's tribe;
we're behind because of Charlemagne's descendant
whom I know.
I know what it is to have our head cut off,
    worth pounds to a poor man,

because of [the loss of] a fleur-de-lis of kings;
he was like three sallets on a target
and he was like three birds and a bull.
The bull and the cock from all the lands of yore

and the white lion from the north
and Owain Gwynedd's swallow
from the ends of the earth went to the grave.
The grave is like many pits,

this world is at an end,
the sigh, and it's not much better,
the woe is in every part of Wales.
Woe to valiant Welshmen yonder,

our griffin's end,
Edmund, earl of Richmond, loved peace.
God placed two

earls under one yoke,
one of the two best men went to lie.
King Henry's brother,

nephew to the Dauphin's sister's son,
son of Owain from the lineage of sons of the feast.

Cutting in every knoll

every man's head
was the cutting of an oak from the apogee of nobility.

Cutting the brave world

is the cutting of the string
of all Gwynedd's land on the day it was taut.

There'll be and there was

a sad day and a black day,
we were breached because of [the loss of] our glory.

We used to believe that the man

would free us from inside a tower
from our captivity, the lion from Tewdwr.

There's no hope now,

there's nothing alight
except the foretelling of pestilence and depravity.
Great is the sighing

and flow and weeping
both here in the east and in the lands of Anglesey,
and blood and howling

and sorrowful crying,
and wailing anew in droves.
May disheartened bald outcasts

call now above
for a Briton in the land of mead.
We're all sad,

a tree without our branch,
without roots for even a second, without any bravery.
A fine forest is not so

without numerous trees,
an armoured knight is not so without a cloak nor
        without a sword.
A man, if a man comes, is not so

if he comes without two hands,
a hand that weighs is not so without the fingers.
We're without a hand,

without a leader, each and every man,
without a soldier of a man and of compassion.
Without a kingly lineage

here we are, forsaken,
without a royal knight, without truth.
From the land of the river Ieithon

a vapour went as far as Anglesey,
a true Briton went to lie in their recumbent state.
England turned into a worthless ford,

France lost its colour,
all Wales went from the waking world to the grave.
His grave was fashioned into a wall

of marble in Mynyw;
there's a tomb on the ground
in Cwrt y Brodyr [= the Brothers' Court] for the monarch;
in the tomb where he's placed
may the old Tewdwr be placed also.
A leader from the lineage of Tewdwr on his brother's soil,

he was laid to rest;
there's the world filling the grave,
and there's the earl from Gwynedd.
For Gwynedd there was no wizardry

by any host of fairy-folk, except sorcery;
there was poetry yonder that was fashioned
from mist into prophecy.
He was so easily made an earl,

he who was taken from the kingship;
a Welshman's earl, he was the apogee yonder,
Edmund, lord Richmond, who was on the sea-shore.
Earl and emperor of every governance,

he wore golden clothes in every earldom;
his death on the bier, twice worse than the sea's force,
was the death of the south.
Our fine stag is dead, we are distressed,

the chequered dice are crumbling deceivers,
our stake is empty like an earldom above,
Wales is an empty house, we are worse.
Empty is the land without control,

empty is the house without both a bed and youth,
empty is the town without palaces, empty is the beach without
    water,
empty is the household without a feast, without mead, without
    nourishment.
Empty is the churchyard without a prelate, without protection,

empty is the tower without a soldier and a bow and arrow,
empty is the home without smoke, and it's worse without a
    fire,
empty is the wide region without tenancy.
England is empty and it polluted me,

Wales is emptier because of the news,
France is totally empty because of [the loss of] an
    eloquent flower,
brave Scotland is without support.
A thorn was thrust into Britain, it went through her,

so too ache and pain and longing tenfold,
Rhodri Mawr's lineage was struck down in its valour,
so too the descent of a bud of a leader.
Farewell to hawks and to riding on horseback,

farewell to nine coursers, the time has passed,
farewell to Wales and to goldsmithery of falseness,
farewell to our nobility if we have no leader.
Farewell to the lending of aristocracy,

farewell to happiness, farewell to order,
farewell to the Briton, who went to perish,
farewell to the conquering of the enslaved land of Wales.[1]

---

1   'Elegy for Edmund Tudor, earl of Richmond', in (D. Johnston (ed.), *Gwaith Lewys Glyn Cothi* (Caerdydd, 1995), poem 10. Trans. by Eurig Salisbury.

APPENDIX F
Prophetic Poem by Dafydd Nanmor

If an earl's visage is in the grave,
another earl was born last year;
God the almighty overseer
will make him, small bud of an earl, a noble man.
I prophesized in song
that he'd become a lad of ancient renown.
They'll receive him as a centenarian
lord of Somerset with the silk mantle.

The sapling from the old timber,
        he'll be a great oak descended from kings.
Henry, grace of Edmund, senior earl of Richmond,
was received as a massive oak;
this tree's branches and roots
[extend] as far as the Sea of Greece, kingly lad.
He'll win the land of Maine by sea,
so too the land of Germany by another sea.
If three emperors were received
in Paris yonder in the land of the fleur-de-lis,
Henry comes from the yonder land,
whence the three emperors come.
The stag of the three crowns
will come from the son of Owain of Anglesey's buck;
of the hundred kings he's the first

to combat before his horns are grown.
A fountain from Anglesey is in fosterage
in its forefathers' river;
is there a river as far as Rhone that flows
except one river from Ednyfed?
During summer every river
turned into dry earth, yet this one remains;
the river from Goronwy won't disappear
until the sea turns to land for ever more.
This man who owns us blazes
to form the candle of Owain Gwynedd,
and the candle, unless I'm mistaken,
will spark a fire in our land,
and from the bud of sovereignty
we'll have wheat to lead us from captivity.
Even though the old hay
was taken off the land from the place of reaping,
his lineage will survive in the bud
(with no less growth).
He's seed-wheat to be sown
as far as the Red Sea, he's a great seed,
as an earl's son (who was an orchard)
he's an offshoot with fine blond hair.
From this man I'd grow every month
a fair tree like the king of Paris;
from the cub that was born
a lion will come, a tawny conqueror.
With his claw from the riverbank
he strikes fear into the city of Rome;
the soldiers of Anglesey will receive an eagle,
so too the crown will receive its chick,
and its two wings will fall
over the sea and the land, if he desires it.
Alexander of yore rose in the wind
above men like an eagle,
two Birds of Llwch Gwin [= griffins] placed him
everywhere above the wind;
from the ground his two uncles raise him
higher than the branches of an oak.

May Henry after Edwin
be the Birds of Llwch Gwin's earl above Gwent.
If he's not an earl at the end of his life
after living for three ages,
may he (no less a Welshman)
have sovereignty in his old age![1]

1

T. Roberts and I. Williams (eds.), *The Poetical Works of Dafydd Nanmor* (Cardiff and London, 1923), poem XVI, trans. Eurig Salisbury.

APPENDIX G
Elegy for Owen Tudor

The great host couldn't do more
in England, in the Valley of river Lugg,
with the mole [= Edward] so destructive,
and their own men behind them.
Grievous enemy, we were found weeping
because of this treachery against Britons.
Calamity came from the battle of Hereford,
revenge will come at once on the men of the North!
In a dispute I'm unruly
– I'd get over it – I'm a wild one;
understandably I lament because of losing him,
Owen my lord.
If it came to pass that some were sad
in battle because of the son of Maredudd,
I could never be happy,
less would be my cry below.
The earls' father from Tudur's lineage
was caught (what's more uncertain?);
in health he was placed
to depart from the world through pain.
Weakness spread too fiercely,
he was easily sold yonder;
Gwynedd would place for him
his weight in gold upon the grave;

a king's wealth was forthcoming to buy him
and to issue a fine.
An Englishman [even] would hesitate somewhat
before shortening this man's life (we won't excuse it).

The poem and all the prophecies of yore
were false and futile (what poetic exuberance are they?)
because it was not possible to crown the man from
    Gwynedd,
peace is rare.
Fluent anger, I express outrage
against Adda Fras's prophecy;
if precedence was given to Heinyn Fardd's sermon,
it was a mistake;
the prophecy of the wizard who was in pain's turmoil
on the spear [= Merlin] is futile;
as for a nun's son [= also Merlin],
I'll burn his prophecy, no less;
Taliesin's wise songs, good poetry,
are no more genuine.
Woe to us for prophesizing Owain!
The pride that created these is unwise.
Woe to the prophets of Gwynedd
because of Englishmen, their adversaries!
Owain Lawgoch the prince,
Owain y Glyn [= Owain Glyndwr],
    roarer with an ashen spear,
Owen Tudor, Anglesey's protector,
and now this man bore the name;
so those men were caught,
we were deprived of our three Owains.

Hope remains for our people
and life has become hopeful.
Having heard that Owen Tudor was killed
by arms, it caused death,
I look to Jasper and Harry,
his son and grandson.
Between me and Monmouth I don't desire,
if this is my task, to say more [than this]:
may God from now on keep these alive,
and commit Owen to heaven! [1]

1   'Elegy for Owen Tudor', in I. Daniel (ed.), 'Gwaith Ieuan Gethin' (Aberystwyth, [unpublished]), poem 7. Exclusively translated for this book by Eurig Salisbury.

APPENDIX H
Elegy for Owne Tudor by Robin Ddu

Interminable treachery! I used to prophesize,
[but] what I prophesized is [now] dissolute.
Gwynedd (her praise was sung),
here's throwing her in death's sweep.
There was no bitter loss for Anglesey
compared to now, because of what happened;
the land went to weep water
by lamenting its son of prophecy.

There was no [worse] cry of pain in the day
than [for] Owen Tudor's life;
he was the prophecies' dragon of a swallow
and a man of Gwynedd's mettle,
an eminent kinsman to Arthur
and a father to earls, he'd work with steel.
Woe to me if a great clan was slain
through vengeance against a family!
He suffered without complaining,
Nudd's loss, he went to the gates of heaven.
St John [= the Baptist] – elegant manner –
was beheaded by unholy men of yore;
St Peter, by the wrath of an evil host of men,
was killed in Jesus's cause;
Owen was killed, beloved lord,

being a gallant and blameless man.
Although the swallow's head was hewn,
the earl remains, great eagle;
our son of prophecy is brown [haired],
blessed are we, the man is from North Wales!
He's the land of Cornwall's horned bull
– with the three horns – from the three lineages.
The promise is the wrathful knight,
that [= promise] is in two halves.
His sustaining army won't be less
in battle than an empire.
The Britons will pull together in a host
to anoint [= possibly 'with blood'] his enemy;
a bird in another country,
may you seek the sea, wise move!
Ride her [= the sea], and this is a necessity,
without a feast for five half years;
the bird will bring the other birds
from afar to avenge the indignation,
and a fleet will be set loose
– the wind will take them to the land of Kent –
and the treachery will come from Scotland
when this happens, it would go to Pembroke;
the Isle of Man in flames, a joint leap of pain,
[and] Dublin in the same predicament;
there will be both a great figure and deformity,
Anglesey's fair will flee to the mountains.
At last the noble white one
will come by wind in anger;
a pleasant eagle for Snowdon
will come; and if he comes, he won't leave.
Who's the one above the soil who cares about
why the five bow down?
The six who raise every Ovid to his work completely
are a visitation.
May we all keep watch so we can have feasts for food
because of the one who was buried!
When the great yellow bull comes
through the trees and oaks because of this,

[there will be] an impudent white dragon laying siege
and a red dragon will break the collar;
there will be a war and widespread shattering
for four years without peace,
and we'll all have the brave man and gentle gem
who bears the name Owen,
and an end and finish to the work,
and all our island as one nation! [1]

1   Robin Ddu ap Siencyn Bledrydd of Anglesey, CeinionLlenyddiaethGymreig, ed.
     Owen Jones (London, 1875), pp. 219–20. Exclusively translated for this book by Eurig
     Salisbury.

APPENDIX I

In praise of Jasper, earl of Pembroke
- Dafydd Nanmor

He'll receive a promise on land and sea
(may Jasper be an emperor!)
to conquer and disperse
both straw and trees, savage and civilized.

He draws to him every civilized person, every land, every manor,
every mountain and valley,
every armoury, every border,
every large town, he desires every region.

He desires every glen as well as the coastline from Anglesey
to the Alps,
this man's course is to subjugate
from Caledonia to the river Cleddau.

Lively Germany's swords and helmets will be received,
and spears from Spain,
the Outer Isles' and Brittany's bows
and great guns and stone-throwing engines of war.

He desires the castles of Maine, Paen and Penial,
Eifionydd and Mathrafal,
the fort of Radyr, the extremities of Italy,
Carno, Gower, Cornwall and Yale.

Yale, the forts of Sandal and Sandwich will be seized,
and Paris opened,
and Cologne and Venice captured,
and so too precious France.

Friesland and Holland also; Scotland's claimant
and Zeeland's sealer,
Iceland's and England's expounder,
all Ireland on the water's edge.

From the water [comes a] conqueror of forts; conqueror,
may you conquer all the countries
and the towers of Rhone and its free land,
so too the houses of Rome and its towns.

May the town of Lleon Gawr [= Chester] follow him freely,
and the towns of Bath and Wigmore,
Rome, Trefor,
York and great Troy.

The forts of Maelor (great fort), Meirion, Winchester,
Caer-went, Worcester,
Cydweli and Caerleon,
the great forts of Ceri and Anglesey.

Caernarfon, the forts of Anglesey, the Isle of Man, Cardiff,
Dyfi, Ludlow,
fair Coventry and Canterbury yonder,
the great fort of Ystwyth, the fort of Bristol.

May he be an earl in Bristol with his mind set on the towers
of the east in their might,
an earl owns the earls and their lives,
he's an earl that owns the whole world.

Earl of the whole world with no equal on land,
earl of both the east and the north,
earl of Pembroke, it's he who owns,
earl of the water and of all the lands.

A horse will be received earnestly through the grass,
one that will with his lances cause some men to be placed in a
     grave,
if it comes to pass, as well as fleeing in the fray,
to seize the word with his spear and sword.

One lifetime will be given, and two or three,
to the earl that will be received, because of [his] appearance
and because of the cross that was the relic of God the pure,
the Virgin Mary and the Man who owns [us].

He owns numerous kinds of wealth
like an oak tree of the mountains, abundant nobility,
great vineyards on the hillside of churchyards,
orchards last year.

A host of white horses in folds,
a thousand corpses deep in riverbanks,
a host of machines, a thousand pieces,
pale faces, many men alike.

Suplication, hospitality,
he knows hunstmanship, he knows a good deal,
he knows warfare, he knows learning,
he knows about the treachery of England's lands.

Seemly Solomon on a day of feasts
for plains of a thousand animals
and his portions of Preseli,
may [his] rowels reach as far as Yr Heledd [= Northwich,
     Middlewich and Nantwich].

Golden tassels in every corner,
we'll rejoice for his wars,
with the crossbow arrows, the mangonels
and the battles, may there be revenge.

Prestigeous ones, with his blows,
earl from grandfathers, he'll lead the banishment
in droves, chancelfuls
and floorfuls homewards.

In shiploads, boatfuls,
cartfuls, men to their own country,
may they go in crowds without souls
at the point of death, great is the glory!

He comes as an igniter (he's never a scoundrel)
and an irreprochable man against the houses of Gwynedd,
piercer of multitudes, consoler of towns,
good designer through a state of righteousness.

One who kisses Dyfr, divider of Dover,
scatterer of Englishmen, water is their abode,
plotter of steel, brave purposer,
man of prophecy from the land of Gwynedd.[1]

---

1   'In praise of Jasper, earl of Pembroke', in The Poetical Works of Dafydd Nanmor, ed. T. Roberts and I. Williams (Cardiff and London, 1923), poem XIV. Exclusively translated for this book by Eurig Salisbury.

APPENDIX J

In praise of Gruffudd Fychan ap Gruffudd of Corsygedol by Tudur Penllyn

The young stag who'll be honoured,
if the ship arrives, according to the tall earl's desire,
you're Gruffudd Fychan, a circle of ruby gold's crimson hawk
from a load of old gold,
son of Gruffudd, his staff is made of beech,
by necessity, Einion's handful.
Three hundred men stand because of love [for]
Rhuddallt's towe
r from Rhydderch's blood.
You know how to align yourself with [Jasper]
the hour the black eagle comes;
he'll come over Anglesey's foaming water, over the sea
of the Isle of Man and through Ardudwy.
When the lord of Pembroke (he didn't know)
went from Abermo [= Barmouth] to the boat,
you didn't leave the earl's side at all
until afterwards (you brought two [staffs of] hazel),
pledging [your] allegiance too soon
and turning his ship to shore once more.
Afterwards there was a pledge from Corsygedol
as far as France in your honour.
Because of a prophet there's a sign from Brittany

between a lord and his man:
a seal and a signature
and the golden earl on the page,
between Jasper and another,
the ship's image and one hand in the other.
Gruffudd, keep watch for the boatman,
keep watch for wine that arrives by water;
keep your corner closed for yourself
and open the door when he comes;
keep Ardudwy's gap closed by day,
wooded hills, keep Meirionnydd;
Cae Annun's [= Harlech] stag from Einion,
maintain peace yourself
from Conwy to the shallow river Efyrnwy,
from Gwyddelwern to the river Dulas.
[...]

From Rhuddlan as far as Gwanas,

long may you keep grey Harlech's host!
Keep the front line of Britain's battle
for the earl, break Sir Rhys's spear,
and may you keep it (and you're one who keeps)
until the greyish black Owain comes![1]

---

1 'In praise of Gruffudd Fychan ap Gruffudd of Corsygedol', in Gwaith Tudur Penllyn ac
Ieuan ap Tudur Penllyn, ed. T Roberts (Caerdydd, 1958), poem 2, lines 1–36, 55–60)
Exclusively translated for this book by Eurig Salisbury.

APPENDIX K

In praise of Gruffudd Fychan ap Gruffudd's house Ty Gwyn – Tudur Penllyn

Full estuaries support the court
Of Jasper's well known estuary;
It's there he'll come as a joyous lord,
it's there that he left fair Gwynedd.[1]

---

1 'In praise of Gruffudd Fychan ap Gruffudd's house Ty Gwyn' in Gwaith Tudur Penllyn
   ac Ieuan ap Tudur Penllyn, poem 16, lines 31–4. Trans. by Eurig Salisbury.

APPENDIX L
*Prognostic poem for Henry Tudor
by Robin Ddu*

This is the time [when] we will be delivered
so that our little bull can challenge the world;
he'll overthrow the tame-looking mole [= Richard III]
and wreak vengeance on him throughout the earth,
[making him] a boar whose poison is thick
– a feeble-bodied one – a Jew
[and then] a raven as he [= Henry] aims
towards the place he goes with his black plumage.
If he goes to Dublin once
as he begins the journey – curse the day! –
the wild Irishmen's defects are [their] strength
(may this [city suffer] hunger),
this is the first of the three genuine vengeances
– they aim towards peace –
and then a hundred men in battle –
the world, for the most part, is at an end.
My lord believes that this is the year
that work will tear the White Tower;
it's guessed that the bones of the three ribs
will break before two or three leaps.
The stag's head with an eagle's action

ahead of a company, he shatters passionately.
I aimed towards their cries,
the moon in a heavy battle yonder.
The eagle's black chick succeeds
in bearing the crown, his tone is just,
and although it's borne, I wouldn't cry,
for this man won't have long to live.
The ox will upturn the nation
at once – Rhonwen and her lineage –
and dwelling with him [will be]
a wrathful lion leading a black [host].
A great man will tear the seas
with a fierce call, a very harsh shout.
Woe three nine times to the hearts of blind men
because of that day [of] new Troy!
Red roses endure and are shown where he comes
in great pomp.
The river Thames will run with blood
from the water after that day – [our] redeemer –
and it's there we'll make our stand –
may this day be their last!
An Englishman won't go to the second field
after him now because of my attacking.
There's great longing for Harry,
there's hope for our nation;
his name is from the mountain,
he'll be a powerful, double-edged man;
and the ancestries from high land
and his swords bear the prize.
May you conquer the pagan world
for Christendom of the cross before you die!
This man is the boar, he finished this,
Cologne's old partner.
If he makes his home in heaven,
may he have mercy and a good end![1]

---

1   Prognostic poem for Henry Tudor by Robin Ddu, in Ceinion Llenyddiaeth Gymreig,
    ed. Owen Jones (London, 1875), pp. 220–21; Exclusively translated for this book by
    Eurig Salisbury.

APPENDIX M
Gwaith Lewys Glyn Cothi

God, He gave fortune, yes, and may He give long life
to King Henry the Seventh;
he knows well after deliverance
the task of bearing the cross and presenting it to Christendom.
Throughout Christendom three sallets have founded the pursuits
of Pembroke's Julius Caesar;
Anglesey's bull goes to the land of his choice,
he'd endeavour to great Troy.

He, earl of Pembroke, against every defamation and anger,
Jasper earl of Bedford;
his nephew took the old, blessed round table
from the fort of Newport.

Milford [= Milford Haven] and Newport and St Non's land,
    tall man,
[are] under Henry and his crown;
the North, the five regions of Ireland
and the South are secure under his staff.
His two pikestaffs throughout Britain bore
both Uthr and Emrys's seal;
it's good to take a part of both Tewdwr and Rhys
from the water for an unruly land.

Rhys's kin throughout the island will bury a desolate savage
under the earth's nape;
controlling both wild men and civilized, generous men
is Jasper's concern.

Jasper, King Henry
from St David's land,
born from a royal branch.

From kingship's kin,
he who interweaves lineage,
Henry, that man took the bench.

Like a giant yesterday
Pembroke took (it doesn't trouble me)
the second chief seat, some finely built lion.
Henry yonder is our bull,
and [he's] good and gentle,
he above is our old stag from a kingly branch.

Come earth and water
over the kin of Tewdwr's region,
if the two men desire it none shall escape.

May England also count
for these men a long spell
as well as the walls and appearance of both Wales and France.

Nine hosts,
one body of nine hundred men,
or a hundred heads or pen and ink

cannot all fashion as one letter
of gold inscribed earldom
the work of a nephew and his uncle who remain forever young.

At the end of my life
we were honoured, young and old,
and God provided a prophet
to keep the peace, Gwynedd's dragon.

He's a beast from Gwynedd, praiseworthy man,
and an oak and bull from Arthur's blood,
an affluent king from the body of Gwladus Ddu
whom, as it happened, hails from Dardanus.

He took the gallant hat by Tulius's [= Cicero's] word
and the great joy of Merlin's word,
and he's a man who's loving and fair
and his men are the honourable twelve.

Henry from Beli, free from worry,
Henry is the king in Brennus's [= Brân's] land,
also throughout the known world this man bore
the valour of old Carolus [= Charlemagne].

Ceredig's kin with loving authority,
kin of a man with nine antlers, Corineus's kin,
Dardanus's kin, a shield, a bull of three kingdoms,
Troy's kin also and Troilus's kin.

One man of the repute of a seventh Henry
is the brave and fair bull from the three Edwards;
the mole [= Richard III] went obediently into the net,
the day he was struck was a happy one.

It's good fortune for a nobleman to bear a leopard
and two just lions, Alan's father,
as well as Tewdwr Mawr's lion in a dark-blue gown of lyre,
and to live in Albanactus's fair land.

The patron's name from this man is St Peter,
the second pillar afterwards is St Paul;
St Andrew, St Matthias, St Matthew and St Machreth
bless him also before Saul's beloved.

There in the peaceable army
may Henry be crowned, endeavouring stag;
honour of All Saints' Day, against the planet's fear
may he be crowned again, Locrinus's kin.

The kingdom below by the name of Jesus
belongs to King Henry, wise champion;
from there through skilful kingship
he'll keep the rule of Cadwaladr.

He's the tall buttress from Brutus,
him after Solomon from Silius's blood,
from the men of Troy, successful pedigree,
and from Gwynedd's side and from Ascanius.

From Ascanius, Cynan's side,
our king was honoured there;
from great Troy over from Anglesey
the fortune is both brave and pleasant.[1]

---

1   *Gwaith Lewys Glyn Cothi*, ed. D. Johnston (Cardiff, 1995), poem 14. Previously unpublished translation made exclusively for this book by Eurig Salisbury.

APPENDIX N

A prophetic poem for Jasper Tudor
(Source: D. Johnston (ed.), Gwaith Lewis Glyn Cothi
(Carded, 1995), poem 13, translated by Eurig Salisbury

(Probably composed during Jasper's first exile years)

The last letter of the language
is called 'I'
    [='J', or 'Y', the last letter of the Welsh alphabet];
I read twenty languages,
[but] that 'I' from the old language,
the Irish capital 'I',
is the 'I' that remains over the land.
The 'I' is on the cold sea,
with nine inlets afraid of her.
A concealed 'I' that will come
from a laying down to give battle from hiding.
The upright 'I' from the wave
that was illuminated by a fair element.
Her brother placed in her land
the forefather's gold on her.
Gwynedd recognizes a hundred times

the gold's colour to steer a nation;
afterwards it recognizes how civilized
the colour black is to steer the world.
Three colours are read,
so too the long 'I' derives from three parts:
from the part of Cynan's land of wine,
from the blood of Rouen, from Edwin's part.
In the glen of Scotland and its land,
as in the Welsh people's prophecy,
the Northerners will read 'I',
the men of the North will serve her.
Not one Englishman as far as Windsor
desires to mention the 'I' over a sea.
'I' went as a man with joyful renown
to the sea to Mary and her son.
A star rose above for 'I'
in the valley with her light;
there's a shining star above St Non's land
for another 'I' now
that lights St John's feast
like fire before a fair 'I'.
It was above all of the river Daugleddau
like the world's candle for a second.
To the shore in the candlelight
he'll come to avenge his treachery.
On two altars the gold from his fist
will spell 'I' for St David.
'I', he went over the sea,
'I' will journey from three seas.
The dark 'I' will go under his finger
along with the island.

(

APPENDIX O

A prophetic poem for Jasper Tudor
Source: D. Johnston (ed.), Gwaith Lewys Glyn Cothi
(Caerdydd, 1995), poem 12) Translated by Eurig Salisbury

(Probably composed during Jasper's first exile years)

May the leopard place two spurs
in Anglesey the mother island's side;
may a swan learn where an old polecat
lands and where its land is.

The polecat will be troubled
by a squirrel and one foal,
by a female donkey with her lowered spear,
by a snake and one who's descended from Idwal.

The third is a bull who's descended from Idwal
throughout the earth after the bath has cooled,
his three darts, London's leopard,
will pull deceivers from their falseness.

The portcullis's false thought,
a ragged staff and a bunch of roses,
eight bears and seven female bears
poisoned our island.

Nine islands and their contentions
will strike the boar, him and his standard,
a lion and a buck, the boar's piglet,
a bison and lings, a lamb and a wolf.

The wolf and his son will be slain,
so too the ape, the serpent and the viper
and the young mole from the earth
and a miserable dog and an eagle chick.

Woe to the eagle and woe to the heron
and woe to the drake and woe to the dragon,
woe to the moon from the west,
woe to the whole company, woe to Kent's old men.

Along with the old beans and the wheat
Rhos below will fall;
the magpie will perish as always,
the one who'll kill it is the cat's claw.

The speckled cat's three nations were a gift,
three hundred will burn London;
may the bull from Gwynedd's three leaps
break the walls of its hall.

He's Taurus Cornutus with three natures
after king Arthur:
from the bank's deer, from pure England,
from Idwal's blood, from Tudur.

From Tudur there is in Italy
a forest cockerel who'll play dice
with his two slender wings that are a payment that grows
and matures soft feathers of gold coins.

From Brittany to land without much hindrance
he'll fly with the diligent ones;
from southern Wales to the walls of London
he'll sing a morning prayer over the Vale
    [=the Golden Vale].

And the first cry of song over Mathrafal
and the second from Sandwich to the edge of Sandal,
the third over Cardiff as a payment for Jasper
will his birds sing, Idwal's chicks.

His long and sharp beak like an enamel crook
will leave its mark tomorrow on the great fort of Yale
    [=Tomen y Rhodwydd];
the mark of his two wings from Yale to Yr Heledd
    [=Northwich, Middlewich and Nantwich],
the mark of his claws on Lyneal.

And there the next day because of Oldhall's kin
will Owain's kin come as a royal bull
and he'll turn that place as far as Devonshire into
    pasture with his blade
as well as heather and moorland as far as the
    fort of Kendal,

and he'll avenge fickle men's wrongs,
and after the avengement he'll break the earth
and break castles with his intense vigour
and divide Powys with his bull horns,

and he'll save York and Caer Dubal
    [=Caerdubalum]
and bear England's banner to Pennal,
and come to land on the brow of the Severn Sea
    [=Bristol Channel]
and drive the woman Rowena to the old lair,

and the English women into the soft water,
and the Englishwoman's oppression to the
    town of Kinsale,
and the weak, raucous English language
    to the ocean's lair,
as well as the black English people,
    he'll surrender almost nothing.

May he not delay [coming to] Dyfed, carefree country,
nor its fair gravelled land nor its three ground-walls;
may he make a mark on an unstable world from
    Milford [=Milford Haven],
may he draw near to Ynys Dudwal with his birds.
    [=St Tudwal's Island]

May he be an emperor where the apple is,
the hair and the brow are Britons' soul;
may Jasper have long life, amazing kinship,
also the same appearance and material as
    Brân ap Dyfnwal.

Like Brân ap Dyfnwal with a dart to capture
both half of France and Lombardy,
and God will better under His guard
the fortune of the leopard's spear.

APPENDIX P

In praise of Henry Tudor, Earl of Richmond
(T. Roberts and I. Williams (eds.), The Poetical Works of Dafydd
Nanmor (Cardiff and London, 1923), poem XVII)
Translated by Eurig Salisbury

(Composed around 1458)

Marvelously miraculous St Mwrog granted Henry
– he'll have long life
and Christ's abode, the cross's torrents –
Edmund's son, life for five ages.

England's honourer was always essential,
luminary of Tewdwr's nation;
may it not be necessary to fear a traitor
nor a wild tide nor a lion nor any man.

No man can kill him, nor tower nor thunderbolt nor dragon,
nor viper nor lightning;
may no snake terrify him, silk shirt,
nor treachery nor water nor fire.

May he not be struck by poleaxes nor
spears thrown from horseback,
may he not be worse off because of fire
nor poisoned food
nor an Englishman's pike nor the point of his arrow.

May he not be worse off because of an arrow
    nor a white dragon nor a lance
or a sword, nor a knife
nor a horse's knee nor a cart-wheel,
nor muscular pain nor a bubo.

Beautiful one, a bubo doesn't harm him, nor does a bow
nor an axe nor a ravenous wolf,
nor a spear nor a steel halberd,
nor his dog's fierce jaws nor a wolf.

Nor the South's wolves or an Irish steward
nor a Jew nor a Lombard,
nor a lively ostler nor a baselard,
nor a stone from a tower nor a dart's blade.

Nor a leopard nor a dart nor a monster's fang,
nor a big old boar,
nor a stag's horns nor pain nor disease,
nor death except old age.

Old age with regard to this island's saints,
they'll allow Henry to grow old for a long time;
may Mary take part, and so too Gabriel, Sariel,
    Thomas, Uriel,
Michael and Rhiniel.

May both St Benedict and St Bernard bless him
    wherever he gives judgement,
and may God and St Dyrnog bless him,
and so too St Brothen and St Sulien and St Silin,
St Buan, St Celynnin, St Beuno of Clynnog.

St Cynin and his servants, St Cynan, St Asaph,
St Cawrdaf, kinsman of Eudaf son of Caradog,
St Collen, St Elian's and Llywelyn's care,
St Cynwyd, Cynfelyn, St Cedwyn and St Cadog.

St Cadfan and St Dyfnan, St Ust and St Dyfnig,
St Caron and St Curig, St Patrick, St Pedrog,
St Peris, St Cristiolus, St Dennis, St Dwynwen,
St Peter, St John, St Gwynnen, St Padarn, St Gwynnog.

St Fagan, bishop St Afan, Ifor,
St Gregory, St George, St Môr and St Mwrog,
St Clare, St Ilar's and Cynddylig's blessing,
St Dominic, St Peblig, St Meilig, St Maelog.

St Dochwyn and St Tecwyn, him and St Tygwy,
St Dochdwy, St Winifred and St Tyfrïog,
St Derfel and St Dwyfel and St Gredifel,
St Dogmael, St Daniel and St Dwynog's blessing.

St Deiniol and St Seiriol and St Saeran's blessing,
Dardanus, St Stephen, St Cynan, St Cynog,
St Deiniolen, Llawdden, St Cathen, St Ceitho,
St David of Mynyw, St Dyfaenog's blessing.

St Tybïe, St Einion and St Non there,
St Tegla, St Agatha, St Anna, St Enoch,
St Tanwg and St Trinio, St James, St Egwad,
St Tysilio, St Lleuddad, St Tysul, St Llawddog.

St Lawrence marked him with the sign of the cross,
St Mark and St Richard, St Luke,
St Lambert, St Edward and St Tyfrydog,
and St Tydecho, St Teilo and St Telyddog
grant him good health.

As the lord of Richmond, yonder lord, he rushes,
as the lord of Somerset who has faith in the cross,
as an ordained knight we'll choose him,
golden-cloaked one, an earl of renown.

A duke, to behold him (new collar),
until he's chosen to be a prince
and a king, leader of the west,
and St Mwrog will make him an emperor.

APPENDIX Q

In praise of Jasper Tudor, earl of Pembroke
(D. Johnston (ed.),
Gwaith Lewys Glyn Cothi (Caerdydd, 1995), poem 11)
Translated by Eurig Salisbury

(Composed shortly after the Battle of Northampton, 10 July 1460)

All the land and the twisting fresh water known to man
[are] under Jasper, earl of Pembroke;
let the south and two Gwynedds
for ever be under him.

It went under him, by St James, bud of Deheubarth,
queen Catherine's hawk;
one brother who'd provide wine for us,
this man has the same heart as his king.

King Henry, like the passage of good weather,
he leads the play, him and the crown;
prince Edward without treaties
keeps the island with an unwavering spear of steel;
thirdly Jasper, [from] Penmynydd in Anglesey,
will gain the man's affection, by the authority of St Caron!

Henry of Richmond will go from Caerleon
to Llifon after his uncle.
Like Meirchion of yore, Jasper is a knight of the garter
who loves his excellent men;
he's called a target from here to Anglesey,
he's considered an earl with a good heart.
Jasper of Talebolion is [like] Beli,
he's a bleaunt of gold in the place where Dôn's children once
   were.

May the men of Aberdaron go to Jasper
and this will lead to victory over old Arfon
and the fort of Tegeingl and Ceredigion
and the limits of Llywel and Chester.

The land of Cymaron will go to Jasper,
the one who'll reanimate the old memories,
and the eight nations will come to the island
to Rhyd Goch on the river Ieithon in the time of his father.

In his time the wooden horses and the oars of the men of
   Rhone
will come as guests,
and he'll play like a righteous thunderbolt,
he'll play with steel throughout Uwch Aeron.

He'll play chess above with the English,
he'll lead the play, him and the faithful ones;
he'll play dice with knights,
the man will win as far as Caereinion;
he'll play chevy between the Marches and Anglesey,
he'll kill a thousand men there;
he'll take the land that was once pleasant,
that was once Uthr Bendragon's territory.

May our proverbs not be forsaken,
the brave men's proverb is true:
an old man, black ashen spear,
is better than the blood-feud of old enemies,
and he'll claim by the old rights
the stubborn acre for his grandchildren
as well as the fortified towns and the knights
and the wheat fields and the white towers.

White towers and great, excellent houses
are in his full grasp;
is there a yoke for the dark-haired Welshman?
Yes, generous Jasper's long spear.

For Jasper, who likes the cannon-balls,
there's a place on the king of Aragon's bench;
we'll see his seal for land,
his fair host too under this man's saplings.

Verdant saplings from Owain's side,
he gathers birds, a talent for a loyal man,
his royal blood as far as Darowain
and from Owain won't delay.
His counsels night and day
and his great excellences are loved;
from the Maelors and the manors
the best earl is the truthful lion.

Everlasting faithful one, a man who eases
and avails men with sweeping ermine.
Everlasting, fair lineage, he'll be blessed
by Jesus's word by confessing.
A strong, complete hawk for a land of roses,
a splendid goshawk in a place of resting.
A man with a large following, castles with many courtyards,
the men of the two shires' courageous goshawk.

One who's sought after by shires, who's the root of drinking,
Dyfed's St Sulien, we're tamed below.
Many are under the seal of Ednyfed who's sought after,
a drinking cellar, many are counted.
A serpent's gestures, a saint's souls,
the basis of his movements are recognised on a Sunday.
His grandfathers have many supporters
and many kinds of hosts across the south.

Lands – under him men pierce –
are demanded through earnest requests.
A crowd sings – blessed towns,
circular towers – for the long-horned bull.
Through Darowain to Trefowain
and through Cedowain yonder he's allowed.
He obtains a province, Ednowain's forehead,
a tower [descended] from Owain with the very long spear.

There are tall soldiers for this Beli
from Cydweli, a battle that causes mourning.
Without weaklings, without barriers,
from the sea above [he'll] set sail.
Long, pleasant summer, Twrcelyn's stag,
they all see this man, a name that causes weeping.
Llywelyn's lineage as far as Cynfelyn
drive the enemy towards the man with the long spear.

This man's supporters are numerous like lush leaves,
the man on a field's ridge who loved truth.
The man who counts the men on a field's ridge,
who's this man but tall Jasper?
The conspicuous men will come where he goes,
the land of Ardudwy will come to his father.
May the whole world go under his seal like a ball,
the verdant earth will go to him.

BIBLIOGRAPHY

Primary Sources

Amundesham, I.

Archives De La Loire-Atlantque, Nantes, Series B en E.

Ballad of Bosworth Field, online version. www.r3.org

'Benet's Chronicle of the Years 1400 to 1462', ed. G.L. Harriss and
M.A. Harriss, in *Camden Miscellany*, vol. 14, Camden Society,
4th series, vol. 9 (1972), pp.151–233.

BL, Additional MSS.

BL, Egerton MS.

BL, Egerton Rolls.

BL, Harleian MS.

BN, Clairambault 473, f. 213

BN, Huntingdon Herald, MS Fr. 18441, f. 112.

BN, Fonds Francaise

Brut or *The Chronicles of England*, ed. F.W.D. Brie, The Early English
Text Society (London: Kegan, Paul, Trench, Trübner, 1906).

Calendar of the Close Rolls

Calendar of the Charter Rolls

Calendar of the Fine Rolls

Calendar of the Patent Rolls

Calendar of the State Papers Milan.

Calendar of the State Papers Venice.

Calendar State Papers and Manuscripts in the Archives and Collections of Milan, (1385–1618), ed. Allen B. Hinds (1912.).

Calendar of the State papers Relating to English Affairs in the Archives of Venice, vol. 1 (1201–1509), ed. R. Brown, Bentinck et al. (1864).

Cardiff Central library MSS.

Chester Recognisance Rolls D.K.R., XXXVII, pt. II, 285 (1876).

Chronicles of England, Scotland and Ireland, Raphael Holinshed, 6 vols. (London, 1807–8).

The Chronicles of Enguerrand de Monstrelet, trans. Thomas Johnes Esq. (London, 1853).

The Chronicles of London, ed. C.L. Kingsford (Oxford, 1905).

Chronicle of the Six Ages and NLW Manuscript 3054D, Elis Gruffydd.

Chronicle of the White Rose of York, Hearne's Fragment, ed. J.A. Giles (London, 1845).

Chroniques de Jean Molinet, ed. G. Doutrepoint and O. Jodogne, 3 vols. (Brussels, 1935–37).

Commynes, Philippe de, Memoires; *The reign of Louis XI, 1461–83*, trans. M.C.E. Jones (Harmondsworth, 1972).

——, *The Historical Memoires of Philip de Comynnes* (London, 1817).

——, *Memoires de Messire Philippe de Comines* (1747).

Croyland Chronicle Continuations 1453–1486, 11 vols., Richard III Society Online Library. www.r3.org.

——, Davies, Cliff,(ed.), 'Information, disinformation and political knowledge under Henry VII and early Henry VIII',*Historical Research* 85, no. 228 (May 2012), pp. 228–53.

Dafydd Llwyd, Cardiff MSS.

Dugdale, William, *The Baronage of England,* vol.3, (London, 1676).

Edward Hall's *The Union of the Two Noble and Illustrious Families of Lancaster and York*, ed. Henry Ellis (London, 1809).

An English Chronicle of the Reigns of Richard II, Henry IV, V, VI, ed. J.S. Davies, Camden Society, old series, LXIV (London, 1856).

Exchequer, E.R., Issue Roll.

Exchequer, E.R., Warrants for Issues.

Fabyan, R., *The New Chronicles of England and France*, ed. H. Ellis (London, 1811).

——, *The Great Chronicle of London*, Robert Fabyan, ed. A.H. Thomas and I.D. Thornley (London, 1938).

The Fastolf Relation, College of Arms, Arundel MS 48, folio 342.

Foedera, Conventiones, Literae..., ed. T. Rymer, 3rd ed., 10 vols (The Hague, 1739–45).

Foedera, ed. Thomas Rymer, 20 vols. (London, 1704–35; reprinted Farnborough, 1967).

Gairdner, James, *Gregory's Chronicle 1461–1469* or *The Historical Collection of the Citizens of London in the Fifteenth Century*, Camden Society, new series, XVII (London,1876).

——, *The Paston Letters* AD 1422–1509, 6 vols. (London: Chatto & Windus, 1904.

Giles, J.A. (ed.), *incerti scriptoris chronicon angliae* (1848).

Guenée, B., *Les Grandes Chroniques de France: Le roman aux rois (1274–518)* (Paris, 1986).

Guto'r Glyn; Ceinion Llenyddiaeth Gymreig.

Gwaith Ieuan Gethin, ed. I. Daniel, Aberystwyth, [unpublished].

Gwaith Lewis Glyn Cothi, The Cymmrodorion, 2 vols., Oxford 1837.

Haut Jussé, B. A. Pocquet, *Francois II, Duc de Bretagne, et L'Ángleterre* (1458–1488).

History of the Duchy of Lancaster, I, 1265–1603, ed. R. Somerville (London, 1953).

Historical MSS. Commission Report.

H.M.C., Beaufort and Donoughmore MSS., Twelfth Report.

KB27/908, Rex. Rot. 8. *Norfolk Archaeology*, vol. 38 (1981–83).

Leics RO, BR II/3/3.

Leland, John, *Itinerary in Wales*, ed. L.T. Smith, 5 vols. (London, 1906–1910).

——, *The Itinerary of John Leland*, ed. L. Toulmin Smith, 5 vols., (London, 1964), vol. 3.

Letters and Papers Illustrative of the wars of the English and France during the reign of Henry the Sixth, etc., ed. J. Stevenson, RS, 2 vols. in 3, incl. the pseudo- William Worcester Annals (1861–64).

A Life of Guto'r Glyn, E.A. Rees, (Ceredigion: Y Lolfa Cyf, 2008).

Lord's Report, IV, 932; V, 293.

Mancini, Dominic, *The Usurpation of Richard III*, ed. C.A.J. Armstrong, 2nd edition (Oxford, 1969).

Materials for a history of the reign of Henry VII : from original documents preserved in the Public Record Office, ed. William Campbell, 2 vols.,(London: Longman & Co., 1837).

NA, C81/1392/6

NLW, Badminton Deeds and Documents. 1194.

NLW, Mostyn MSS.

Owen, George, *The Description of Pembrokeshire,* ed. Henry Owen, Cymmrodorion Record Series, 4 vols. (London, 1892–1936).

The Parliament Rolls of Medieval England, 1275-1504, vol. 15: *Richard III, 1484-1485; Henry VII, 1485-1487,* ed. Rosemary Horrox (London, 2005).

The Parliament Rolls of Medieval England, 1275-1504, vol., 16: *Henry VII, 1489-1504,* ed. Rosemary Horrox (London, 2005).

The Paston Letters and Papers of the Fifteenth Century, ed. N. Davies, 2 vols. (Oxford, 1971–76).

Pepys, Samuel, *The Diary of Samuel Pepys 1659–1669,* ed. R. Latham and W. Matthews (London: HarperCollins, 2000).

——, *Diary and Correspondence of Samuel Pepys; F.R.S.,* vol. 3, ed. Lord Richard Braybrooke and Rev. J. Smith (London: Henry Colburn, 1849).

Poetical Works of Dafydd Nanmor, ed. T. Roberts and I. Williams (Cardiff/London: University of Wales Press Board, 1923).

Political poems and songs relating to English history: composed during the period from the accession of Edw. III. to that of Ric. III, Thomas Wright (London, 1859).

Proceedings and Ordinances of the Privy Council, ed. N.H. Nicholas, 7 vols., Record Commission (1834–37).

PRO, Chancery, Ancient Deeds, Series C.

PRO, Chancery, Inquisitions post mortem, series, I, C.139, C.40, C.141.

PRO, Chancery Parliamentary and Council Proceedings, C49/62/12, C49/31/2-3, C49/32/12A.

PRO, Chancery, Parliamentary Rolls.

PRO, Chancery, Warrants for the Great Seal.

PRO, Duchy of Lancaster, Chancery Rolls.

PRO, Duchy of Lancaster, Ministers' Accounts.

PRO, Exchequer, Warrants for Issues.

PRO, King's Bench, Ancient indictments.

PRO, King's Bench, Plea Rolls.

PRO, Privy Seal Office Warrants.

PRO, Proceedings of the Privy Council.

PRO, Special Collections, Ancient Correspondence.

PRO, Special Collections, Court Rolls.

Registrum Abbatiae Johannis Whethamstede, ed. H.T. Riley, R.S., 2 vols. (1872-73).

Ricart, Robert, *The Maire of Bristowe is Kalendar,* ed. L.T. Smith, Camden Society, V (London, 1872).

Robin Ddu ap Siencyn Bledrydd of Anglesey, *Ceinion Llenyddiaeth Gymreig,* ed. Owen Jones (London, 1875).

Rotuli Parliamentorum.

John Ryland's Library, Latin MS 113.

Six Towns Chronicles, ed. R. Flenley (Oxford, 1911).

Somerset Medieval Wills (1383–1500), ed. The Rev. F.W. Weaver, *Somerset* Record Society vol.15 (London, 1901).

Special Collection of Ancient Correspondence.

Scofield, C. L., *The Life and Reign of Edward IV* (London, 1923).

Stow, John, *Annales, or a Generall Chronicle of England,* ed. Edmund Howes (London 1615, 1631).

——, *The Annals of England* (London, 1592).

——, *Survey of London by John Stow* (1598), ed. William J. Thoms (London: Whittaker & Co, 1842).

——, *Three Fifteenth Century Chronicles,* ed. James Gairdner, Camden Society New Series XXVIII (London, 1880).

Strickland, A., *Lives of the Queens of England,* 8 vols. (London, 1840–48).

Thomas, S.R., 'The Political career, estates and connection of Jasper Tudor, Earl of Pembroke and Duke of Bedford (d. 1495)' , PhD dissertation, Swansea University, 1971.

Vaessen, J., *Lettres de Louis XI, roi de France,* vol. 2 (Paris, 1883–1909).

Vergil, Polydore, *The Three Books of Polydore Vergil's English History,* Camden Society (London, 1838).

——,*The Anglica Historia of Polydore Vergil AD 1485–1537,* ed. and trans. D. Hay, Camden Society, 3rd series, 74 (London, 1950).

Warkworth, J., *A Chronicle of the First Thirteen Years of the Reign of King Edward the Fourth by John Warkworth,* Richard III Society, Camden Society, 9 vols. (London, 1839).

Waurin, Jehan de, *Recueil de Chroniques et Anchiennes istories de la Grant Bretaigne*, ed. W. Hardy, 5 vols. RS (London, 1864).

Westminster Abbey Muniments.

William Worcestre Itineraries, ed. John Harvey (Oxford, 1969).

Wynne, John, *The History of the Gwydir Family* (Oxford University, 1878).

Secondary Sources

Accession of Henry VII; EHR, cii 1987.

Allanic, J., *Le Prisonnier de la Tour d'Elven, ou la jeugnesse du Roy Henry VII d'Angleterre* (Vannes, 1909).

Allen, E, 'The Tomb of the earl of Richmond in St. David's Cathedral', *Archaeologia Cambrensis*, 5th series, XIII (1896).

Annuaire-Bulletin de la Société de L'historire de France, vol 2 (1867), pp. 179–80

Archaeology Cambrensis, vol. 1.

Ashdown-Hill, John, *Royal Marriage Secrets: Consorts & Concubines, Bigamists & Bastards* (Stroud: The History Press, 2013).

Entrée de Charles VIII à Rouen en 1485, ed. Robinet Pinel and Charles de Beaurepaire (Rouen, 1902).

Armstrong, C.A.J.,'Politics and the Battle of St. Albans, 1455', *Bulletin of the Institute of Historical Research*, vol. 33, no. 87, 1960,

Bagley, J.J., *Margaret of Anjou* (London: Herbert Jenkins 1948).

Beltz, G.E., *Memorials of the most noble order of the Garter*, (London, 1841).

Bennet, Michael, *Lambert Simnel and the Battle of Stoke* (New York: St Martin's Press, 1987).

Blaauw, W.H., 'On the effigy of Sir David Owen in Easebourne Church near Midhurst', *Sussex Archaeological Collections*, VII (1854).

Blacman, John, *Henry the Sixth A Reprint of John Blacman's Memoir with Translation and Notes*, ed. M.R. James (Cambridge University Press, 1919).

Boardman, Andrew, *The Fist Battle of St Albans 1455* (Tempus: Stroud, 2006).

Burke, John, *A general and Heraldic dictionary of the peerage of England, Ireland and Scotland* (London; H. Colburn and R. Bentley, 1831).

Busch, Wilhelm, *England under the Tudors*, I, King Henry VII (London, 1895).

Calmette, J. and Perinelle, G., *Louis XI et L'Angleterre, 1461-83* (Paris, 1930).

Chrimes, S.B., 'The landing place of Henry of Richmond, 1485', *Welsh History Review*, II (1964–65).

Church Book of St Mary the Virgin, Tenby (Tenby, 1907).

Dictionary of National Biography.

Dictionary of Welsh Biography (Bangor University: Honourable Society of Cymmrodorion etc, 1959).

Driver, J.T., *Cheshire Men in the Later Middle Ages* (Chester, 1971).

The Early Chronicle of Shrewsbury 1372–1603, ed. W.A. Leighton (1888).

Ellis, Sir Henry, *Original Letters illustrative of English history*, series 2, 4 vols. (London, 1827).

Evans, H.T., *Wales and the Wars of the Roses* (Cambridge University Press, 1915).

Fenton, Richard, *A Historical Tour through Pembrokeshire* (London, 1811).

Freeman, A., *The Battles of Wakefield* (1894).

The funeral sermon of Margaret, Countess of Richmond and Derby, mother of King Henry VII, and foundress of Christ's and St John's College in Cambridge, preached by Bishop Fisher in 1509, ed. J. Hymers (Cambridge University Press, 1811).

Gage, John, *The History and Antiquities of Hengrave in Suffolk* (London, 1822).

——, *The History and Antiquities of Suffolk: Thingoe Hundred* (London, 1838).

Miscellanea Genealogica et Heraldica, 4th series, vol. 5, ed. G. Grazebrook and. J. Ballinger (1914).

The Complete Peerage of England, Scotland, Ireland and Great Britain..., vol. VI, ed. George Edward Cockayne. (London: George Bell and Sons, 1895).

Gill, Louise, *Richard III and Buckingham's Rebellion*, (Stroud: Sutton Publishing, 1999).

Griffiths, R.A. and Thomas, R.S., *The Making of the Tudor Dynasty*, (Stroud: Sutton Publishing, 2005).

——, *The Reign of King Henry VI* (Stroud: Sutton Publishing, 1998).

——,*Sir Rhys ap Thomas and his Family, A Study in The Wars of the Roses and Early Tudor Politics* (Melksham: Cromwell Press, 1981, 2014).

——, *Welsh History Review*, Vol. 2 (1965).

——, 'Queen Katherine of Valois and a Missing Statute of the Realm', *Law Quarterly Review*, 93 (1977).

Guto'r Glyn, www.gutorglyn.nl.

Halsted, C.A., *Life of Margaret Beaufort, Countess of Richmond and Derby* (London: Smith, Cornhill Elder and Co., 1839).

Hammond.

Heywood, Thomas, *The most pleasant song of Lady Bessy* (London: Richard Taylor, 1829).

Hicks, Michael, *Warwick the Kingmaker* (Wiley-Blackwell, 2002).

Higginbotham, Susan, *The Woodvilles, The Wars of the Roses and England's Most Infamous Family* (Stroud: The History Press, 2013).

Historie of the Arrivall of Edward IV (London: Camden Society, 1838).

History of the Family of Mostyn of Mostyn, London 1925.

The History of King Richard III, in *The Complete Works of Thomas More*, Vol. II, ed. Richard S. Sylvester (New Haven and London, 1963).

Hodges, G., *Ludford Bridge & Mortimer's Cross* (Herefordshire: Lagaston Press, 2001).

Johnson, P.A., *Duke Richard of York 1411–1460* (Oxford: Clarendon Press, 1991).

Jones, M.K. and Underwood, M.G., *The King's Mother: Lady Margaret Beaufort, Countess of Richmond and Derby* (Cambridge University Press, 1992).

Jones, W.G., *Welsh nationalism and Henry Tudor* (London; The Cymmrodorion, 1916).

Kendall, P.M., Richard III(W. W. Company and Co 2001).

Laws, E., 'Notes on the Fortifications of Medieval Tenby', *Archaeologia Cambrensis*, 5th series, vol. VIII (London; The Bedford Press 1896), pp. 177–94.

Letters of Queen Margaret of Anjou and Bishop Beckington and others, Camden Society, 1st series (1863).

Markham, C.R., 'The Battle of Wakefield', *Yorkshire Archaeological and Topographical Journal* , vol. 9 (1886).

Merrick, Rice, *A Book of Glamorganshire Antiquities etc..* ed. J.A. Corbett (London, 1887).

Morice, Dom. H., *Memoire pour servir de preuves a l'histoire ecclesiastique et civile de Bretagne*, Vol. 3, cols. 266–70 (Paris, 1742–46).

De Lisle, Leanda, *Tudor: The Family Story* (London: Chatto & Windus, 2013).

Davies, C.S.L. Davies, 'Richard III, Brittany and Henry Tudor', *Nottingham Medieval Studies*, 37 (1993).

Norton, Elizabeth, *Margaret Beaufort, Mother of the Tudor Dynasty* (Stroud: Amberley, 2011).

Norris, Charles, 'A Historical Sketch of Tenby and its Neighbourhood', plate no. 3 in *Etchings of Tenby* (1844), in the possession of Tenby Corporationhood'.

Owen, H. and Blakeway, J.B., *A History of Shrewsbury* (London: Harding, Lepard and Co., 1825).

Page, William, *The Victoria History of the County of Buckingham*, vol. 3 (London: The St Catherine Press, 1925).

Palgrave, F., *The Ancient Kalendars and Inventories of His Majesty's Exchequer*, vol. 2 (1836).

Penn, Thomas, *Winter King, The Dawn of Tudor England* (London: Allen Lane, 2011).

Ramsey, James H., *Lancaster and York, A Century of English History AD 1399–1485* (Oxford: The Clarendon Press, 1892).

Raymond, Paul, *Correspondence inedite de Louis XI avec le duc de Bretagne, 1463 et 1464.*

Reports from the Lord's Committees Touching the Dignity of a Peer of the Realm, Vol. 4, p. 940 (London, 1820–29).

Rosenthal, R.T., 'Estates and finances of Richard Duke of York', PhD thesis, University of Chicago; 1963.

Ross, James, *John de Vere, Thirteenth Earl of Oxford 1442–1513*, (Woodbridge: The Boydell Press, 2011).

Santiuste, David, *Edward IV and the Wars of the Roses* (Barnsley: Pen and Sword, 2011).

Skidmore, Chris, *Bosworth, The Birth of the Tudors* (London: Weidenfeld & Nicolson, 2013).

Storey, R.L., *The End of the House of Lancaster* (Stroud: Alan Sutton Publishing, 1999).

Stubbs, W., *The Constitutional History of England*, Vol. 3 (Oxford: Clarendon Press, 1903).

Sudbury, P.G., 'The Medieval Boroughs of Pembrokeshire', unpublished thesis, University of Wales, 1947.

Sussex Archaeological Collections, Illustrating the History and Antiquities of the County, vol. 7, ed. John Russell Smith (London, 1849).

Thomas, D.H., *The Herberts of Raglan and the Battle of Edgecote 1469* (Freezywater Publications, 1994).

Thornton, Tim, *The Channel Islands 1370–1640, Between England and Normandy* (Woodbridge: The Boydell Press, 2012).

Wedgwood, J.C., *History of Parliament, Register of the ministers and members of both houses, 1439–1509* (London, 1938).

Weir, Alison, *Britain's Royal Families, The Complete Genealogy* (Vintage, 2008).

Williams, L., *Ancient and Modern Denbigh: A Descriptive History of the Castle, Borough, and Liberties* (Denbigh, 1850).

The Works of Sir John Fortescue, ed. Lord Clermont (London, 1869).

Wroe, Ann, *Perkin, A Story of Deception* (London: Vintage, 2004).

LIST OF ILLUSTRATIONS

Index

A

B

D

E

MADEGLOBAL PUBLISHING

Non-Fiction History

- The Fall of Anne Boleyn - **Claire Ridgway**
- George Boleyn: Tudor Poet, Courtier & Diplomat
  - **Claire Ridgway**
- The Anne Boleyn Collection - **Claire Ridgway**
- Sweating Sickness in an Nutshell - **Claire Ridgway**
- The Anne Boleyn Collection II - **Claire Ridgway**
- On This Day in Tudor History - **Claire Ridgway**
- Two Gentleman Poets at the Court of Henry VIII
  - **Edmond Bapst**
- The Merry Wives of Henry VIII - **Ann Nonny**
- A Mountain Road - **Douglas Weddell Thompson**

Historical Fiction

- The Claimant - **Simon Anderson**
- The Truth of the Line - **Melanie V. Taylor**

Other Books

- Easy Alternate Day Fasting - **Beth Christian**
- 100 Under 500 Calorie Meals - **Beth Christian**
- 100 Under 200 Calorie Desserts - **Beth Christian**
- 100 Under 500 Calorie Vegetarian Meals - **Beth Christian**
- Interviews with Indie Authors - **Claire Ridgway**
- Popular - **Gareth Russell**
- The Immaculate Deception - **Gareth Russell**
- The Walls of Truth - **Melanie V. Taylor**
- Talia's Adventures - **Verity Ridgway**
- Las Aventuras de Talia (Spanish) - **Verity Ridgway**

PLEASE LEAVE A REVIEW

If you enjoyed this book, *please* leave a review at the book seller where you purchased it. There is no better way to thank the author and it really does make a huge difference! *Thank you in advance.*